Alluring New Mexico

Alluring New Mexico

Engineered Enchantment
1821–2001

Marta Weigle

Museum of New Mexico Press
Santa Fe

Project editor: Mary Wachs
Design and production: David Skolkin
Map by Deborah Reade
Composition: Set in Bedoni Book with Brush Script display
Manufactured in United States of America
10 9 8 7 6 5 4 3 2 1

Library of Congress Cataloging-in-Publication Data
Weigle, Marta.
Alluring New Mexico : engineered enchantment, 1821-2001 / by Marta Weigle.
p. cm.
Includes bibliographical references and index.
ISBN 978-0-89013-573-0 (clothbound); ISBN: 978-089013-574-7 (paperbound)
1. Tourism—New Mexico—History. 2. New Mexico—Description and travel. I. Museum of New Mexico.
Press. II. Title.
G155.U6N66 2010
338.4'791789—dc22
2010018592

Museum of New Mexico Press
PO Box 2087
Santa Fe, New Mexico 87504

Contents

Preface 7

Part One
Trail: The Tourists' Shrine 12

❖

1. Birthplace of Montezuma 17 *2. Land without Law* 29
3. Land of Heart's Desire 43

Part Two
Rail: The Great Southwest 52

❖

4. Land of the Well Country 57 *5. Indian Detours, the Real Southwest* 65
6. Land of Pueblos 75

Part Three
Road: The Strange and Different 86

❖

7. Land of Enchantment 91 *8. Land of Sunshine* 101
9. The Colorful State 113 *10. Carlsbad Caverns, the Eighth Wonder* 125
11. The Volcano State 139 *12. 2001—Route 66, Essence of Enchantment* 151

Part Four
Air: The Science State 160

❖

13. The Space State 164 *14. The Atomic State* 177

Conclusion
New Mexico's Engineered Nineteenth- and Twentieth-Century Enchantment 193

References Cited 203
Credits 217
Index 219

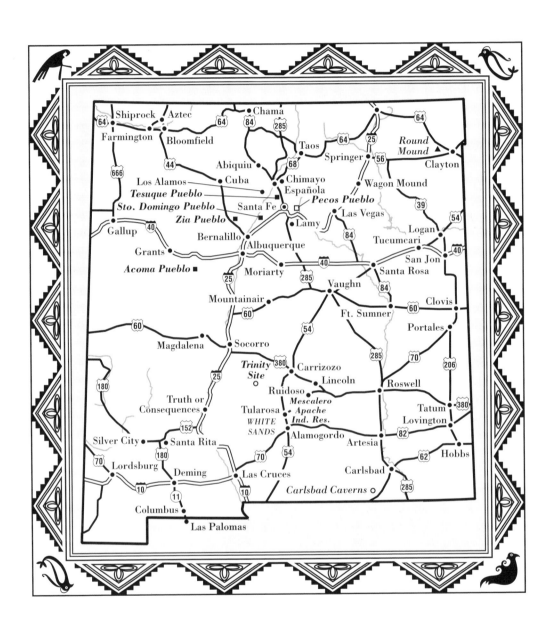

Preface

On November 16, 1821, Captain William Becknell, the Father of the Santa Fe Trail, and five other American traders arrived in Santa Fe from Franklin, Missouri. The trail's subsequent "commerce of the prairies" flourished until eclipsed by Colonel Cyrus Kurtz Holliday's Atchison, Topeka and Santa Fe Railroad, which first reached the Territory of New Mexico over Raton Pass in December 1878, Albuquerque in April 1880, and the Arizona border in July 1881. What in the twentieth century became The Great Southwest of the Santa Fe Railway and the Fred Harvey Company was, in turn, supplanted by U.S. Highway 66, launched in 1926 between Chicago and Los Angeles. The Father of Route 66, Cyrus (Cy) Stevens Avery, dubbed it the Main Street of America in February 1927. By the time it was decommissioned on June 27, 1985, it was better known as the Mother Road, John Steinbeck's designation in his 1939 novel *The Grapes of Wrath*. The Diamond Jubilee of Route 66 was celebrated in 2001.

The Mexican province of New Mexico became part of the United States following the 1846–48 Mexican War. Congressional legislation established the Territory of New Mexico in 1850. Known as the Land of Sunshine, the territory was recognized as the forty-seventh state on January 6, 1912. In 1934, when Florida appropriated the Sunshine State as its sobriquet, the New Mexico State Highway Department, and after May 1935 the State Tourist Bureau, began calling New Mexico the Land of Enchantment. "Land of Enchantment" first appeared on license plates in 1941. However, despite efforts in 1947 and 1999, it was not designated the state's official nickname until Governor Bill Richardson signed enabling legislation on April 6, 2003.

Alluring New Mexico: Engineered Enchantment, 1821–2001, is a narrative historical overview of provincial, territorial, and state identities constructed along trail, rail, road, and from the air. The book's parts are organized chronologically: (1) "Trail: The Tourists'

Shrine," covering the nineteenth-century Mexican and Territorial periods; (2) "Rail: The Great Southwest," the Atchison, Topeka and Santa Fe Railroad (after 1895, Railway) and the Fred Harvey Company's corporate image-making from the 1880s through the 1930s; (3) "Road: The Strange and Different," which begins with the first issue of the State Highway Department's *New Mexico Highway Journal* (July 1923) and concludes with a discussion of Route 66, 1926–2001; and (4) "Air: The Science State," constellated around the Trinity Site detonation on July 16, 1945, and the Roswell Incident of July 1947. These constructed identities are reviewed in the concluding section, "New Mexico's Engineered Nineteenth- and Twentieth-Century Enchantment."

The chapters, too, are organized chronologically from the initial constructed identity. Most carry the subject forward into the late twentieth century, if not to 2001. The core subjects and sites in each chapter are: (1) "Birthplace of Montezuma," Pecos Pueblo and missions; (2) "Land without Law," Clayton (Black Jack Ketchum), Fort Sumner, and Lincoln (Billy the Kid); (3) "Land of Heart's Desire," the 1915–16 San Diego Panama-California Exposition and the 1933–34 Chicago Century of Progress Exposition; (4) "Land of the Well Country," Las Vegas Hot Springs; (5) "Indian Detours, the Real Southwest," Santa Fe's La Fonda; (6) "Land of Pueblos," Albuquerque's Alvarado Hotel and Zia Pueblo; (7) "Land of Enchantment," the New Mexico State Tourist Bureau; (8) "Land of Sunshine," art colonists in Taos, Santa Fe, and Abiquiú; (9) "The Colorful State," Chimayó and the 1940 WPA *New Mexico: A Guide to the Colorful State*; (10) Carlsbad Caverns, the Eighth Wonder," the caverns, White's City, and the Waste Isolation Pilot Plant; (11) "The Volcano State," Shiprock and Four Corners; (12) "2001 – Route 66, Essence of Enchantment," the Diamond Jubilee year and the fall advertising campaign; (13) "The Space State," Galisteo Junction, Columbus, Roswell, and Alamogordo; and (14) "The Atomic State," White Sands, Trinity Site, and Los Alamos.

Each chapter is an orchestration of contemporary voices, many from newspapers and ephemeral promotional materials, and the published words of historians, journalists, writers, and others reflecting on those times. The newspaper and ephemeral materials are identified in the text. A bibliography of published "References Cited" concludes the book.

Alluring New Mexico was conceived as "The Lure of New Mexico," a companion to *The Lore of New Mexico*, written with my University of New Mexico colleague Peter White and first published in 1988, followed by an abridged edition in 2003. In 1992, first in the American Studies Department and then in the Anthropology Department, I began teaching a course entitled "New Mexico Folklore/lure" and subsequently "New Mexico Lore and Lure." My students in all those classes have contributed importantly. Graduate research assistant Carol Lambourne did expert work at a crucial time.

In 1985 the University of New Mexico Departments of History and Anthropology received a generous endowment from Santa Feans James and Georgia Snead and Jerry and

Mary Carole Wertheim. I was fortunate to hold the Snead-Wertheim Research Lectureship during the 2004–2005 academic year. This book benefitted greatly from that research help.

By their steadfast commitment to St. John's College, in Annapolis from 1949 and after 1960 also in Santa Fe, my parents, Richard D. Weigle and Mary D. Weigle, gifted me this state. Through them, during the early days of the Santa Fe campus, I met many of the people I now know to have been significant participants in fashioning a twentieth-century New Mexico cultural discourse. Here I wish especially to acknowledge John Gaw and Faith Meem for their superlative contributions, evident and intangible, to St. John's College Santa Fe, to the University of New Mexico where I have taught since August 1972, and to the State of New Mexico.

When my parents first brought my sister Connie and me to Santa Fe in 1961, we stayed in the guesthouse of Sallie Wagner and her then husband William J. Lippincott, who was acting treasurer and business manager for the new campus. From 1938 until 1950 Sallie and Bill had operated a trading post on the Navajo Reservation at Wide Ruins, Arizona. Sallie took us "everywhere" and introduced us to all manner of Santa Feans, to the pueblos where she continued to trade, and to the "high road" Hispanic villages from Chimayó to Taos. On that road she acquainted me with the Penitente Brotherhood, ten years later the subject of my doctoral dissertation at the University of Pennsylvania. Her guidance thus made it possible for me to fulfill the seventeenth-birthday wish I made to myself on her mirador overlooking Santa Fe on July 3, 1961: to find a way to return to New Mexico to stay.

The first offices of St. John's College Santa Fe were at La Posada Inn, then billed as "Santa Fe's Motor Hotel in the Center of Old Santa Fe, New Mexico." Manager Harvey Durand kindly hired me to live there upstairs in the Staab House and work behind the desk and as hostess in the dining room that first summer and several following. La Posada opened to me the city of Santa Fe and the world of tourism in northern New Mexico. The worlds of anthropology and of the Navajo were opened because Florence Kluckhohn stayed there one summer and offered me work sorting her late husband Clyde Kluckhohn's papers and typing the manuscript of his and W. W. Hill's *Navaho Material Culture* (Harvard University Press, 1971) throughout my sophomore, junior, and senior years at Harvard.

In between morning and evening shifts at La Posada, I sought the company of book people two blocks down Palace Ave. in the Sena Plaza at The Villagrá Book Shop and at Ancient City Bookstore. Robert Kadlec, who owned the latter, had just started Ancient City Press that first summer. Twenty years later, in 1981, I and several others were privileged to become partners in that press, which flourished under the leadership of Mary Powell until she and I sold it to Gibbs Smith Publisher in June 2005. Bob introduced me to a rich lore of books and New Mexicana, as well as New Mexicans native and newcomer, including Lorenzo de Córdova (Lorin W. Brown) and, during a very brief book-related visit to her home in Abiquiú, Georgia O'Keeffe, who tolerated my unwelcome presence there no better than when my father had first introduced me to her in downtown Santa Fe. Most important is that Bob introduced me to Diana and Joe Stein and their marvelous La Galeria de los Artesanos bookstore on the plaza in Las Vegas, New Mexico. The wealth of their new, used, and out-of-print "Books of the West," seemingly endless ephemera, and wonderful "shop talk" through the years proved invaluable to this and many of my other books.

My longtime friend and irreplaceable University of New Mexico colleague Sylvia Rodríguez's wit and acumen about tourism, interethnic relations, and countless other matters in her native Taos and my adopted Santa Fe changed everything. Other good New Mexico friends also truly know this travel/travail: Mary Powell, Minrose Gwin, and Ruth Salvaggio. What Kay Hagan knows is a marvel, and I delight in the folk detective agency now and again out and about in this engineered enchantment. Jean Hess, a student in my first anthropology class following my car accident semester, knows the rigors of the road and the Georgian gossip. Elizabeth Kay, too, knows Our Lady of Mount Pedernal *et alii* but also the tinker woman and much, much more. This book began in Santa Fe at Julia's in July 1961, and thanks to Liz's keen vision and astonishing midwifery it resumed there some forty years later.

Alluring New Mexico

The Great Seal of the Territory as it appears on the title page of
The Legislative Blue-Book of the Territory of New Mexico, *25th Session,*
1882, compiled by W. G. Ritch, Secretary of the Territory.

Part One
Trail: The Tourists' Shrine

Health *for the afflicted everywhere, in the pure air and water, in the equitable temperature and altitude and in the medicinal hot springs.*

Comfort *and pleasure at the many new and well appointed hotels.*

Scenery *on natures [sic] grandest scale in all parts of the Territory.*

Fishing, hunting and camp-life, *to satisfy the most ambitious, in the mountains and mountain parks.*

Antiquarians and archaeologists *can satisfy their most fastidious tastes over pre-historic ruins and the remains of the hundreds of thousands of industrial and village population of the 16th centuary [sic].*

—*The last five of twelve "Opportunities in Brief," cover of* New Mexico the Tourists' Shrine: Health, Wealth, Home, *Territorial Bureau of Immigration, 1882*

*F*ather of the Santa Fe Trail Captain William Becknell placed his fateful advertisement in the Franklin *Missouri Intelligencer* of June 25, 1821, two months before the Treaty of Córdoba was signed on August 24 and a newly independent Mexico opened its northern borders that Spain had kept closed to trade. Captain Becknell, "a noted Indian fighter and veteran of the War of 1812," sought "the enlistment of seventy men willing to join and invest in an expedition whose purpose was to trade for horses and mules and trap fur-bearing animals 'of every description.'" Six traders and their pack animals left

Franklin, Missouri, on September 1 and were welcomed in Santa Fe on November 16 with "apparent pleasure and joy" (Simmons 1996, 68, 72). The next day New Mexico's provincial governor Don Facundo Melgares received Becknell and remarked: "Well informed and gentlemanly in manners; his demeanor . . . courteous and friendly, . . . he asked many questions respecting my country, its people, their manner of living, & c.; expressed a desire that the Americans would keep up an intercourse with that country, and said that if any of them wished to emigrate, it would give him pleasure to afford them every facility" (Beachum 1982, 29).

In the summer of 1822 Becknell returned to Santa Fe with twenty men and three wagons carrying three thousand dollars in goods. He entered New Mexico via the more level Cimarron Cutoff rather than the mountainous Raton Pass through which he, his horsemen, and their pack animals had come the previous fall. Many others followed that summer and throughout the next quarter-century while Mexico controlled the western end of a trade that "within a short time . . . ballooned into a million-dollar-a-year business, pouring Mexican silver coin and raw products into the state of Missouri and precipitating a minor economic boom in what heretofore had been a depressed area on the American frontier" (Simmons and Jackson 2001, 1–2; also Hyslop 2002, 43).

Josiah Gregg chronicles this prosperous period, during which the trail was surveyed, in his two-volume *Commerce of the Prairies: Or the Journal of a Santa Fé Trader, during Eight Expeditions Across the Great Western Plains and a Residence of Nearly Nine Years in Northern Mexico*, first published in 1844. Gregg made his four round-trips and did his residencies between 1831 and 1840. On all his journeys he carried pocket notebooks to record his experiences and observations, which John Bigelow edited for publication. According to historian Paul Horgan (1979, 11), Gregg's only book "became the monument to his life, and a guide to other travelers who took to [the] Far West with the benefit of his information." It went through fourteen printings, seven of them posthumous, from presses in England, Germany, and the United States (Gregg 1954, xxxii).

On May 11, 1846, President James K. Polk asked Congress for a declaration of war against Mexico, and such was legislated on May 13. Brigadier-General Stephen Watts Kearney led the Army of the West into Santa Fe on August 18 of that year, and Acting Governor Juan Bautista Vigil y Alaríd surrendered New Mexico. The Mexican War ended when the Treaty of Guadalupe Hidalgo was signed on February 2, 1848, then ratified by the U.S. Senate on March 10 and by the Mexican Congress on May 26. The Organic Act of the Territory of New Mexico was part of the Compromise Bill passed by Congress on September 9, 1850.

Thirty years later, on February 15, 1880, the Territorial Legislature authorized the Territorial Bureau of Immigration whose "object" was "to prepare and disseminate accurate information as to the soil, climate, minerals, resources, productions and business of New

Mexico, with special reference to its opportunities for development; and the inducements and advantages which it presents to desirable immigration and for the investment of capital; to have prompt replies sent to all inquiries relative to the above subjects that may be addressed to it, and to publish and distribute such pamphlets and documents as in its judgment shall tend to promote the objects of the organization." The bureau was organized on April 15 with officers, commissioners, and an "Office in Adobe Palace [of the Governors], Santa Fe" (*Resources of New Mexico* 1973).

Two pieces by William G. Ritch, who served as Secretary of the Territory (1873–84), interim governor (1875), and secretary of the Bureau of Immigration (1880–89), anchor the October 3–8, 1881, inaugural Territorial Fair's *Resources of New Mexico: Prepared under the Auspices of the Territorial Bureau of Immigration*: a ten-page "Introductory. New Mexico. A Sketch of Its History and Review of Its Resources" and the fourth revised edition of the "Chronological Annals of New Mexico, Etc.," from 1325, when "City of Mexico founded by the Aztecs," to July 1881 (*Resources of New Mexico* 1973). These two, with the chronology extended to December 20, 1881, were appended to Ritch's *The Legislative Blue-Book of the Territory of New Mexico* for the Twenty-fifth Session in 1882, the first handbook of New Mexico government (Ritch 1968).

For the Blue-Book's cover, Ritch designed and copyrighted an embellished territorial seal. According to *The Daily* [Santa Fe] *New Mexican* of January 1, 1882:

> The design of the Great Seal of the Territory is the eagle, as represented in the coat of arms of the republic of Mexico, perched on a cactus bush, under the protective or shadowing wing of the eagle, as represented in the coat of arms of the United States, with the Latin motto '*Crescit Eundo*,' and the date 'MDCCCL,' the latter dating the organic act [of territory]. . . . In the vignette, Mr. Ritch has added a sunrise scene for a background, with an Aztec standing upon the top of his house, his hand shadowing his eyes, watching with interest for the coming of Montezuma, and which tradition has assured him he will some time, with the rising of the sun. The wreath surrounding the above scene is suggestive of the possibilities of New Mexico in viniculture and horticulture. The scenes to the right and left are mineral and pastoral, mountain and plain, and speak for themselves.

This seal appeared for a time on government and Bureau of Immigration publications, but legislation on February 1, 1887, removed the surrounding vignette and authorized only "the Mexican eagle, grasping a serpent in its beak, the cactus in its talons, shielded by the American eagle with outspread wings, and grasping arrows in its talons. The date MDCCCL under the eagles; and under that, on a scroll, the motto: *Crescit Eundo* [It grows as it goes]" (Tórrez 1993, 85–86).

From 1880 until statehood in 1912 the Territorial Bureau of Immigration produced over 126 county and state publications. Between 1880 and 1885, for example, it "issued six editions (27,000 copies) of Ritch's *Illustrated New Mexico*, a book that grew with each edition until it reached a length of nearly 250 pages," while "between April 1909 and April 1910, [it] distributed 142,000 pieces of printed matter; during the next twelve months, 183,000" (Lang 1976, 207). Bureau materials were also carried by railroads like the Chicago, Rock Island and Pacific, the Denver and Rio Grande, and the Atchison, Topeka and Santa Fe, with the latter sometimes using excerpts from bureau publications in its own extensive promotional literature (Dye 2005, 18, 21–22).

By the twentieth century, according to historian John M. Nieto-Phillips (2004, 119, 120), the Bureau of Immigration "had succeeded in creating among Anglo Americans outside New Mexico a popular image of Pueblo Indians as docile, sedentary, and semicivilized, and Nuevomexicano villagers as descendants of the conquistadores," thereby making "the territory more alluring to tourists and migrants." Depicting a place "wherein peace-loving Pueblo Indians and noble Spaniards had coexisted for centuries . . . catered to American tourists' search for the primitive while assuaging their concerns for their safety":

> Very early in the bureau's existence, its visionaries had come to comprehend tourism—the temporary visitation of New Mexico's places and peoples—as a profitable industry unto itself. Tourists, like migrants, had material needs. They were consumers, with an appetite for ethnic cultures. The railway allowed individuals—at least those who could afford a ticket—the freedom of travel, and it initiated an era of migration and leisure travel that grew steadily into the twentieth century. New Mexico's Bureau of Immigration merely sought to capture as much westward traffic as possible, hoping to persuade visitors to plant themselves and buy land in the territory. One 1883 Las Vegas Hot Springs brochure summarized this new recreation, saying, "Among the principal objects of tourist travel are health, rest, [and] recreation . . . but the chief aim of the tourist is to see something new, interesting and instructive."

1
Birthplace of Montezuma

TRADITION/ A written record of which is to be found in some of the pueblos, is that Pecos pueblo was the birth-place of Montezuma; that after he had grown to man's estate he showed himself possessed of supernatural powers; that he at a certain time assembled a large number of his people and started from New Mexico on a journey south, Montezuma riding on the back of an eagle; and thus riding in advance, was to his people, as was the star to the wise men of the East. Wherever the eagle stopped at night there was planted an Indian pueblo. The sign of arriving at the site of the great city and capital of the Aztec nation was to be the 'alighting of the eagle upon a cactus bush and devouring a serpent.' This event took place when the eagle arrived at the site of the present city of Mexico, then first made a city and capital.

—William G. Ritch, "Introductory. New Mexico. A Sketch of Its History and Review of Its Resources," appended to the Legislative Blue-Book *for the Twenty-fifth Session of the Territorial Legislature, 1882*

In addition to the prehistoric wonders of the eight National Monuments and the natural wonders of the eighteen Indian Pueblos, the tourist will see the deserted Indian Pueblo of Pecos, 23 miles southeast of Santa Fe. When Christopher Columbus discovered America, Pecos was the largest city on the continent. It was founded about 800 A.D., and contains the world's biggest apartment house, having from 1,500 to 2,000 rooms and in its prime housed 2,500 people or more. Each year new discoveries throw the time of this historic city back a few centuries, and it is believed that it may have existed during the days of Christ.

—New Mexico Today and Tomorrow, *Bureau of Publicity booklet, 1925*

7he Aztec ruler Montezuma was "born" along the Santa Fe Trail at Pecos Pueblo, some twenty-five miles southeast of Santa Fe. In his 1844 *Commerce of the Prairies* Josiah Gregg (1954, 188, 189) reports: "What with the massacres of the second conquest, and the inroads of the Comanches, they [the Pecos] gradually dwindled away, till they found themselves reduced to about a dozen, comprising all ages and sexes; and it was only a few years ago [1838] that they abandoned the home of their fathers and joined the Pueblo of Jemez." Gregg then recounts "a tradition that was prevalent among them" about Montezuma's "holy fire" and vouches for his "curious" tale: "I have myself descended into the famous *estufas*, or subterranean vaults, of which there were several in the village, and have beheld this consecrated fire, silently smoldering under a covering of ashes, in the basin of a small altar." Archaeologist Frances Levine (1999, 28) calls Gregg's account "a staple of Santa Fe Trail travelers": "The story, embellished to astonishing lengths by some and abbreviated to its essentials by others, claims that the Pecos were obliged to keep huge sacred fires burning in their kivas, and their labors in keeping an adequate wood supply and stoking the fires, compounded by the struggle of breathing the noxious fumes, caused their demise."

In September 1839, the year following the abandonment of Pecos, "the irrepressible Matthew [Matt] C. Field, actor, journalist, and rover, spent the night with Dr. David C. Waldo in the Pecos church" and wrote an article about the "dilapidated town called *Pécus*" for the New Orleans *Picayune*. An old man fed them "a supper of hot porridge made of pounded corn and goat's milk, which we drank with a shell spoon from a bowl of wood, sitting upon the ground at the foot of the ruined altar by the light of a few dimly burning sticks of pine." The old man told of a summertime "pestilential disorder" that left only three people to tend the Sacred Fire—a chief, his daughter, and her betrothed. The chief died. Just before the couple died the young man took a brand from the fire and led his betrothed outside the cave. "A light then rose in the sky which was not the light of morning, but the heavens were red with the flames that roared and crackled up the mountain side. And the lovers lay in each other's arms, kissing death from each other's lips, and smiling to see the fire of Montezuma mounting up to heaven."

He told it in glowing words and with a rapt intensity which the writer has endeavored to imitate, but he feels that the attempt is a failure. The scene itself—the ruined church—the feeble old man bending over the ashes, and the strange tones of his thin voice in the dreary midnight—all are necessary to awaken such interest as was felt by the listeners. Such is the story, however, and there is no doubt but that the legend has a strong foundation, in truth; for there stands the ruined town, well known to the Santa Fe traders, and there lives the old man, tending his goats

*Cochiti Pueblo pottery called "Rare Specimens Ancient Montezuma Pottery," for sale
by L. Fisher, ca. 1881. Photo by Ben Wittick.
(Museum of New Mexico Neg. No. 16296)*

on the hill side during the day, and driving them into the church at night.... It
was imperative upon us to leave the place before day light that we might reach our
destination (San Miguel) early the next morning, so that we could not gratify our
curiosity by descending the cavern ourselves, but we gave the old man a few bits
of silver, and telling him that the story with which he had entertained us should
be told again in the great United States, we each pocketed a cinder of the sacred
fire and departed. (in Kessell 1979, 459, 461, 462)

This "Montezuma Legend" figured in early Territorial Bureau of Immigration literature, according to historian John M. Nieto-Phillips (2004, 122, 123):

Between 1880 and 1885, William Gillette Ritch ... authored a series of publications, with titles such as *Illustrated New Mexico: Historical and Industrial* (which went through five editions) and *Santa Fé: Ancient and Modern, Including Its Resources and Industries*. "The Territory of New Mexico," wrote Ritch in the former work, "is anomalous, in that it is the seat of the antipodes of civilizations upon the continent." In this land, "modern energy, enterprise and prosperity, with the coming of steam transportation ... has here peaceably met, face to face, mediaeval conservatism, and the crooked stick plows and industrial methods of the Ptolemies." According to Ritch, New Mexico was the meeting ground for the modern Americans, the descendants of "the old Latin civilization" and the "native [Pueblo Indian] races." It was precisely this convergence that made New Mexico unique in all the United States, he claimed.

Ritch "insisted" that Santa Fe "was the very birthplace of the great Aztec Empire [and] between 1880 and 1885, virtually all of the bureau's publications alluded to Ritch's Montezuma Legend, and to Santa Fe as the birthplace of Aztec civilization."

In 1885, Ritch went so far as to change the name of his most popular publication from *Illustrated New Mexico* to *Aztlán: The History, Resources and Attractions of New Mexico*. Besides embellishing the material and climatic wonders of New Mexico, Ritch recounted the then-famous Montezuma Legend, which gained notoriety in the 1870s and 1880s. It fixed the birthplace of Montezuma I, founder of Tenochtitlán, or contemporary Mexico City, in the city of Santa Fe or nearby Pecos Pueblo. As recounted by Ritch, Montezuma I was said to have been born into poverty in the vicinity of Santa Fe. Endowed with a magical rattle, he blessed hunters with special powers, garnering for himself status and fame, and eventually power as the monarch of the Pueblo people. One day, as prophesied by the Great Spirit, an eagle appeared before Montezuma. On mounting it, he flew off into the horizon, trailed by a procession of followers. In AD 1325, after stopping several times and establishing many settlements, Montezuma arrived at Lake Tenochtitlán, the promised destination, and here founded the great Aztec civilization that later [1519–21] was defeated by the Spaniard Hernán Cortes.

The Swiss-American archaeologist/ethnologist Adolph F. Bandelier, "pondering Montezuma's alleged birth at Pecos and his vow to return, ... ascribed the tale to 'an evident mixture of a name with the Christian faith in a personal redeemer, and dim recollections of Coronado's presence and promise to return'" (Kessell 1979, 472). In September 1880

Bandelier did fieldwork at Pecos, which he (in Kessell 1979, 476) reports first glimpsing from the train:

> ... to the left, the towering Mesa de Pecos, dark pines clambering up its steep sides; to the right, the broad valley, scooped out, so to say, between the *mesa* and the Tecolote ridge. It is dotted with green patches and black clusters of cedar and pine shooting out of the red and rocky soil. Scarcely a house is visible, for the *casitas* of adobe and wood nestle mostly in sheltered nooks. Beyond Baughl's [siding], the ruins first strike his [the tourist's] view; the red walls of the church stand boldly out on the barren *mesilla*; and to the north of it there are two low brown ridges, the remnants of the Indian houses.

Historian John Kessell adds that "to alert the less observant tourist, the Santa Fe Railway Company later erected on the north side of the tracks opposite the ruins an immense signboard proclaiming Pecos a wonder of the Southwest."

The Atchison, Topeka and Santa Fe Railroad and the Fred Harvey Company drew on Pecos in naming their luxury hotel and hot springs spa near Las Vegas the Montezuma. Miguel Antonio Otero, then former territorial delegate to Congress and acting vice president of the Santa Fe and later territorial governor of New Mexico, "alluded to the railroad as the reincarnation of Montezuma" when he addressed "a crowd of dignitaries and tourists" at its opening on April 17, 1882 (Nieto-Phillips 2004, 124):

> The [nearby] Pecos Indians ... implicitly believed that their mighty ill-fated emperor, the glorious Montezuma, disappeared from view amid the clouds of their native mountains, that he promised to return ... [and] that he would come in glory from the east.... The last remnant of the faithful old tribe has disappeared ... but we who fill their places, have lived to see the return of the mighty chieftain.... [T]onight we hail his coming in the new and splendid halls of the Montezuma!

On May 15, 1926, the Santa Fe/Harvey Indian Detour began operating guided automobile tours between their station-platform hotels, the Castañeda at Las Vegas and the Alvarado at Albuquerque, via La Fonda on the Santa Fe Plaza. The December 1927 *Indian-detour Santa Fe Harveycars* booklet describes the group's journey from Las Vegas to Santa Fe, "seventy-five miles to the westward along the historic Santa Fé Trail. Our route is that of pack train and covered wagon, of pony riders and Indian fighters; of the first overland mail, in '49, and of the swaying Concord coaches that in the early '60s made the run from Independence, Missouri, to Santa Fé, in two to three weeks and for a fare of $150." Pecos Ruins at Cicuyé follow views of Kearney's Gap, Starvation Peak, and the "Spanish-American" villages of Tecolote and San José:

"Ruins of the Ancient Pecos Mission." The drivers of two Indian-detour Harveycars
await the Courier-guided groups touring the mission.
Indian-detour *booklet, October 1929.*

By 11.30 we reach Cicuyé, to spend a full hour among the partly excavated ruins of a great pueblo continuously inhabited for 1,200 years. Here the Spaniards found the largest settlement in New Mexico, a community of five plazas, sixteen kivas and 2,000 inhabitants. Succeeding centuries, however, brought the ravages of siege, battle and pestilence; of bloody struggles with the Conquerors and truceless war with the Comanches. Cicuyé's doom was sealed with the final ambush and massacre of its man-power by the latter and the ancient pueblo was abandoned by the pitiful remnant of its people in 1838.

Near by stand the massive walls of the old Spanish church, built before the Landing of the Pilgrims. In the martyrdom of its priests it, too, has chapters penned in blood. Partly destroyed in the Pueblo Rebellion of 1680, the church was repaired in later years, only to be itself abandoned in 1792.

Luncheon draws us to the wide comfort of Apache Inn, at Valley Ranch, the open gate to the famous game country of the Upper Pecos. This is an all-year tourist ranch, with opportunities for horseback rides and hill-climbing as well as trout fishing. The modern village of Pecos is on the way to Apache Inn.

By December 1927 Santa Fe Railway passengers could disembark at Rowe, a few miles from the "Pecos Ruins," and stay at Tex Austin's Forked Lightning Ranch, which was both a "tourist" and a working ranch near the pueblo. According to *The Forked Lightning Ranch: Tex's "Dudes" to Texas Cattle*, a December 2005 Pecos National Historical Park brochure, rodeo producer Tex Austin had changed his name from Clarence Van Nostrand to John "Tex" Van Austin when he left his St. Louis home in 1908 to work on New Mexico and Texas ranches.

> From his first rodeo in El Paso in 1917 to his last in London, England, in 1934, Tex was known for his generosity and showmanship. When he produced the first Madison Square Garden Rodeo in 1922, the prize money was a record $25,000.
>
> Tex had other "firsts": First recorded indoor rodeo in Wichita, Kansas (1918); first rodeo ever held in Chicago Stadium (1926); and the first contest rodeo to go overseas. Some 114,000 people attended his 1924 rodeo in London's Wembley Stadium.

Known as the "Daddy of Rodeo," Austin was named to the Rodeo Hall of Fame at the National Cowboy and Western Heritage Museum in Oklahoma City in 1976.

Austin purchased "parcels of land on the old Pecos Pueblo Grant" in 1925 and named "his 5,500 acre holdings The Forked Lightning Ranch." It included "the remains of Kozlowski's Stage Stop and Tavern on the Santa Fe Trail (1858–1880) ..., which Tex converted into ranch headquarters and a trading post." According to historian Marc Simmons and geographer Hal Jackson (2001, 211–12):

> Martin Kozlowski, a Polish immigrant, entered New Mexico after 1846. Later he acquired this site on the SFT and constructed ranch buildings using materials scavenged from the ruined Pecos mission and Indian pueblo 1 mile away. Meals provided to stage passengers by his wife, including fresh trout from the Pecos River, were said to be the best on the western end of the trail.

In October 1925 (Bunting 1983, 160) Austin hired Santa Fe architect John Gaw Meem to design and build the main ranch house. The park brochure describes it as rectangular, with all the rooms facing "a grassy patio" and "its defining touch ... a huge, specially sculpted steer head mounted outside on the chimney." In his advertising he called it "the most complete, modern and comfortable ranch house in the West," which "was less than two days by train from Chicago: 'Thirty-four hours, and you're out where the West is—and will be for some time.'" Each of the eighteen guests sharing the nine bedrooms paid $125 per week and received "all proper service ... to insure the comfort and friendly atmosphere of a country home." The venture lasted only seven years; "the last guests left in May 1933." Austin's rodeo ventures also began to fail, and he sold the ranch to W. C. Currier in 1936 and moved to Santa Fe. There he "opened the Los Rancheros Restaurant near the Plaza" and in October 1938 committed suicide. "Rumor at the time was he had been told he was going blind." In 1941 W. C. Currier sold the Forked Lightning Ranch "to E[lijah] E. 'Buddy' Fogelson, a Dallas oil man and rancher. Over the next 25 years, [Col.] Fogelson purchased land to the south, expanding the ranch to 13,000 acres. The Forked Lightning became a small cattle ranch and Tex's ranch house the Fogelson summer home. After Fogelson married the actress Greer Garson in 1949, the ranch house became a center for gracious entertaining." Journalist Keith Easthouse (in the *Santa Fe New Mexican*, June 28, 1998; also Troyan 1999) begins an article on the National Park Service's renovation of the ranch house: "What do J. Edgar Hoover, Gregory Peck, Charles Lindbergh and Art Linkletter have in common? They all stayed at the Forked Lightning ranch near the village of Pecos. To be more specific, those luminaries slept at the ranch's centerpiece—a 72-year-old John Gaw Meem hacienda-style structure that still stands on a majestic bluff above the confluence of Glorieta Creek and the Pecos River."

Pecos Pueblo and mission was proclaimed a state monument on February 20, 1935. Authorized as a national monument on June 28, 1965, it was transferred to the National Park Service on December 13 of that year. (It was redesignated Pecos National Historical Park on June 27, 1990.) The Fogelsons played a crucial role in the development of the national monument, according to Secretary of the Interior Donald P. Hodel (in Bezy and Sanchez 1988, 10–11):

In June 1965, the pueblo and mission of Pecos were designated as a national monument, culminating a thirty-year effort by the Fogelsons to obtain Federal protection for the site. In 1964, they donated 279 acres from their Forked Lightning Ranch to form a buffer zone around the original sixty-two acres of the ruins. This zone excludes any commercial activity in the area, and benefits each visitor who walks the ruins trail and experiences being part of this historic and natural scene.

Fifteen years later they donated an additional twenty-three acres including the Forked Lightning Ruin, which dates back to A.D. 1150 and is a vital link in the occupational chain of the Pecos Valley. In 1981 their hard work and generosity were finally recognized when they were awarded the Conservation Service Award—the highest honor bestowed by the Department of the Interior.

The Fogelsons had long dreamed of building a visitor center and museum at the site of the ruins on their ranch. The Department of the Interior under President Ronald Reagan's administration welcomed the idea as an opportunity for Government and private citizens to cooperate in a civic project, and in 1984 Secretary William Clark dedicated the E. E. Fogelson Visitor Center, which provides an interpretive facility that will be enjoyed for countless generations to come.

*Pecos National Historical Park souvenir patch in cellophane wrapper
with "Made in China" sticker. The text on the back reads: "For centuries Pecos
Pueblo dominated the pass linking the Rio Grande Valley with the Great Plains, a
thoroughfare for hunters, traders, soldiers, and settlers. Ruins of the pueblo and its
Spanish missions are preserved at Pecos National Historical Park in New Mexico."
Purchased by the author for two dollars on March 12, 2001, at the Fogelson Visitor
Center. The National Park Service employee selling it called the figure in the sky,
taken from a pot excavated on the site, "El Capitan," considered "the mascot"
of park operations. The pot was on display in the center's museum with
a bilingual label: "Pecos tradition continued through Spanish times as can be seen
by the serpent figure on this Glaze V [1600–1700] bowl." A photo
of the bowl (in Bezy and Sanchez 1988, 39) is captioned: "The distinctive 'Awanyu,'
thought to be a feathered serpent, was a popular design found on Pecos pottery for
hundreds of years."*

The plaque at the entrance reads: THE NATIONAL PARK SERVICE/ GRATEFULLY
ACKNOWLEDGES/ THE GENEROUS SUPPORT OF/ COLONEL E. E./ AND/ MRS.
GREER GARSON FOGELSON,/ WHO HAVE GIVEN THE SURROUNDING LANDS/
AND CONTINUING ASSISTANCE TO/ PECOS NATIONAL MONUMENT.

After Colonel Fogelson's death in 1987, according to the 2005 National Park Service brochure, "the Forked Lightning was divided along the old southern boundary line of Tex's original Forked Lightning. Greer Garson Fogelson received the 'old' Forked Lightning Ranch and Mr. Fogelson's son [Gayle] inherited the southern portion." Both became the focus of a land development brouhaha in the winter of 1990.

The story was broken by the weekly *Santa Fe Reporter* in its "Happy Holidays!" issue of December 20–26, 1989: "Developers Seek Greer Garson Ranch for Huge Resort City Near Pecos." Capital Developers International, Inc., of Orlando, Florida, headed by Greek developer Jerassimos Crassas, was negotiating with Garson's representatives for a complex to be known as Santa Fe East 2001. A spread of 11,892 acres (including Los Trigos Ranch, owned by Fogelson's son Gayle), it was to encompass an airstrip, a 300-room hotel on 92 acres, ranch-size and "higher density" residential housing on 7,234 acres, "extended stay" cabins on 480 acres, an athletic center on 729 acres, a convention center on 160 acres, a hunting preserve on 1,776 acres, a health clinic on 100 acres, two 18-hole golf courses on 448 acres, and a shopping center called "World's Fair Today" and featuring "goods and commodities from around the world" on 454 acres.

Crassas, interviewed for the *Santa Fe Reporter* of January 3–9, 1990, claimed to be trying only to "ease the pressure of growth in Santa Fe." His envisioned "satellite town" was "the wave of the future" in "this type of development." He is quoted as saying: "What we are trying to do here . . . is to try to be instrumental in keeping the atmosphere of Santa Fe by taking the pressure of growth out. Creating a satellite city a little elsewhere without disturbing the picture, *per se*, of Santa Fe." His purported concern provoked outrage, however. Local sentiment was captured in a cartoon by Jon Richards (in the *Santa Fe Reporter*, January 17–23, 1990). Entitled "The Last Picture Show," it depicts a poster for what is "coming soon" to the Pecos Cinema: "Santa Fe East 2001: a wide-open spaces odyssey starring Greer Garson and Jerry Crassas, a terrifying vision of the future!"

That particular future was not actualized. The same issue of the *Reporter* carried an announcement: "Crassas, a Greek citizen, also has been convicted of crimes in Greece 48 times, according to Greek law enforcement authorities. And he is listed in federal computers as 'excludable' from the United States, a designation reserved for aliens deemed undesirable and possibly subject to deportation proceedings." Columnist Robert Mayer concluded: "Our local Greek tragedy has run its course. The deal for the Forked Lightning Ranch most certainly is dead; Greer Garson has never been a woman who consorts with gentlemen wanted by the police." Nevertheless, the *Albuquerque Journal North* of February 7, 1990, reported that Crassas was planning a similar project near Washington, D.C., claiming that, despite losing the Pecos opportunity, "one of our interests is to buy a hotel within Santa Fe proper . . . so we don't have to face any laws or environmental problems or opinions of the neighborhoods. An existing business might suit us better." In January 1991 Greer Garson Fogelson sold her Forked Lightning Ranch to The Conservation Fund, which in turn donated it to the National Park Service to become part of Pecos National Historical Park.

Key, pioneering archaeological work that led to Pecos becoming a state and later national monument was done by Alfred V. Kidder beginning in 1915, when trustees of the Phillips Academy, Andover, Massachusetts, "resolved to excavate a site in the Pueblo area 'large enough, and of sufficient scientific importance, to justify work upon it for a number of years'" (Kessell 1979, 480–81).

In the course of ten summers at Pecos between 1915 and 1929, two events broadcast the coming of age of American archaeology. The first was the publication in 1924 of Kidder's *An Introduction to the Study of Southwestern Archaeology, with a Preliminary Account of the Excavations at Pecos*, which has been called "the first detailed synthesis of the archaeology of any part of the New World." The second, in August 1929, was an informal, precedent-setting reunion of Southwestern field researchers at what became known as the "Pecos Conference." Here, at Kidder's invitation, he and his colleagues reached fundamental agreement on cultural sequence in the prehistoric Southwest, definitions of stages in that sequence, and standardization in naming pottery types. When the fiftieth anniversary Pecos Conference convened in 1977, there was high praise for Alfred Vincent Kidder, who in pursuit of his vision made Pecos the most studied and reported upon archaeological site in the United States.

Archaeologist James E. Snead (2001, xvi) begins his *Ruins and Rivals: The Making of Southwest Archaeology* at Pecos National Historical Park, where tourists can "stroll the concrete pathways maintained by the National Park Service, and find themselves viewing a powerful symbol of the heritage and identity of the Southwest."

Less than a mile from the mission, still within the monument's boundaries, is another ancient pueblo, its adobe walls leveled and made nearly invisible by centuries of wind and rain. Parked in a grove of juniper and piñon pine at the center of this ruin is the wreck of a Model-T Ford once owned by the archaeologist A. V. Kidder. Left behind after a summer's excavations in the 1920s the pickup sits, gradually flaking into rust. Amidst a scatter of potsherds nearby and obscured by grass, a flat plaque marks the graves of Kidder and his wife Madeleine. Interred [on October 21, 1981,] at Forked Lightning Ruin the Kidders, along with the truck they once called "Old Blue," are now inextricably bound up with Pecos and its past, part of the archaeological record they devoted their lives to revealing. The symbolism of Pecos, its public monuments and the hidden record of its exploration, captures the complex relationship between archaeology, society, and identity in the American Southwest.

Ruins are as central to the modern image of the Southwest as are its mountains and deserts. Chaco Canyon, Mesa Verde, Bandelier, Hovenweep, Casa Grande, Montezuma Castle, and other relics of the past appear on calendars and coffee mugs and are major tourist destinations. The combination of stark landscapes and tangible reminders of a prehistoric past form visual touchstones of great power.

2
Land without Law

Captain Aubry approached our tent and told us that we were now [1852] in New Mexico territory. "This is the place," he said, "where only the brave and the criminal come. It is called 'The Land without Law.'"

— Mrs. Hal Russell, "Memoirs of Marian [Sloan] Russell," 1943

The Territory of New Mexico, in the mid-1870–80s, experienced a wave of rampant lawlessness, unparalleled in the history of the United States. One must walk a mile in their shoes before coming to conclusions about the lives of men and boys of that era.

Henry McCarty, alias Kid Antrim, alias William H. Bonney, alias Billy The Kid, born in the east, came to New Mexico in the 1870's and started out on his own from Silver City. Go where you will over the trails he rode, and you will agree, he is alive today.

In Lincoln, he became involved in the famous Lincoln County War. This was a time of political strife and financial power struggles. In most cases, one must kill or be killed....

...[In] Old Fort Sumner..., on July 14, 1881, Pat Garrett, in the Maxwell house, killed the famous Outlaw. In the old fort cemetery a vagrant wind whisks across the plain, a tiny dust devil will spin for a moment madly, futilely, and is swallowed up in nothingness. This was the life of the Kid, and certainly, he is buried there, in Old Fort Sumner.

— Billy the Kid Pat Garrett Trail, *Billy the Kid Outlaw Gang brochure, Taiban, New Mexico, 1989 ("Our purpose is to preserve, protect and promote Billy The Kid/Pat Garrett history in New Mexico.")*

*I*n 1852, as a child of seven, Marian Sloan accompanied her mother Eliza St. Clair Sloan and older brother William Hill Sloan on the first of five trips over the Santa Fe Trail. Normally the journey would have cost them $500 ($250 for adults and half-price for each child), but they traveled without charge as far as Fort Union, New Mexico, because Eliza Sloan agreed to cook for three young army officers in the government train that joined theirs for safety. Their caravan was led by famed, Canadian-born Santa Fe Trail freighter and explorer François (Francis) Xavier Aubry, who befriended the children, making them "promise him never to stray too far from the camp [so] gradually we came to know that everyone was torn between joy at making the great overland trip and terror of the Indians" (Russell 1943, 88; epigraph quote, 95).

The Sloans' caravan entered New Mexico via the Cimarron Cutoff in the vicinity of what today is Clayton thirty years after William Becknell made his second trip to Santa Fe with twenty men, three wagons, and three thousand dollars in goods. In 1930 "the Colorado & Southern Railway built a large marker three miles south of Grenville to show where the first wagon trains came over the Old Santa Fe Trail in 1822, crossing the strip on which its track was to be laid nearly a hundred years afterward. [Such] century-old ruts, worn by ox-drawn covered wagons, are visible today in Union county [and] can be followed from Moses in the northeastern corner of the county along past the Rabbit Ear mountains to the Colfax county line" ("Marking the Old Trails" 1931, 34; also Simmons and Jackson 2001, 181). The bronze plaque in a white obelisk trackside reads: "FIRST WAGONS USED ON/ SANTA FE TRAIL/ CROSSED HERE IN 1822/ ERECTED BY/ COLORADO & SOUTHERN/ RAILWAY/ J. D. WALKER, SUPT. – ROBT. RICE, V.P. & G.M./ 1930."

The Becknell monument is found on a highway pull-off with a single, covered picnic table along U.S. 64/U.S. 87 some twenty-three miles west of Clayton. From this vantage Round Mound (Mount Clayton), a tourist spot for Santa Fe Trail travelers, is visible directly to the south and slightly west. Josiah Gregg (1954, 68, 69, 71) recalls how in July 1831

> we were now approaching the 'Round Mound', a beautiful round-topped cone, rising nearly a thousand feet above the level of the plain by which it is for the most part surrounded. We were yet at least three miles from this mound, when a party set out on foot to ascend it, in order to get a view of the surrounding country. They felt confident it was but half a mile off – at most, three-quarters; but finding the distance so much greater than they had anticipated, many began to lag behind, and soon rejoined the wagons.... At last, some of the most persevering of our adventurers succeeded in ascending the summit of the Round Mound, which commands a full and advantageous view of the surrounding country, in some directions to the distance of a hundred miles or more.

"American Pioneers Followed the Flag to . . . ," Santa Fe Trail ruts and Fort Union.
Trail text reads: "No less fascinating than the history of the Spanish and Mexican
periods is the record of American frontier days in New Mexico. As early as 1821,
when New Mexico was still a Mexican province, the great wagons of sturdy American
traders rolled westward over the famous Santa Fe Trail, some climbing over Raton
Pass and then either heading straight for Santa Fe, or swinging up beautiful Cimar-
ron Canyon toward Taos. Others used the route that entered New Mexico near the
present town of Clayton. Traces of the old Butterfield Stage route which, about 1858,
made the trip from St. Louis to California in twenty-five days, may still be found in
Southern New Mexico. A full-color map, locating the early Spanish and American
Trails, is supplied free by the State Tourist Bureau, Santa Fe." New Mexico "Land of
Enchantment," *State Tourist Bureau booklet, 1941.*

If the modest prominence of Round Mound were indeed "nearly a thousand feet above the
level of the plain" it would loom almost as high as Shiprock. Still, it afforded a valued
panorama of "hills, plains, mounds, and sandy undulations" and, to the northwest, "low
on the horizon a silvery stripe . . . upon an azure base, resembling a list of chalk-white
clouds . . . , the perennially snowcapped summit of the eastern spur of the Rocky Mountains." Tourists like those in Gregg's party could also overlook their fellow travelers: "As

the caravan was passing under the northern base of the Round Mound, it presented a very fine and imposing spectacle to those who were upon its summit" and could hear "the unceasing 'crack, crack,' of the wagoners' whips, resembling the frequent reports of distant guns, almost [making] one believe that a skirmish was actually taking place between two hostile parties."

Round Mound was renamed Mount Clayton in 1887 and the townsite near Apache Spring so named in 1888. *Clayton New Mexico: In the Heart of Dinosaur Country*, an undated, eight-panel Clayton/Union County Chamber of Commerce brochure from the late 1980s, proclaims "a vast and colorful history" that begins with "Dinosaur Tracks":

> The dinosaur tracks visible on the spillway of Clayton Lake [created by the State Game and Fish Commission when building a dam in 1955 and made a state park in 1967], a short distance from the parking area, were first discovered in 1982. More than 500 tracks have been identified. At least two sets of tracks are quite exceptional. One is a set of handprints from a flying creature known as a Pterodactyl. Another is a set of prints left by a web-footed dinosaur as yet unnamed.

The town is also touted as a place where Coronado searched for the Seven Cities of Gold in 1540, "the Cimarron Cutoff of the Santa Fe Trail—the oldest regular land route across the Great Plains—bisected Clayton," and where "Black Jack Ketchum, one of the last old-fashioned train robbers, who was hanged in Clayton in 1901," is buried.

In his account of cowboy-turned-train-robber Thomas "Black Jack" Ketchum historian Marc Simmons (1990, 43, 44–45) notes that "Clayton in the far northeastern corner of New Mexico possesses little in the way of tourist attractions" except the train robber's grave "located in the center of the municipal cemetery." In August 1899 Ketchum bungled an attempt to rob a Colorado & Southern Railway train south of Folsom and was shot in the right arm. Ketchum was eventually held at the penitentiary in Santa Fe, where his arm was amputated. After various trials, appeals, and postponements he was executed in Clayton on April 26, 1901.

> Without a doubt the hanging of Black Jack in 1901 was the most celebrated event in Clayton's history. A photographer [from John Wheatley Studio] was on hand for the occasion and made a series of startling pictures.
>
> Copies of these pictures are on display today in the bar of Clayton's Eklund Hotel. They have been published many times in popular outlaw books. The most grisly of the lot shows the body of the outlaw with his head cradled under his arm.
>
> You see, no one in Clayton had ever performed a hanging before, and several mistakes were made.... The result was that when he hit the end of the rope, he was decapitated....

THE BLACK JACK STORY

A cowboy who went wrong

The Black Jack Story: A Cowboy Who Went Wrong, compiled by Sue Richardson, n.d. (purchased by the author at the Herzstein Memorial Museum, Clayton, August 12, 2004). The front cover shows one of the copyrighted John Wheatley Studio photos of the April 26, 1901, hanging of Thomas "Black Jack" Ketchum. The back cover shows the outlaw's then unmarked grave in the middle of Clayton Memorial Cemetery. According to Richardson, when Ketchum's remains were disinterred on September 10, 1933, "the coffin was opened and [his] body was found to be well preserved. [Clayton's Col.] Jack Potter, who had known Tom during his trail drive days, placed flowers in the casket with a card that read, 'to a cowboy who went wrong.'"

After time was allowed for local folk to pose with the headless corpse and have their pictures made, the undertaker was brought in to put things right. He sewed the head to the torso and the body was placed in a pine box. Burial followed in Boot Hill on the outskirts of town, where the less desirable were banished.

Simmons (1990, 46) "learned in Clayton" that "Ketchum's coffin was dug up in 1933 and moved to the new town cemetery." There, "for many years" it "was left unmarked." However, "not long ago a new headstone was installed, so now visitors can easily find it." That Clayton Memorial Cemetery headstone (photographed in August 2004) reads: THOMAS EDWARD "BLACK JACK" KETCHUM/ OCT. 31, 1863 APR 26, 1901/ AND HOW HIS AUDIT/ STANDS WHO KNOWS/ SAVE HEAVEN WILLIAM SHAKESPEARE.

Clayton's dinosaur prehistory and its outlaw history clashed for the hundredth anniversary of Ketchum's death. A headline on the front page of the February 25, 2001, *Albuquerque Journal* announces: "Dead Outlaw Trumps Dino," with the subtitle: "Town of Clayton plans to abandon festival for long-vanished iguanodon in favor of one for notorious and poorly hanged train robber." Staff writer Fritz Thompson reports that the Union County Historical Society, the Clayton-Union County Chamber of Commerce, and a retail merchants committee "earlier this year" decided to abandon the annual June Dinosaur Days, begun in 1989, and inaugurate the Black Jack Ketchum Festival in the centennial year of the outlaw's hanging. Mindful of the lucrativeness of celebrating outlaws like Billy the Kid and eager "to court more business and to entice visitors into staying longer," they "recommended for a $1,400 appropriation by the Clayton Lodgers Tax Committee," began application for a $2,000 grant from the New Mexico Endowment for the Humanities, and started looking for private donations. Thompson claims that "it's figured that the botched hanging will be a bigger drawing card for Clayton than the iguanodons' footprints ever were." He also denies that the hanging itself was a tourist event: "Contrary to some inflated claims, tickets were not sold, vendors did not hawk garroted dolls hanging from a stick, Ketchum's head did not fly over the crowd and land in the street, and his head is not preserved in a jar somewhere. His body—all of it [though minus the right arm]—is buried in Clayton Memorial Cemetery."

The events of September 11 caused organizers of the first festival to reconsider the celebration, and by 2004 they had abandoned Black Jack for "Dinosaur Daze / Community Fun Day" on the first Saturday in June. Nevertheless, when journalist Toby Smith (in *Albuquerque Journal*, August 15, 2004) went "Off the Beaten Path" to Clayton that August, he "toured the Herzstein Memorial Museum and met one of Clayton's nonpareils, D. Ray Blakeley":

> With his brambly-wild gray beard and great sense for the dramatic, Blakeley resembles a 19th-century stage actor. A Clayton native, he reported for the weekly Union County Leader for ages, and these days runs the museum....
>
> Much of the museum is a repository for items gathered from area attics, including a stuffed salmon caught in Alaska by a Claytonite. As might be expected, the museum has renderings of Rabbit Ear Mountain and sepia-colored shots of Black Jack's final moments on the gallows.
>
> "Not everyone around here enjoys seeing a reprobate glorified," D. Ray lectured. "But you see, Black Jack attracts visitors. He's surely done for us what that worthless punk Billy the Kid has done for Fort Sumner."

The first report of a Billy the Kid grave marker in Fort Sumner is from the *Las Vegas Daily Optic* of January 16, 1882: "To the southwest of the abandoned and decaying Fort Sumner lies the graveyard, surrounded by what was once a good adobe wall, but from decay and neglect is now merely an outline, surrounding an acre of ground. We enter on the north, walking over the remains of the once handsome gate.... To the right of the entrance lies the grave of Billy the Kid, marked by a plain board, with the stenciled letters: 'BILLY/ THE/ KID'" (in Simmons 2006, 175). According to Marc Simmons (2006, 151, 161, 164), "by the end of the nineteenth century, the historic cemetery was without markers of any kind," and Billy's grave remained so until 1931:

> In that year, a large stone block incised with the names of Tom O'Folliard, William H. Bonney, and Charlie Bowdre, including the death dates of each [O'Folliard and Bowdre, Dec. 1880; Bonney, July 1881], was placed over their communal burial.

"...in the Days when the West was Young," Billy the Kid "Pals" monument, Fort Sumner, and Kit Carson House, Taos. The text reads: "At Lincoln town, former seat of Lincoln County, is the very courthouse from which Billy the Kid, famous outlaw and leader in the Lincoln County Cattle War, who had been tried at Old Mesilla, escaped after killing his guards. His grave is at Ft. Sumner. It was to Ft. Sumner that Kit Carson took the captured Navajo nation after conquering them in the campaign of 1863. (They were allowed to return to their reservation in 1868.) Kit Carson's former home and burial place are at Taos." New Mexico "Land of Enchantment," State Tourist Bureau booklet, 1941.

A one-word heading at the top read simply, "Pals." This monument represents the first substantial effort to permanently mark the site....

Almost at once the monument came under the assault of souvenir hunters. "Chunks from fist size down to small pebbles have been knocked off the sides and top of the granite marker," lamented the *Fort Sumner Leader* on October 14, 1932. Unless a Society for the Prevention of Damage to Desperado Graves can be formed soon, it editorialized, the monument will have to be replaced within a year. Protection was soon provided by surrounding the grave-site with a nine foot high chain link fence.

The "Pals" monument is set in the middle of the three graves. In March 1940, with "cooperation" from the Fort Sumner Chamber of Commerce, the Warner tombstone was set in place inside the fence atop Billy's grave alone. Carved by James N. Warner of Salida, Colorado, "an accomplished stone cutter and proprietor of the Warner Memorial Service Co.," it "was eagerly photographed by thousands of visitors, many of them probably believing that it was the original marker because of its 'antique' look." As Simmons (2006, 164–65) describes it:

On the globe or triangular cap appear the words "Truth and History" above crossed pistols cut into the stone. Below there is a row of 21 chiseled bullets for the 21 men legend claims Billy killed.

On the main body of the tombstone's dark granite, large letters read: "Billy the Kid" followed by his supposed birth date of November 23, 1860 (sic) and the confirmed death date, July 14, 1881. At the bottom, visitors see: "The Boy Bandit King. He Died As He Had Lived."

The Warner tombstone's fate is told on a sign next to the iron-bar-caged graves within the walled enclosure behind the building that in January 2006 carried the name OLD FORT SUMNER MUSEUM/ *"Authentic* GRAVESITE of BILLY the KID":

BILLY THE KID'S ELUSIVE TOMBSTONE
Billy the Kid's Tombstone was stolen in 1950. For 26 years it remained a mystery until 1976, when it was recovered in Granbury, Texas by Joe Bowlin. Stolen again on Feb. 8, 1981. Recovered Feb. 12 in Huntington Beach, Calif. Gov. Bruce King arranged for De Baca County Sheriff "Big John" McBride to fly to Los Angeles, Calif. via Texas International Airlines to return the marker. Chamber officials with Jarvis P. Garrett [Pat's son] officially reset the marker in iron shackles May 30, 1981.

The "elusive" Warner tombstone inspired the Billy the Kid Tombstone Race during Fort Sumner's Old Fort Days Celebration the second weekend in June, according to journalists Kathy Kincade and Carl Landau (1990, 69–70), who put annual attendance at 10,000 for the sixteen-year-old event:

> A tombstone race? This bizarre event is called "the world's richest (and probably only)" race of its kind in the world. It's a relatively simple event – a running race over a 100-yard obstacle course – with one slight complication: you must carry an 80-pound tombstone (40 pounds for the women) with you wherever you go! T-shirts are awarded to all survivors, and the winner takes home the grand prize of $1,000.

The 1940 WPA New Mexico Guide, sponsored by the Coronado Cuarto Centennial Commission and the University of New Mexico, includes a "Coronado Cuarto Centennial Folk Festival Calendar (Giving Principal Events from May 15 to November 1940)" with two Billy the Kid-related dates: June 17 "A Day in Old Lincoln" with the "entire community participating in depicting customs and traditions of early Anglo and Spanish settlers in Lincoln" and August 20, 21 at Fort Sumner's "De Baca County Festival, in form of dramas, 'Coronado's March to Quivira' and 'Saga of Billy the Kid'" (Workers of WPA 1940, xxxiv, xxxvi). The Lincoln festival was

> an elaborate historical pageant…that used the whole town as its stage. New Mexico artist Peter Hurd played the role of Billy the Kid in this reenactment of the Kid's [April 28, 1881,] escape from the Lincoln County courthouse. World War II then intervened, but the outdoor folk pageant, *The Last Escape of Billy the Kid*, resumed in 1948 at the pageant grounds just west of the actual courthouse. This is sponsored annually by Lincoln Pageants and Festivals, with local people acting the roles. (Wilson 1993, 29–30)

In the 1940 WPA Guide the main attractions of Lincoln ("named…for the Civil War president") itself, "(5,600 alt., 438 pop.), …the county seat until 1913, when the seat was transferred to Carrizozo," are:

> Lincoln County Court House State Monument (*open 9 to 5*) [which] has been restored and is administered by the Lincoln County Society of Art, History, and Archeology as a branch of the Museum of New Mexico. It once held the Murphy-Dolan store, downstairs, while the second floor contained the courtroom, jail, and bedrooms. The courtroom upstairs is now the auditorium and one of the bedrooms

is an art gallery, in which exhibits of local artists as well as traveling exhibits from the Museum of New Mexico are shown. The two rooms on the first floor house historical and archeological material. The History Room includes economic exhibits, such as mining and cattle raising as well as mementoes of the Lincoln County War. The Archeology Room represents the Mescalero Apache, pueblo ruins, cave ruins, and cave dwellings. Cases of exhibits are installed in both rooms, and above the cases are dioramas explaining the use of the items....

Near the site of the McSween house, on the same side of the street [on the opposite side from the courthouse] is the Torreón (*caretaker next door west; 10¢ customary*), built by early settlers in 1852 for protection against Indian raids. It is of red-brown adobe brick, three stories in height, with loopholes in each floor and gun embrasures on the roof. Ascent is by a ladder inside. It was restored by the Chaves County Historical Society of Roswell in 1935. (Workers of WPA 1940, 384–85)

After the county seat was moved in Carrizozo in 1913, the Lincoln County courthouse was used as a high school until exodus from the area meant declining enrollments and the school was moved to Capitán in 1931. The building stood vacant until 1937,

when a group of county residents organized the Lincoln County Society of Art, History, and Archaeology. Through their efforts, the courthouse was deeded to the state. Renovation began the next year under the direction of J. W. Hendron from the Museum of New Mexico in Santa Fe, with funds provided by the Works Progress Administration. The intention was to restore the building as nearly as possible to its appearance at the time Billy the Kid made his famous escape in 1881. Governor John E. Miles dedicated the old courthouse as the Lincoln County Museum on July 30, 1939....

The *torreón* and courthouse were the beginnings of Lincoln State Monument, which now includes the Tunstall Store, the José Montaño Store, the Convento (the first courthouse), San Juan Church, and four other properties. The Lincoln County Heritage Trust, formed in 1976, administers the Wortley Hotel [burned in 1934, rebuilt on the same foundations in 1960], the Dr. Woods House and Annex, two other houses, and two store locations in addition to their Historical Center. Few buildings in town postdate the early 1900s. A Lincoln County Historical Ordinance, approved in 1972, ensures the architectural integrity of the village. (Wilson 1993, 29)

In 1976 author John Sinclair (in Tatum 1982, 4) declared: "You can dissolve a marriage, separate an egg, split a deck of cards and take a boy from the country – but down in

Lincoln town they just can't shed themselves of Billy the Kid." This was clearly the case in July 1929, when the New Mexico State Highway Commission booklet *Roads to Cibola: What to See in New Mexico and How to Get There* promised automobile tourists:

> A turn or so following the green-banked Bonito brings the traveler through a rich ranch country to sleepy old **Lincoln** town, meditating in the soft, wild-flower scented air on the glories of its heydey. The ruins of the old fort which was once maintained here, the remainder of the store from which Billy and his gang and honest but misled McSwain issued forth into the flaming night to meet Murphy's bullets, the old Murphy store, later courthouse and jail where Billy was incarcerated, and now a school all still stand.
>
> Most any friendly townsman will take the tourist over the scenes of one of the most dramatic and colorful episodes in the never dull history of New Mexico. Here

The caption reads: "'Billy the Kid Escapes' from the old Lincoln jail, from a painting by Manuel F. Moseley depicting this incident in the life of the Southwest's most famous outlaw. 'A Day in Old Lincoln' is part of the Coronado program at Lincoln on June 17." The Coronado Magazine: The Official Program of the Coronado Cuarto Centennial in New Mexico, *New Mexico Coronado Cuarto Centennial Commission, 1940.*

is the old hotel where Bob Ollinger ate. Here is the old saloon whose walls heard Garret's voice and were not infrequently punctured by the bullet of some obstreperous cowwaddy. A day dreaming over the past in Lincoln Town is well spent.

The Lincoln pictured is along U.S. Highway 566, which "might well be termed The Outlaw Trail as over its course one of the most famous bandits in the southwest rode many times and in his wake came other gentlemen who did not approve of questions as to their past, right name, or where they were going. Today, it exists in itself as a famous beauty route."

Some seventy years later, Billy the Kid National Scenic Byway (NM 48, NM 220; U.S.70/380; 84.2 miles) was among the scenic and historic byways listed by the New Mexico Highway and Transportation Department: "Follow the trails of famous lawmen, outlaws and warriors through the rugged beauty of the one million acre Lincoln National Forest." Along the byway is Lincoln, "established in the 1850's, [which] has remained virtually the same since the Lincoln County War was fought here. Now a National Historic Landmark and a State Monument, visitors tour the Courthouse where The Kid made his last escape. The Lincoln County Heritage Trust operates the Historical Center where visitors enjoy exhibits of the Apaches, Spanish, Western Black Cavalry (Buffalo Soldiers) and the Lincoln County War. Lincoln offers a unique opportunity to experience firsthand the many cultures that created Lincoln County and New Mexico." Also along the Kid scenic byway is Ruidoso, "a cosmpolitan village with restaurants and lodging facilities ranging from rustic to luxurious. It offers fine galleries, shops and five area golf courses. Skiing, biking, hiking, horseback riding, casino gaming and wagering on the horses are just moments away." The gambling is at nearby Ruidoso Downs Racetrack, "home of The World's Richest Quarter Horse Race, the All American Futurity, [which] operates mid-May through Labor Day" (Arellanes n.d., 42, 43).

The Billy the Kid National Scenic Byway Visitors Center is near Ruidoso Downs. According to its 1999 brochure, *Billy the Kid National Scenic Byway*, the center

primarily orients visitors to the area encompassed by the Scenic Byway. Exhibits explore some of the many stories of the region and provide information visitors need to plan a stay in Lincoln County; exploring the communities along the Byway.

Secondarily, regional attractions within an easy day's drive of the Byway are highlighted since they are available to visitors staying in Lincoln County. You will also find a shop featuring items relevant to the Byway. The Center is adjacent to the Hubbard Museum of the American West ... just east of Ruidoso Downs Race Track.... This magnificent museum boasts a collection of over 12,000 horse related artifacts including saddles, carriages, wagons, Indian artifacts and fine western art. The Museum is also home to the Ruidoso Downs Race Horse Hall of Fame. The grounds in front of the Museum are marked by one of the nation's most remarkable equine sculptures, "Free Spirits at Noisy Waters." The monumental sculpture features seven breeds of horses each created at 1 and 1/2 times life size.

"Horses, horses" (*Santa Fe New Mexican, Pasatiempo*, August 23/29, 2001) further notes of the Hubbard Museum:

> The core collection was founded in 1960 by Anne C. Stradling, in Patagonia, Ariz., as the Museum of the Horse in 1990. Stradling donated her artifacts to the Hubbard, which formally opened in 1992.
>
> The collection is stabled in the refurbished Chaparral Convention Center near Ruidoso Downs racetrack and [Billy the Kid] casino. An immense outdoor sculpture of flying mustangs by [Dave] McGary, *Free Spirits at Noisy Water*, catches the eye as you turn in off U.S. 70....
>
> The museum also operates the Billy the Kid National Scenic Byway Visitor Center just down the highway, and the annual Lincoln County Cowboy Symposium ...at the racetrack, [with] cowboy poetry, music and storytelling, horsemanship demonstrations, and a chuck wagon cook-off and demonstration.

Kansas-raised R. D. Hubbard, who "formed glass-manufacturer AFG Industries in 1978 through the merger of two companies [and] built it into one of the nation's largest companies before selling to Japanese interests in 1992," was worth "just under $193 million by June 2000, according to a financial statement filed with the Racing Commission" (Thomas J. Cole in *Albuquerque Journal*, September 15, 2002). Besides "gaming interests," these holdings "included $49 million in real estate investments, a $29 million art collection and a $15 million airplane."

> Hubbard paid $2.6 million in cash and assumed $9 million in debt to obtain control of Ruidoso Downs in 1988. As a horse owner, he had been racing there since the 1960s.
>
> "Ruidoso was always the big leagues," Hubbard said in an Albuquerque Journal interview in 1990. "That's where you wanted to come."
>
> Within a few years, he and his minority partner at Ruidoso Downs had made improvements to the track and begun development of a golf course in Ruidoso.
>
> Hubbard also lobbied the Legislature for years to get a law allowing casino gambling at the track. He succeeded in 1997 in getting slot machines [for the Billy the Kid Casino].

By 2001 R. D. Hubbard was embroiled in a new Lincoln County War, one fought not over mercantile interests, government contracts, grazing rights, and land but over recreation and water. According to Rene Romo (in the *Albuquerque Journal*, February 4, 2001), Hubbard had bought a 745-acre ranch in March 2000 and in August "gained approval to change the well location for 53 acre-feet of water from the Hondo area" in order to develop "a world-class, 18-hole [7,300-yard-long] golf course in the Angus area called the Hideout of Lincoln County." In January 2001 four new applications "seeking approval for changes in well locations for an additional 260 acre-feet of water" were filed.

Opponents were "the U.S. Bureau of Land Management, which acquired 1,020 acres of land along the Rio Bonito in the Lincoln Valley in 1995; Lincoln, home to the legendary Billy the Kid and now a state monument listed on the National Historic Register; the neighboring town of Capitan; and a 493-lot subdivision near Alto called the Ranches of Sonterra." Hubbard's representatives claimed that "the Hideout will use state-of-the-art water conservation techniques, but the BLM argues, in its protest to a well move for 150 acre-feet of water, that another golf course is not in keeping with water conservation." Three public (Hubbard's Links at Sierra Blanca, semi-private Cree Meadows Public Golf Course, the course at the Mescalero Apaches' Inn of the Mountain Gods) and two private (Alto Lakes Golf and Country Club, Kokopelli Golf and Tennis Club) courses already were operating in the Ruidoso area. "Lincoln native Alfred Sanchez, whose great-grandfather settled in the valley, said five golf courses is enough. But in Ruidoso, Kokopelli golf pro Jeff Chapman said adding another golf course would make the mountain hamlet more attractive to visitors, and that would help real estate values."

3
Land of Heart's Desire

Under a sky of azure,
Where balmy breezes blow;
Kissed by the golden sunshine,
Is Nuevo Mejico.

Home of the Montezuma,
With fiery heart aglow,
State of the deeds historic,
Is Nuevo Mejico.

—First verse of "O, Fair New Mexico," the official state song, adopted in 1917;
written, composed, and copyrighted in 1915 by Elizabeth Garrett, daughter of Pat
Garrett and Apolinaria Gutiérrez Garrett

New Mexico is both a winter and summer resort. It is in addition a land of a thousand wonders,—scenic, historical, archaeological. No other state has such tourist
attractions. Its mission churches are 150 years older than those of California, and
many of them are shrines for worship to the present day. Cave and cliff dwellings
number tens of thousands and are vestiges of a culture thousands of years old.
Indian pueblos and hogans are as quaint and mysterious as any of the ancient
habitations of the Orient. Indian dances, such as may be witnessed in New Mexico,
and church ceremonials, are more interesting and as full of poetic and symbolic
meaning as any of the Greek mysteries. New Mexico has been the meeting place of
successive cultures, of many races and tribes and each has left its imprint, each has
its survivors, making the land a treasure trove for archaeologist and ethnologist.
Nowhere else in the United States can be found so great a variety of unique sights,
glimpses of Old Spain and of scenes that hark back to prehistoric times. It is Egypt
and Babylonia, Spain and Mexico, Colorado and California, Switzerland and the
Orient, combined. Stupendous mountain masses, the loftiest peaks more than
13,000 feet high, are accessible by easy trails to their very pinnacles; shadowy

canyons, flower spangled mountain meadows, picturesque waterfalls, whispering pine forests, babbling trout streams, vast game preserves, the all-pervading sunshine, the mystery of the desert, the invigorating atmosphere of the higher altitudes, the unique aspects of irrigation, the smile of orchards and alfalfa fields, the unspoiled hospitality of flat-roofed adobe homes in which the mellifluous Spanish is spoken, are all spanned by perfect turquoise skies that rival those of Naples and Andalusia. Yea, verily, here is a land of delight, of myriad charms, of the heart's desire, well worth a visit and a stay.

—Paul A. F. Walter, "'The Land of Heart's Desire': Commerce: For the Tourist," New Mexico The Land of Opportunity: Official Data on the Resources and Industries of New Mexico—The Sunshine State, *1915*

During the San Diego Panama-California Exposition of 1915–1916, the main exhibit in the New Mexico Building's central Hall of the Governors was entitled *Landmarks of the Santa Fe Trail*. "Large sepia portraits of New Mexico's governors from the military occupation of 1846 to statehood" hung on the walls. Arrayed on tables in the center were Museum of New Mexico staff member John Percy Adams's models of "ancient buildings, churches, pueblos, and other edifices prominent in New Mexico's long history" (Miller 1985, 15). Among these was "a sixteen-foot-long model of the [Pecos] mesa top showing reconstructed church, South Pueblo, and main Quadrangle" (Kessell 1979, 477), a major landmark of the trail and by then popularly ensconced as the birthplace of the Aztec ruler Montezuma.

At Governor William C. McDonald's request, blind musician, singer, and composer Elizabeth Garrett and her "escort," friend Elizabeth (Beth) Roe, were invited to San Diego to serve as hostesses in the New Mexico Building. Garrett was also to give a "daily program of entertainment" presenting "the songs of Old Mexico, cowboy ballads, and Indian chants." She "closed with a group of her compositions which told of mountains and valleys and apple orchards, of summer showers on mesa and desert, the *Paisano*, the roadrunner; her own songs of New Mexico." Former president Colonel Theodore Roosevelt attended a special program in his honor and afterward expressed his "great pleasure to meet the daughter of my old friend, Pat Garrett, ...the most noted sheriff of the Southwest, in territorial days.... In fact, I feel that he was the man who introduced law to the territory" (Hall 1983, 116).

Elizabeth Garrett, who "once said: 'My father tried to bring peace and harmony to our country with his guns; I would like to do my part with my music'" (Hall 1983, 9), wrote, composed, and copyrighted "O, Fair New Mexico" in 1915. McDonald was pleased with the popular reception for the state's "First Lady of Song" and with "O, Fair New Mexico," which was adopted as the official state song in 1917. Born on a ranch at Eagle Creek in Lincoln County in 1884, three years after Billy the Kid's death, Elizabeth Garrett died in Roswell on October 16, 1947, some three months after the Roswell Incident. She is buried in the cemetery there under a marker with the inscription "ELIZABETH GARRETT/ 1947/ O FAIR NEW MEXICO."

New Mexico had become the forty-seventh state in the United States of America at 1:35 p.m. on January 6, 1912, when President William Howard Taft signed the proclamation of statehood in the White House. The following year the new state was invited to participate in the San Diego Panama-California Exposition scheduled to open in 1915. Governor William Calhoun McDonald, the first of statehood, and "other state officials saw the exposition as an excellent opportunity to promote the state's resources, enhance the economic development of its citizens, and take advantage of the millions of dollars expected to be spent in San Diego — in return for a comparatively small investment by the tax paying citizens of the state" (Miller 1985, 13). A legislative act created the Board of Exposition Managers; its five members elected Santa Fe historian and attorney Ralph Emerson Twitchell as their chairman. Albuquerque's A. E. Koehler Jr. served as commissioner of publicity on the board's executive staff.

Twitchell and Koehler designed a flag to fly over the New Mexico Building in Balboa Park when the exposition opened on January 1, 1915. It was presented to the Second State Legislature and adopted as New Mexico's first flag on March 19, 1915, in House Bill 319:

A flag or banner with a turquoise blue field, emblematic of the blue skies of New Mexico; a flag of the United States of America in miniature in the upper left hand corner of the field, designating the loyalty of our people, in the upper right hand corner the figures No. 47, the forty-seventh star and state in the American Union, in the lower right hand corner the great seal of the State of New Mexico, and upon the field running from the lower left to the upper right hand corner in white the words "NEW MEXICO" be and the same hereby is adopted as the state flag or banner of New Mexico.

Publicity Commissioner Koehler solicited advertising for and edited the 254-page *New Mexico The Land of Opportunity: Official Data on the Resources and Industries of New Mexico—The Sunshine State*, published as an "Official Souvenir of the State of New Mexico" by the Press of the Albuquerque Morning Journal in 1915. According to Koehler's foreword, the book is modeled on "the Exposition Book of New Mexico, issued ten years ago for the [1904] St. Louis Exposition, [which] resulted directly and indirectly, in bringing 100,000 new settlers to the State [Territory], who tripled the number of farms in the State, turned the eastern livestock ranges into agricultural country, founded villages and

The first state flag, adopted on March 19, 1915.
(Museum of New Mexico Neg. No. 130798)

towns, created new counties, and inaugurated a new era of growth and prosperity." The 1915 book was prepared with "but one object in view, namely, to acquaint the world with the advantages, resources and progress of the great Sunshine State. Knowledge of the New Mexico of today is certain to result in the influx of tourists, settlers, capital, for no other state in the Union presents so great a variety of attractions for these as does New Mexico."

Koehler calls the San Diego Exposition's New Mexico Building, designed by architect Isaac Hamilton Rapp and his Rapp, Rapp, and Hendrickson firm, "an inspiration." Its exterior "is in greater part a replica of the Franciscan mission church on the Rock of Acoma." The main auditorium inside the church houses "the most unique moving picture theater in the world":

> It has been furnished in mission style and seats six hundred people. Here are shown 30,000 feet of motion picture films and 3,000 stereopticon views, all being explained by expert lecturers. New Mexico's resources, attractions, progress, are the theme of every talk and admission is free to all.

A publicity room "has been made attractive with Indian rugs, comfortable chairs, tables and desks for representatives of commercial organizations and newspapers."

In the convent are the exhibit halls, with the mineral and other exhibits, the wonderful models of historic landmarks, Indian pueblos and mission churches and
various displays, maps, charts, all complying with a standard of beauty and art,
set from the very start for all exhibits. There are cozy rest rooms for women, with
colored transparencies of New Mexico's most beautiful scenery in the windows,
and various offices for exposition officials (12).

Rapp's New Mexico Building served as model for his design of the State Art Museum (now
New Mexico Museum of Art, Museum of New Mexico), which opened on the Santa Fe Plaza
in November 1917 (Sheppard 1988).

New Mexico Board of Exposition Managers member Paul A. F. Walter served as its
publicity secretary. Historian and banker Walter contributed several pieces to *New Mexico The Land of Opportunity*, including the first two on the state: "Historical Sketch of New
Mexico" and "'The Land of Heart's Desire.'" The sobriquet "Land of Heart's Desire"
comes from "the official book for the St. Louis Exposition" of 1904, which Walter quotes in
"A Cordial Invitation" at the end:

New Mexico wants more people, it needs them; it has room and resources for
them. It offers to immigrants a fine climate, free homesteads under the land laws
of the United States, great natural resources; to the healthseeker, health; to the
tourist, scenic, historic and archaeological attractions; to the sportsman, good fishing and hunting; to the summer and winter guests, the best summer and winter
climate on earth, hot and cold mineral springs, mountain retreats, ranch resorts,
good hotel accommodations and the comforts and luxuries of modern communities; ...to the real estate man, cheap lands and a chance to make money, and to
the capitalist, opportunities to make big dividends and to buy anything that his
heart desires, from a gold or copper mine worth a million or more, to a game preserve as big as a European kingdom (30).

Eighteen years after San Diego's Panama-California Exposition opened in 1915
Chicago launched its Century of Progress Exposition, the first of six enormously popular,
depression-era American world's fairs (Chicago, San Diego, Dallas, Cleveland, San Francisco, New York) that became "cultural icons for the nation's hopes and future" (Rydell
1993, 1). Originally scheduled for May–November 1933, at the urging of President
Franklin D. Roosevelt the Chicago Exposition was opened for a second season in 1934.
This enabled New Mexico to vie successfully for exhibition space.

Governor Andrew W. Hockenhull personally raised the requisite financing despite very
difficult times. The governor sought the economic advantages of "added tourist travel" and
an end to what he considered the state's failing: "New Mexico, which for many years has

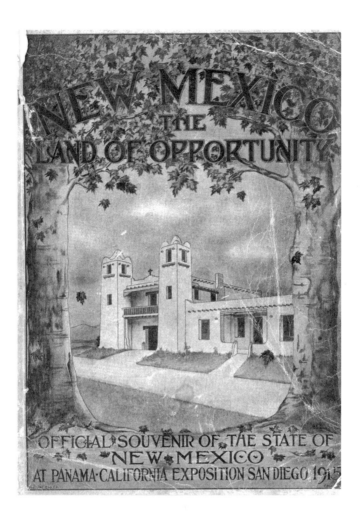

Cover of New Mexico The Land of Opportunity: Official Data on the
Resources and Industries of New Mexico – The Sunshine State, *Press of
the Albuquerque Morning Journal, 1915. This "Official Souvenir of the
State of New Mexico" shows the New Mexico Building at the 1915
Panama-California Exposition in San Diego's Balboa Park. According to
New Mexico Exposition Board Commissioner of Publicity A. E. Koehler:
"The exterior of the New Mexico building is in greater part a replica of the
Franciscan mission church on the Rock of Acoma, a fort and castle-like
structure, almost severe but also magnificent in its simplicity and with
many massive buttresses. In order to lighten the heaviness of the facade,
the balustrade as it is found in the mission church of Cochiti was
reproduced. The church has two characteristic bell towers and is connected
with the convent by an enclosed arcade which serves as a publicity room.
On the roof between the two campaniles there is a tea garden. The Patio is
surrounded by an arched cloister and a fountain plays in the garden,
recalling days of Old Castile."*

been the mecca of those seeking health, recreation and the best of fishing and hunting, never has told the story of the state's almost unlimited attractions as it should have been told" ("New Mexico at Century" 1934):

Due to adverse conditions abroad and the depreciated value of American money in other nations, I feel that the great bulk of travel to be done by Americans for the next year or two will be within the borders of our own nation. For that reason it seems highly desirable for New Mexico to make a bid for a portion, at least, of that travel. We have been endowed by Nature with scenic attractions unexcelled anywhere. Our climate is admirably adapted for those seeking health and rest. The Indians, our quaint Spanish-American villages, Carlsbad Cavern, Chaco Canyon, and myriad other attractions beckon to the tourist. Our chief concern at this time is to see that those attractions are properly advertised so that we may get from them the benefits to which our state is entitled.

When New Mexico's exhibit for the Court of States at the Chicago Century of Progress Exposition opened on July 9, 1934, Exposition President Rufus C. Dawes declared that "I feel as though I had actually stepped into New Mexico itself" while accepting the space from New Mexico Exposition Commissioner Berton I. Staples and Navajo medicine man Hosteen Klah. The latter,

assisted by Pish-li–ki Yazza [Fred Peshlaikai], Navajo silversmith who is working on the exhibit, conducted the Navajo "home blessing ceremony." An invited group of notables watched spellbound as the old Navajo medicine man chanted the weird ceremony and sprinkled the blessing pollen at the four points of the compass. Staples ... welcomed the invited guests and spoke of the allurement that New Mexico has for the thousands of visitors that find health and recreation within the state's borders each year.

Mrs. Margaret Abreu represented the Highway Department, which had dispatched staff engineer O. T. Jorgensen to supervise construction from Santa Fe architect Gordon Street's plans. The Pueblo-style structure boasted "a carpet of the white sands from the famous national monument near Alamogordo ... [a] snow-white floor covering, which presents a striking contrast to the rich brown hue of the *adobe* buildings, [and] is an unending wonder for the thousands who visit the exhibit every day." A corral fence, shed, carved beams, vigas, furniture, and tin light fixtures were Spanish. Both Navajo and Chimayó blankets hung from the walls, which also "displayed paintings by eighteen New Mexico artists, some from Taos and others from Santa Fe, ... valued at $80,000, [which] were hung by Will Shuster of Santa Fe, and a requirement was made by the artists' committee which

Acoma Towers, Front View.

Palace of the Governors.

Rear View.
Reproducing Old Pecos Mission.

From Santa Ana Balcony, Toward Plaza.

Centerfold, The New Museum of Santa Fé, *n.d. (for November 1917
dedication) on the plaza, now the New Mexico Museum of Art, Museum
of New Mexico, modeled after the San Diego Exposition's New Mexico Building.
Upper left: "Acoma Towers, Front View"; lower left: "Rear View, Reproducing Old
Pecos Mission"; upper right: "Palace of the Governors"; lower right: "From Santa
Ana Balcony, Toward Plaza."*

selected the paintings that none should be hung for any artist who had been in New Mexico
less than fifteen years" (Shuart 1934, 10, 11, 12).

Besides showcasing the state's mineral and other resources, the New Mexico exhibit
featured daily demonstrations by two unidentified Hispanic weavers from Chimayó under
one portal and by Navajo weaver Ah-Kena-Bah and silversmith Peshlaikai under the other.
Medicine man Klah, who had demonstrated rug weaving at the 1893 Chicago World's
Columbian Exposition, made daily sandpaintings on a stand in the center space, behind
which were cases of Indian and Spanish jewelry and other handicrafts. Trader Franc Johnson Newcomb (1964, 193) remembers that "Klah and his sand painting were about the
first things visitors saw when they entered the New Mexico building," where he "had a

square about twelve by twelve feet fenced so that curious spectators could not crowd too close to him while he was working or step on the painting when it was finished."

Special Santa Fe trains carried New Mexicans to Chicago for New Mexico Day on August 14, 1934. The governor addressed the crowds attending the program in the big Court of States stadium. According to an Associated Press release in the *Albuquerque Journal* on that day, Governor Hockenhull called his "the most colorful of the 48 states":

> "Oldest in point of settlement and yet the newest in the sisterhood of states, New Mexico has been the land of heart's desire for many peoples for well nigh 2,000 years," [he] said ... [and] spoke of the state's history, its resources and its art, coming down from prehistoric days to the present.... "New Mexico stands unique in that it has maintained its public credit and pays its own way even in these times of depression.... In every sense of the word it is a modern state which at the same time has preserved for future generations antiquities, ancient ways, colorful ceremonies and quaint places which have drawn to it groups of artists and writers of wide renown. In fact in the intangible values of culture, New Mexico may well claim to stand at the head of the procession of states."

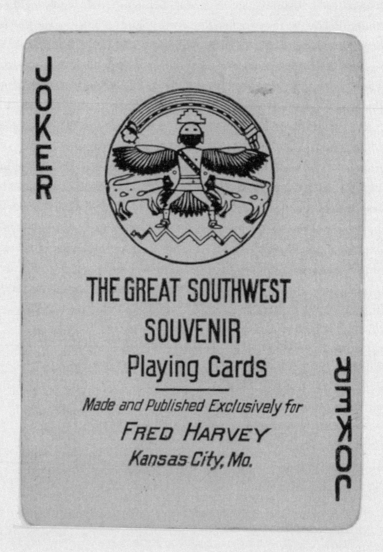

Joker, *The Great Southwest Souvenir Playing Cards*, Fred Harvey.
Beginning in 1911, the Fred Harvey Company produced decks of Souvenir Playing
Cards of the Great Southwest that were distributed by it and the Santa Fe Railway
(Howard and Pardue 1996a, 98–99). This undated deck is from the 1920s
because the Queen of Hearts shows Gallup's Santa Fe/Harvey El Navajo Hotel,
which opened in May 1923. The booklet boxed with the deck gives "Legends
describing subject shown on the face of each card," in this case: "Joker:—The God
of War. The Zuni name for this god is A-tchl-a-la-to-pa, and he is the hero of many
folklore tales. As shown in the picture, he is represented as possessing the human form.
His dress consists of the convential [sic] terraced cap (symbolic of his dwelling in the
clouds), and the badge and ornaments of the Ka-Ka. His weapons are the great flint
knife of war, the arrow of lightning and the bow of the skies (rainbow)."

Part Two
Rail: The Great Southwest

The historic highway known as the Santa Fé Trail has been alluded to. But the road was not first made across the plains and all the dreary reaches of the Llano Estacado by white men. The Indians knew it first. It had been traveled for perhaps thousands of years. What we know as the Raton (Rah-tone) pass was their objective point also. So, when you see the old road from the [railroad] car windows, you may reflect that you are looking upon the unused paths made by prehistoric wanderers over one of the most familiar regions of the world. The roads that lead to Mecca; the sand-drifted highways of the Sahara; the very footsteps of Christ; are not more ancient. As most of those have been abandoned, so has this, to be usurped by that most brilliant and beneficent of human achievements, – a railroad.

—Las Vegas Hot Springs, New Mexico, *"Prepared for the Information of Tourists, Tired People, Invalids of all Classes, and those who seek a Summer or Winter Resort, with the benefit to be derived from Medicinal Baths and Mineral Waters,"* Passenger Department, Santa Fé Route, booklet, 1887

Mile by mile, day by day, the Atchison, Topeka and Santa Fe has built along the Old Santa Fe Trail and moved onward to California. Early stretches of Santa Fe rail reached Hutchinson, then ribboned onto roaring Dodge City, La Junta, Trinidad, then over Raton Pass, and in 1880 it reached old Santa Fe. From there it stretched westward to California, forming a "Path of Empire" along the route of the historical wagon trail of pioneer days.

*When you look out of your Santa Fe train window and watch the land fly by,
you are looking at historic ground:*

There the Conquistador marched, the padre walked, the mountain man
trapped, the ox-team strained, the soldier campaigned, the emigrant toiled, the
engineer surveyed; and over the footprints of them all was built the Santa Fe!

—*"The Steel Santa Fe Trail,"* Along Your Way: Facts about Stations and Scenes
on the Santa Fe, *Atchison, Topeka & Santa Fe Railway booklet, 1948*

ather of the Santa Fe, Colonel Cyrus Kurtz Holliday, personally drafted the char-
ter for the Atchison and Topeka Railroad Company. Since Kansas had no incor-
poration laws at that time, a special act during the territorial legislative session of 1859
empowered the construction, maintenance, and operations of "a railroad, with one or more
tracks, from or near Atchison, on the Missouri River, in Kansas Territory, to the town of
Topeka, in Kansas Territory, and to such point on the southern or western boundary of the
said Territory, in the direction of Santa Fe, in the Territory of New Mexico, as may be convenient and suitable, for the construction of such railroad; and, also to construct a branch
of said railroad to any points on the southern boundary of said Territory of Kansas in the
direction of the Gulf of Mexico." At a November 24, 1863, stockholders' meeting in
Topeka's Chase Hotel, "in an effort to make the name of the railroad more inclusive and
descriptive, 'Santa Fe' was added." Final success came on September 23, 1868, at a New
York City meeting of the Associates. Afterward, the Topeka *State Record* editorialized: "It is
fitting that Col. Holliday should be the final successful negotiator in this enterprise. To no
one man in Kansas can the praise be awarded more surely for fostering and encouraging
the various railroad schemes now making every farmer in the state richer than he was than
to Col. Holliday" (Waters 1950, 26, 31, 36).

The Atchison, Topeka and Santa Fe Railroad broke ground in downtown Topeka on
October 30, 1868. Its founder promised that "those present would live ... to see the line
head far down into Mexico, and meet the broad Pacific on the Gulf of California ... and into
the Rocky Mountains, with their hidden mineral wealth" (Marshall 1945, 20–21). On
April 26 of the following year, at a picnic on Wakarusa Creek outside Topeka to celebrate
completion of the first seven miles of track, Colonel Holliday proclaimed more grandly:
"Fellow citizens, the coming tide of immigration will flow along these lines and, like an
ocean wave, advance up the sides of the Rockies and dash their foamy crests down upon
the Pacific." He concluded with eloquent flourish: "See, there rolls the broad Pacific, and
on its breast are the ships of the Santa Fe riding in from the Orient" (Bryant 1974, 2).

The first Santa Fe train entered the Territory of New Mexico over Raton Pass on December 7, 1878. The line reached Galisteo Junction (later named Lamy) with a spur line opened to Santa Fe in February 1880. On February 15 of that year, according to "Chronological Annals" appended to *The Legislative Blue-Book of the Territory of New Mexico* for the 1882 session (Ritch 1968):

> Completion of the first railroad to Santa Fe, the oldest town on the continent, celebrated by an excursion to the Missouri river in Pullman coaches; given by the railroad company...to the Territorial Officers, Members of the Legislative Assembly and business men. The excursionists visited Lawrence, Kansas City, Leavenworth, Atchison and Topeka and many of the State institutions, manufactories and business houses of these cities: going and returning in five days; where, in 1863, the trip occupied in time one way, by U.S. mail coaches, thirty days. Thus the newest and oldest civilization upon the American Continent were brought together, and the old Santa Fe trail of a verity became the T-rail.

On May 31, 1887, the first Atchison, Topeka and Santa Fe Railroad train arrived in Los Angeles over exclusively Santa Fe trackage. The first to do so to Chicago's Dearborn Station arrived on December 31 of that year. The inaugural run of the California Limited, the Santa Fe's first luxury train and the first to offer any dining car service west of Kansas City, left Dearborn Station on November 27, 1892.

In 1874 the Atchison, Topeka and Santa Fe Railroad had opened a second-floor lunchroom in Topeka. In the spring of 1876 English immigrant Frederick Henry Harvey entered a "gentleman's agreement" with the Santa Fe to lease the lunchroom and provide all future dining and lodging needs for the line. The first formal contract between the two was signed on January 1, 1878, when Harvey opened the Clifton Hotel in Florence, Kansas. In 1883 Harvey, who became known as the "Civilizer of the West," fired unruly male waiters at the Raton, New Mexico, restaurant and hired waitresses, soon replacing all restaurant servers with reliable young women who became famous as Harvey Girls. A second formal contract, signed on May 1, 1889, "granted to Fred Harvey the exclusive right, with some minor reservations, to manage and operate the eating houses, lunch stands, and hotel facilities which the company then owned, leased, or was to lease at any time in the future upon any of its railroads west of the Missouri River, including all lines then leased or operated in the name of the Atchison, Topeka and Santa Fe" (Henderson 1969, 44, 45; also Poling-Kempes 1989; Morris 1994).

The Fred Harvey Company continued as a family operation following its founder's death in 1901. At that time it had interests in twelve states that "included 15 hotels, 47 restaurants, 30 dining cars, and food service on the ferries across San Francisco Bay"

(Bryant 1974, 121). Some fifty years later journalist Dickson Hartwell (1949, 30, 32) extolled the ongoing enterprise:

> If the .45 revolver was the peacemaker of the Southwest, Fred Harvey, founder of the empire, was its civilizer. Working with the vast, longest-in-U.S. Santa Fe railroad—some say the Santa Fe made Harvey, others stoutly declare Harvey made the Santa Fe—he carried Delmonico food standards west of the Mississippi. He gave America the Harvey Girl, immortalized by M-G-M [*The Harvey Girls*, a 1946 musical based on the 1942 Samuel Hopkins Adams novel], and he sold enough Indian curios to put a touch of Navajo or Hopi in every U.S. home.

4
Land of the Well Country

Physicians are often asked by their consumptive patients and by people residing in the frosty regions of the north: "Where can I find a dry and mild winter climate?" To this the inquirers often get an unsatisfactory reply. To say Tangier or Tetuan necessitates crossing the broad Atlantic in cold weather, with none too good accommodations after the long voyage. In view of the facts given above, it hardly seems necessary to say that the place they seek is Las Vegas Hot Springs. Here is a very paradise for people afflicted with lung diseases, and where they can be comfortable the year round.

> —Nature's Sanitarium: Las Vegas Hot Springs Las Vegas New Mexico on the Line of the Atchison Topeka and Santa Fe Railroad *booklet, January 9, 1883*

There is but one Land of the Well Country, and Albuquerque is its heart, metropolis, and capital.... Medical men spent years in investigating and marshalling facts to prove the superiority of the climate of the Southwest over that of all other sections in the cure of tuberculosis.... It has been a natural course of disclosures that has finally placed outside the geographical boundaries of the Well Country such points as Denver and Colorado Springs, because of high humidity, and southern California, and parts of Arizona and Texas, because of low altitude. Generally speaking, we can say that this land of which we are writing extends from Albuquerque, its heart, in every direction a distance of about four hundred miles.

> —R. W. Wiley, Albuquerque: In the Heart of the Well Country, *Health Department of the Albuquerque Commercial Club booklet, n.d. (1890s)*

*7*n *El Gringo; or New Mexico and Her People*, his 1857 "volume mainly written from a diary the author kept during a residence of two and a half years in New Mexico, and the matters contained in it … either drawn from careful personal observation, or other reliable sources," United States attorney and interim territorial governor W. W. H. Davis (1973, v, 295–96) anticipates the climatology that later dominated his century:

> That which most adds to the enjoyment of the [winter] season in New Mexico is the climate, which, in point of salubrity, is not excelled in any part of the world. No country can boast a purer, brighter, and healthier sky, equal in all respects to that which bends over the vine-clad hills of Italy. The atmosphere is dry, pure, and clear, and seldom rains, but when it does, then look to the roof of your house.… There is comparatively little sickness in the country, and fever or fever and ague are diseases almost unknown. Health seems to be the natural condition of man instead of disease, and a larger number of persons live to a great old age than in any other part of our country, and before they die some assume almost the appearance of Egyptian mummies.

Such climatology involved "the belief that climate produces and cures levels of illness, a theory that flourished in the medical community from the 1880s until germ theory eclipsed it around the turn of the century" (Fox 1983, 213). The American Climatological Association was founded in 1884.

During the 1880s and 1890s, Colorado doctors Samuel A. Fisk, Samuel Edwin Solly, and Charles Denison, themselves recovered tuberculars, wrote promotional medical journal pieces describing the "southwest climate as the best-known therapy for tuberculosis, asthma, and hay fever, and hot springs as therapy for rheumatism, eczema, psoriasis, and acne." They "turned promotional travel rhetoric into scientific dogma by describing respiratory cures in articles they published in medical journals all over the country" (Fox 1983, 218, 219). Although New Mexico boosters used these claims, as "poor cousin to other resort areas shrouded under the mantle of the United States," the state struggled to hold its own in the health industry of the late nineteenth and early twentieth centuries, when it, "unlike other western health centers, was still looked upon with suspicion as an alien land" (Shane 1981, 395; also Spidle 1986).

Claims about the territory's salubrity were routinely included in Bureau of Immigration literature. In 1881 Grant County boosters proclaimed: "For all pulmonary complaints there is not a more congenial spot on the top of the green earth. Here you inhale the pure, fresh, lifegiving and invigorating air." Bureau writers reported that the Las Vegas Hot Springs contained "the great national laboratory, that sends gushing from its side those hot and healing waters, limpid and pure, a nectar fit for the Gods themselves. There the halt and the infirm can come and quaff this innocent beverage" (Shane 1981, 389).

Albuquerque advertised itself as "in the heart of the well country." In an undated 1890s booklet prepared for the Health Department of the Albuquerque Commercial Club, forerunner to the Chamber of Commerce, R. W. Wiley sent a "distinctly humanitarian message to those who are sufferers from health impairment, bidding them come to this land and find in its unequaled climate new life and hope and to learn its gospel of health." He claimed: "A few heard the story of the miracle of sun and air and mountains in the time before Koch had discovered the tubercle basillus [*sic*], and when the engineers of the Santa Fe drove the stakes of the first survey in New Mexico, they found there a few men, camped in the hills and on the mesas 'chasing the cure' the best they knew, but with only a limited knowledge of its proper pursuit."

The Santa Fe's climatological promotions were foreshadowed in *Health, Wealth and Pleasure in Colorado and New Mexico, A Reliable Treatise on the Famous Pleasure and Health Resorts, and the Rich Mining and Agricultural Regions of the Rocky Mountains*, a 130-page, 1881 publication by F. C. Nims (1980, 15), ticket agent of the Denver & Rio Grande Railway, "The Scenic Line of America." Its introduction promises climatological wonders to railroad patrons:

> For people from the East who seek health through a change of climate and associations, the country traversed by the Denver and Rio Grande Railway offers inducements that are nowhere surpassed. The pure, dry air of the plains and mountains, rarefied by an elevation of from one to two miles above the sea, and often in a high degree electrical, is bracing and exhilarating to the lungs. For asthma it is an almost unfailing specific, as hundreds of persons, confirmed asthmatics before coming to Colorado, but here able to breathe with comfort, and in the enjoyment of health, will make haste to testify. Those who have weak lungs, or who are in the incipient stages of consumption, seldom fail of relief in this climate, especially if they live out of doors as much as possible, and are not afraid of the sunshine, which is one of the crowning glories of Colorado. Nowhere in America are so many fine days. During some seasons a cloudy day is almost as rare as an eclipse, and there can be no doubt that cheerfulness and bodily and mental activity are promoted by absence of dark days, fogs, mists and dampness. If, as Longfellow sings, "Some days must be dark and dreary," in this climate they are reduced to the minimum, and during some years happily missed from the calendar altogether.

The Atchison, Topeka and Santa Fe Railroad and the Fred Harvey Company entered this commerce in earnest near Las Vegas, New Mexico. Native Americans and later Hispanos had long used the nearby hot springs at Gallinas for various curative purposes. In

1846 the invading United States Army established a hospital there. In 1862 it was sold and converted into the Adobe Hotel, where Billy the Kid and Jesse James dined together on July 27, 1879. A Boston syndicate bought the property and in December 1879 opened a new Hot Springs Hotel, later known as the Old Stone Hotel. The Santa Fe had completed track to Las Vegas that year, and in 1880 it created the Las Vegas Hot Springs Company to purchase the hotel and surrounding property. A spur line was laid to connect with the town and a 270-room luxury resort hotel constructed of wood. Operated by Fred Harvey and named the Montezuma because the Aztec ruler was supposed to have bathed there, it opened to great fanfare on April 17, 1882. The first Montezuma burned in January 1884; the second, built up on the hill rather than by the hot springs, opened in 1885 and burned down four months later. The third Montezuma opened as the Phoenix Hotel on August 16, 1886 (Bowman 2002, 12, 15–16).

A sixteen-page 1883 booklet touts the first Montezuma as the Santa Fe/Harvey "New Winter Resort" with "Accommodations as elegant in Winter as in Summer." Entitled *Nature's Sanitarium: Las Vegas Hot Springs Las Vegas New Mexico on the Line of the Atchison Topeka and Santa Fe Railroad*, it reveals "THE SECRET OF MEDICINAL WATERS" and offers "scientific speculation" about how, "in addition to its dryness and purity, /THE ATMOSPHERE IS ELECTRIC /In an extraordinary degree." It is "A PARADISE FOR CONSUMPTIVES":

"Hot Springs N.M.," AT&SFRR No. 109, n.d. The bathhouse is at the lower left, the Montezuma Hotel upper center. (Museum of New Mexico Neg. No. 137336

During the year 1881 quite a number visited The Springs who had been condemned to die of chest disorders within a short time, but who are now engaged in active business in Las Vegas or other parts of New Mexico. The extreme dryness of the air and the general absence of wind make it really more comfortable and pleasant than the winter thermometer would seem to indicate. It is a matter of experience that one is more comfortable in New Mexico at 58° Fahr. than on the seaboard at 68°, even when in-doors. Out of doors the difference is much more in favor of New Mexico. Elegant little flowers have bloomed on the hillsides all winter and the Mexican laborers employed on The Hot Springs grounds have slept comfortably among them with no protection from the weather but their blankets.

In 1887, when the third Montezuma was open as the Phoenix Hotel, the Passenger Department of the Santa Fe Route published a forty-seven-page booklet entitled *Las Vegas Hot Springs, New Mexico*. Life in the territory is included under the heading "How to Go There":

It may be somewhat startling to state without qualification that New Mexico is a foreign country. It has long been under the American Flag; but it was, until the railroads came, only politically a part of our domain. To any one interested in ethnology, it is, with its sister, Arizona, very foreign and very interesting. The old civilization still remains, and the picturesqueness of old Spain is scattered all over the country. An isolated civilization always produces quaint results, and to the Mexican we may add in this country the still older and stranger civilization of the Aztecs, Toltecs, or whatever they may be decided to be, as represented in the people, who are called Pueblos (Poo-*aib*-lo). The name means simply a settlement, a village, and is given for convenience. All *other* Indians were wanderers. These—not "Indians" at all in our sense—lived always in villages, and cultivated the ground.

"Tesuque (Tay-*soo*-kee)," eleven miles from Santa Fe, is said to be "the nearest pueblo to Las Vegas Hot Springs, or at least the most convenient." At the pueblo, "the ways and doings of these patient, hospitable and long-suffering people may be seen, if not studied, with very little pains, and much in the fashion of a picnic."

The railroad's namesake city of "Santa Fé (Santah Fay)" is described as "the oldest, also the most curious of the cities now inhabited in this country," of which "not the least interesting fact is that it is a religious as well as a civil centre." The section concludes:

Decidedly the most mistaken idea one could imbibe would be that life in this country means personal discomfort. The dominant and penetrating power of the century is American civilization. It has brought everything with it thither, and the

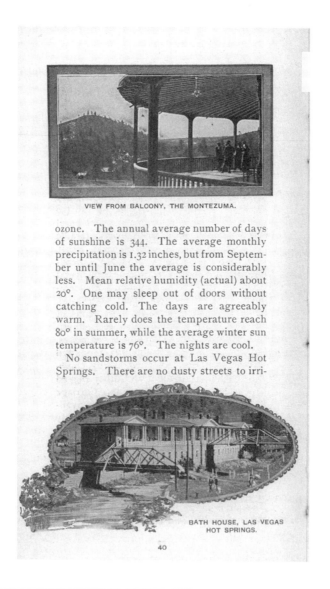

VIEW FROM BALCONY, THE MONTEZUMA.

ozone. The annual average number of days of sunshine is 344. The average monthly precipitation is 1.32 inches, but from September until June the average is considerably less. Mean relative humidity (actual) about 20°. One may sleep out of doors without catching cold. The days are agreeably warm. Rarely does the temperature reach 80° in summer, while the average winter sun temperature is 76°. The nights are cool.

No sandstorms occur at Las Vegas Hot Springs. There are no dusty streets to irri-

BATH HOUSE, LAS VEGAS HOT SPRINGS.

40

Las Vegas Hot Springs, page 40 in New Mexico Health Resorts, *Health-Seekers' Series No. 2, Santa Fe Passenger Department booklet, January 1903.*

most curious feature of the country is that it is the land of the telephone, the electric light and the daily paper; that the little Saxon boys and girls go to school, and look, as they go, precisely as they do elsewhere; that their mothers are precisely as such women are in an Eastern town, and their fathers are unchanged as to dress, demeanor and conversation. And yet beside it all, and running with it, is the stubborn old life of the Spanish peasant, as poor and as quaint as it ever was at home. It is, as ever, "a land where it is always afternoon." You may find it so. Your average countryman has ceased to notice it. He has not time. You have; that is what one goes there for; and the charm of the country, if half invited, will make for you a lasting memory of pleasant days.

The cover of the 1887 booklet carries the title *The Las Vegas Hot Springs and Surroundings near Las Vegas, New Mexico: The Karlsbad of America*. Calling it Karlsbad was the beginning of an ultimately unsuccessful campaign to recoup losses from the first two Montezuma hotels. The Panic of 1893 brought bankruptcy to the Santa Fe. The Montezuma was closed on September 1 of that year, reopening only during the summer seasons of the next decade until the railway shut it down on October 31, 1903.

In the January 1903 Santa Fe Passenger Department Health-Seekers' Series No. 2 booklet, *New Mexico Health Resorts*, Las Vegas Hot Springs is called "practically a village devoted to recreation and the restoration of health":

> The buildings are numerous, were erected at a large expenditure, and consist of The Montezuma, a palatial fire-proof structure of stone and iron with several hundred rooms and all modern conveniences, including elevators; numerous cottages and annexes; bath house, hospital, post office, casino, station house, schoolhouse; also telegraph and express offices, etc. A large park lies in the center. The buildings are steam heated and lighted by electricity.

It is prominent among the "sanatoriums and other special facilities for invalids [which] are found all the year round at Las Vegas Hot Springs, Las Vegas, Santa Fé, Ojo Caliente, Las Cruces, Silver City and El Paso, [while] the others are either summer pleasure resorts, like Jemez Springs, Sulphur Springs and El Porvenir or they are cities and villages, some of which possess certain business advantages, and all of which have New Mexico's universal endowment of pure mountain air." The latter are of interest to some of the sick and some of the healed:

> There are many seekers after health who must make a living while they are getting well. For their guidance a few pages are devoted to data concerning the avocations open to invalids, who can perform light manual labor. This information will also be of value to still another class, who, after having been restored to good health by the climate of New Mexico, must remain in that region in order to avoid a relapse, and who eventually find it necessary or desirable to engage in business.

In any case, however, "invalids should be urged to go in the early stages of disease. Marvelous cures are effected by this climate, but absolute miracles should not be expected."

5
Indian Detours, the Real Southwest

It is the purpose of the Indian-detour to take you through the very heart of all this, to make you feel the lure of the real Southwest that lies beyond the pinched horizons of your train window. In no other way can you hope to see so much of a vast, fascinating region in so short a time.... It is three days and three hundred miles of sunshine and relaxation and mountain air, in a land of unique human contrasts and natural grandeur.

—*Inaugural* Indian-detour *booklet, April 26, 1926*

It is along these old-new trails that we of the Harveycar courier corps would take you.... They lead us and our guests away into the beckoning, foot-loose distances of New Mexico and Arizona. They find out for us buried cities that flourished when Britons crouched in caves, reach medieval Spain dreaming away the centuries in the mountains of America, and string together age-old Indian pueblos where one may "catch archaeology alive." They lead us to the mines, the lumber camps, the open ranges and the painted canyons of the least known and most alluring corner of the United States.

Those who are passing on into the setting sun made the Southwest safe for you and for us. The railroad gave it gateways. Now the Harveycar has let down the last barriers of time and distance, of discomfort and inconvenience, until the Southwest's heart is no longer for the pioneer alone.

—Indian-detours: Most Distinctive Motor Cruise Service in the World *booklet,*
November 1930

7here is no record as to why the last significant Santa Fe/Harvey Great Southwest venture was initially called Indian-detour. On August 21, 1925, the day after the plans had been announced in Albuquerque, the *Albuquerque Morning Journal* carried an editorial on the proposed "Santa Fe Auto Tours":

> It was the genius of Fred Harvey that recognized the historic interest of the land traversed by the Santa Fe and the unique character of the Indian and old Spanish customs and industries. His influence was seen in the architecture of the stations and in the museums which he made a part of them. He collected vast quantities of objects almost priceless and thus saved them from destruction. So far as he could he brought historic New Mexico to the trans-continental traveler. It is appropriate therefore that his company is connected with the latest development of taking the tourist away from the railway directly to the places of scenic, historic or archaeological interest.
>
> Fred Harvey had in fact the true spirit of the collector and antiquarian. He insisted on authenticity. He discouraged the fairy stories that too often passed current to astonish the gullible tourist. If Fred Harvey showed an old Spanish bell there was no doubt of its age. If one of his agents related an historical incident or an Indian legend, its veracity could be relied on. Because of the insistence on authenticity which Mr. Harvey drilled in his organization, we may be sure the planned tours will not be vulgarized. The tourists will not be regaled with fanciful stories and amused with "fake" objects of interest. They will have presented to them the life of New Mexico both as it has been and as it still is.

These "presentations" followed three decades of publicity by the Fred Harvey Company and the Atchison, Topeka & Santa Fe Railway which had bought the failed railroad in 1895.

Atchison, Topeka and Santa Fe Railroad fortunes suffered during the financial panic and depression of 1893–94, and the company was placed in receivership on December 23, 1893. Two years later, on December 10, it was sold to the Atchison, Topeka & Santa Fe Railway, which appointed Edward Payson Ripley as its president and established executive offices in Chicago. "A man with lifelong railroad management experience and one of the leading figures in developing the Chicago World's Columbian Exposition of 1893, Ripley turned the Santa Fe around within six months" and by 1900, according to Santa Fe Railway historian Edward Hungerford (1923, 44), "was recognized as a consummate genius in his profession":

> Ripley at heart was an advertiser. He seized upon [Santa Fe passenger traffic manager W. F.] White's [promotional] plans and ordered them carried forward. He

found the Fred Harvey System a struggling chain of eating-houses along the lines, and his force and inspiration helped the Harvey's, father and sons, to make theirs the greatest organization of hotels and restaurants in the entire world. Ripley rightly regarded the Harvey meals as one of the very finest advertisements that his railroad possibly could have.... Their service quickly became the road's greatest single advertisement.

By 1896 Santa Fe passenger traffic manager W. F. White was exploring means to make the railway more competitive. Ripley strongly encouraged these efforts because, writer and filmmaker T. C. McLuhan (1985, 16–17) contends, he was "faced with the immediate problems of removing the stigma of recent bankruptcy and the railroad's callous image as an arrogant practitioner of nineteenth-century free enterprise" and so turned "to study seriously the possibilities of using advertising to enhance the [line's] image." Under Ripley, W. F. White, and the latter's successor George T. Nicholson,

the Santa Fe began to devote itself to the heritage of America, the wilderness, and the Indians. With patriotic drama and allure, the railroad's advertising became a sustained hymn to *natural* America. The imagination was encouraged to roam into the farthest reaches of the wilderness, where an ideal new world was promised— the exotic and simple life of an earthly paradise.

Until his sudden death in 1900, Charles A. Higgins served as Nicholson's assistant general passenger agent in charge of advertising. Remembered by the Santa Fe as a romantic who "loved the Grand Canyon ... [and] the great Southwest, big with historic, scenic and human interest" and one whose "grasp of the ancient and modern in Indian life (facilitated by membership in one of the most exclusive Moki [Hopi] secret societies), would ultimately have made him prominent among ethnologists" (*Grand Canyon* 1906, 9), Higgins epitomized the railway's new direction.

That direction had been fully realized by 1933 when they eulogized Higgins's successor, William Haskell Simpson, who had worked nearly fifty-two years for the Santa Fe with "three loves": "One was for his family; one for his railroad; one for that vast, indefinable, question-stirring workshop of God that those of us who live in it think of unconsciously as the Santa Fe Southwest" ("William H. Simpson" 1933; Howard and Pardue 1996a, 81). Simpson's corporate importance is emphasized in his June 13, 1933, *Santa Fe New Mexican* obituary:

As an advertising expert and executive, he was in charge of what has been for all these years probably the most elaborate, ambitious and effective program of development publicity ever inaugurated by any railroad. The Santa Fe Company has led the field in the style and character of its printed business propaganda, selling Santa Fe service, and the middle west and southwest territory, its resources and opportunities, to the world.

Art was key to the Santa Fe's new promotions and would prove "the basis for revolutionizing corporate advertising and the development of the first, and one of the most important, corporate art collections in the country." Encouraged by Ripley, traffic manager W. F. White's first advertising success came when he "hit upon the great painting of the Grand Cañon which Thomas Moran had just completed.... The road bought all the rights to the Moran picture [in 1912] and had very careful lithographic reprints made of it. These it framed in handsome gilt frames and then sent them out, first by the hundreds and then by the thousands. It placed them in offices, in hotels, in schools, even in homes – almost anywhere that there was a fair chance of the picture bringing in business" (D'Emilio and Campbell 1991, 3, 8–9). The Santa Fe Railroad had sponsored Moran's initial visit to the Grand Canyon in 1892, the first of many such Southwest trips by him and numerous artists (and writers) whose work then adorned guidebooks, posters, calendars, menus, and other promotional materials.

Photographer William Henry Jackson, who became known as the Father of the Picture Postcard, was first employed by the Santa Fe Railroad in 1892, when he accompanied his friend and collaborator Thomas Moran to the Grand Canyon. In 1897 he became a partner in the Detroit Photographic Company, a mass market postcard publisher which thereby received twenty thousand negatives of his own and other western photographers like Adam Clark Vroman. Jackson toured the Southwest in a specially outfitted Santa Fe Railway car that served as a showroom for the Detroit Photographic Company, which changed its name to the Detroit Publishing Company in 1904, the year it contracted with the Fred Harvey Company and the Santa Fe to produce postcards and other photographs for them. According to art historian Peter B. Hales (1988, 266):

At a time when the Southwest remained one of the few regions tourists still insisted they'd rather travel through at night than during the daytime, Harvey's decision to use the Detroit Photographic Company and the postcard medium as a means of generating a new and more positive image, was brilliant.... Focusing first on the most obvious points of touristic interest, the earlier sets [of views] "worked up" the Grand Canyon, revitalized the Indian as a creature of interest to visitors, and began to market a new Western sublime of the desert.... Harvey's set showed Kit Carson's house, Navajo medicine men, an "Apache War Party," Indians on horseback, Indians in ceremonial garb, Indians in all possible poses designed to suggest to the viewer the possibility of reenacting a mythological Western past without danger to self or property. And this presentation dovetailed with the campaign to present the dry Southwest as a place with an exciting past and a picturesque present.

In 1926 the Santa Fe purchased and leased to the Harvey Company a failed hotel on the southeastern corner of its namesake city's plaza. Built in 1920 on the site of hostelries dating back to the Mexican period, in its two years of operation La Fonda Hotel had used the advertising slogan "Inn at the end of the Santa Fe Trail." The building was the last major commission in Santa Fe for Isaac Hamilton Rapp and his Rapp, Rapp and Hendrickson architectural firm (Sheppard 1988), and they incorporated elements of their design for the 1917 State Art Museum diagonally across the plaza (Wilson 1997, 138–39; also Lynn 1999, 29–46). Architect John Gaw Meem designed the remodel; its interior decoration was the work of Harvey Company architect Mary Colter, who was asked by a friend

if she was at all apprehensive about decorating a major hotel in Santa Fe, a town full of artists. Colter confided, "I'm scared to death of these Santa Fe artists." She needn't have worried. Fred Harvey opened the remodeled La Fonda in 1929, and it soon became a landmark. Not only did it become a mecca for tourists to the Southwest, but it was a haunt for Santa Feans as well. (Grattan 1980, 54; also Berke 2002)

The inaugural July 1929 booklet *La Fonda in Old Santa Fé: The Inn at the End of the Trail* proclaims: "La Fonda of today—the present hotel was completed only in the late spring of 1929—is another Santa Fe-Fred Harvey dream come true; a dream for the fine development of that Southwestern empire carved out in the Trail days that have passed."

Santa Fé's crude *fondas* of other days were famous as the End of the Trail. La Fonda of today was created to be both the End and Beginning of Trails—for those who would step aside for a time from accustomed things, to follow a hundred new and old ways into the hidden corners of a singularly beautiful and interesting section of our country as yet undisturbed and unspoiled by the rush of modern life.

La Fonda served as headquarters for the Santa Fe/Harvey Indian Detours when they began in 1926. The 1929 remodel accommodated new guest rooms for the increased tourist traffic, a Courier Lounge with maps, photographs, books, films, and lantern-slides about New Mexico and Arizona, and an Indian Lecture Lounge where illustrated talks on the Southwest were given nightly. When Harvey opened Winslow, Arizona's, La Posada Hotel in 1930, it became the Arizona fleet base, thus assuring tourists that "the Southwest

La Fonda in Old Santa Fé, *cover design by Santa Fe artist Gerald Cassidy,
Rand McNally & Co., July 1929. The final page begins: "La Fonda, The
Inn at the End of the Trail, and the Indian-detour and Harveycar Motor
Cruises have been developed side by side as means to a definite end. To Old
Santa Fé, the logical capital of those who would know and enjoy the off-the-
beaten-path Southwest, La Fonda brings the utmost in hotel service and
comfort. The Indian-Detour and Harveycar Motor Cruises, in a motor
service of the same high standard, solve all the problems of exploration."*

is theirs to command, from Trinidad and Santa Fe to Yuma; from Grand Cañon to the Carls-bad Caverns, and beyond" (in Weigle 1996b, 48).

With Santa Fe Railway authorization, the Fred Harvey Company's Major Robert Hunter Clarkson had announced in Albuquerque on August 20, 1925, the launch of "an Indian detour rail and motor way which will enable rail tourists from Chicago and California to see points of historic and scenic interest in this state and at the same time to travel on a fixed schedule ... [during] three days of unusual motoring through oldest America, in the New Mexico Rockies between Las Vegas and Albuquerque ... [providing] a pleasant break in the cross continent rail trip the year 'round." The next day's *Albuquerque Morning Journal* sported an enthusiastic front-page spread:

> The section of New Mexico included in the plan and Albuquerque as its most important city, will get the same advertising as has been given to Southern California as a section by the Santa Fe railroad, and as is given to the Grand Canyon as a special trip. When it is realized that the busses at Grand Canyon handled 50,000 passengers last year, an idea of the magnitude of the present undertaking can be had. It will not only bring tourists directly to New Mexico and Albuquerque—something which has never been done before on a large scale, but it will have the far more important effect of introducing easterners to the resources and beauties of New Mexico which can be seen in only few instances from the railroad car windows. It will, in a sense, be an announcement of the "open door" to New Mexico. It will result in thousands of monied people seeing the possibilities of the state where only a very few see them now. (in Thomas 1978, 45, 50–51)

The first Indian Detour—two Harveycars, each with a male chauffeur in "cowboy" uniform and a female courier guide in "Navajo" uniform, and each carrying four tourists, called dudes—left the station-platform Harvey Castañeda Hotel in Las Vegas at 9:00 a.m. on Saturday, May 15, 1926. They stopped at the Pecos Pueblo ruins on the way to a tour of Santa Fe and two nights at La Fonda. The second day included visits to Tesuque, Santa Clara, and San Juan Pueblos and the Puyé cliff dwelling ruins. The third day brought them down La Bajada through Santo Domingo Pueblo to Albuquerque's station-platform Harvey Alvarado Hotel, from which they took afternoon trips to Isleta Pueblo and the city's Old Town. After dinner at the Alvarado there was a conducted tour of the adjacent Indian Building (Thomas 1978, 117–21). More and more tours were added in subsequent years, and the November 1930 booklet *Indian-detours—Most Distinctive Motor Cruise Service in the World....* lists a variety of custom-designed ones, as well as eight fixed trips: Frijoles-Puyé, Taos, Raton-Taos-Santa Fé, Carlsbad Caverns, Sierra Verde, Santa Fé-Grand Canyon, Hopi, and Navajo.

Centerfold map designed by artist Gerald Cassidy, Indian-detour,
Atchison, Topeka & Santa Fe Railway booklet, December 1927.

Like the Harvey Girls before them, young women trained as courier guides were considered crucial to the service. In the first *Indian-detour* booklet (April 1926) "Miss Erna Fergusson" is introduced as director of couriers: "The Courier Service has been inaugurated and the personnel trained with a view to providing visitors with interesting and authentic information on the archaeological and ethnological history of the Southwest. The couriers are women whose lives have been mostly spent in the region and who have intimate knowledge of its exceptional interest." Its six advisory board members and their credentials are listed: archaeologists Dr. Edgar Lee Hewett, School of American Research, Dr. A[lfred] V[incent] Kidder, Phillips Andover Academy, and Dr. S[ylvanus] G[riswold] Morley, Carnegie Institution; ethnologist F[rederick] W[ebb] Hodge, Esq., Museum of the American Indian; author Dr. Chas. F[letcher] Lummis of Los Angeles; and historian Paul F. Walter, Esq., president of the Historical Society of New Mexico. The board did not change until 1928, but Fergusson resigned her post in September 1927.

Erna Fergusson was a veteran at guiding tourists, whom she called dudes, via automobile: "When the war ended I began to dude-wrangle [and] dragged tourists all over New

Mexico, Southern Colorado, and Arizona to see Indians and Indian ceremonials." Together with her friend Ethel Hickey, also a native New Mexican, from 1921 until 1926 she operated Koshare Tours. Named "after the Pueblo dancers who, as emissaries of the gods, were called the 'delight makers' by [Adolph F.] Bandelier" in his 1890 novel *The Delight Makers*, according to literary historian Robert Franklin Gish (1996, 53; also Weigle 1992): "One of the early Koshare promotional brochures—almost as interesting for its advertisements as for its timetables and descriptions—announced to prospective customers the purpose of the company as envisioned by these two Southwestern entrepreneurs: 'Koshare Tours were created to reveal to you the delights of a land as yet but little known to the travelers, to invite you to get away from the railroad and shake hands with a thousand years.'" Fergusson's experience was invaluable to the Santa Fe/Harvey enterprise because, as the November 1930 *Indian-detours* booklet declares: "Yet nowhere on earth is that old, old business of intelligent guidance more essential. The whole land cries out for interpretation, from the gigantic masterpieces of Nature to the arts and crafts and curious customs of unspoiled native races and the tumultuous, unwritten frontier history that lurks behind every bush."

Major Clarkson hired well-known freelance travel writer Roger Williams Birdseye to head Detour publicity and advertising. In September 1926, Birdseye (1926, 8–9) announced "a fresh campaign of enlightenment" about the "new Indian-detour and allied motor services." In "Selling New Mexico Right" he advocates "intelligent exploitation [that] need never 'spoil' New Mexico, as some are prone to claim," because "economists tell us that scenery, 'atmosphere' and climate, in combination, form one of the greatest cash crops in America today." Birdseye claims: "Neither the State government nor any community or group of communities within the state, is today in a position to undertake a campaign of similar magnitude and diversity. The development of the Grand Canyon by the Santa Fe-Fred Harvey interests has meant much to Arizona as a whole; the development of the Indian-detour along contemplated lines will pay far greater dividends, directly or indirectly, to the people of New Mexico."

In 1928 Birdseye produced a fifty-six-page booklet for Indian Detours and the Passenger Department of the Santa Fe Railway. Entitled *They Know New Mexico: Intimate Sketches by Western Writers*, it contains essays by Dr. Charles F. Lummis, Alice Corbin Henderson, Mary Austin, Witter Bynner, Eugene Manlove Rhodes, and Elizabeth Willis De Huff, plus twenty-two poems in "And the Poets: A Little Collection of Verses about New Mexico, edited by Alice Corbin." In the lead essay, "The Golden Key to Wonderland," Lummis claims: "There is no other State in the Union of such centuried Romance as New Mexico; nor other town so venerable as Santa Fé, nor other road with half the history or a tenth the tragedies of the old Santa Fé Trail," concluding that "the ideals, the insight, the actual sanity—on top of the Harvey efficiency—which motivate this gallant plan, make it not only the happiest thing that ever happened for the traveler, but perhaps also for the Southwest":

Today the laziest traveler can not only see, in Pullman comfort, many of the wildest and noblest sceneries on this continent, and the most picturesque and fascinating types of humanity—but he can see *comprehendingly*, with guides so charming and so authentic as were never available before ... [who] give the tourist such insight and understanding as not one traveler in 500 ever got before. Through their trained and sympathetic eyes the tourist sees in the Pueblos not "funny mud houses" and "savage dances," but the immemorial architecture and dramatic rituals of the oldest American Aristocracy. And in the Mexican towns the quiet, high-bred heirs of the oldest Aristocracy in Europe—heirs whose own unbraggart heroism tamed this remote wilderness a generation before the Pilgrims landed, and has held it against vastly greater odds through the three centuries since; with their architecture, so sane and logical for the Southwest that it is eagerly copied by the intelligent among us. The Babbitt sneers at the adobe house; the artist or cultured millionaire buys an old one if he can, and fixes it up; or next-best, builds him a new one, near to the art of the old as possible—and never quite equals it!

6
Land of Pueblos

The State Flag of New Mexico has a modern interpretation of an ancient symbol of a sun design as seen on a late 19ᵗʰ century water jar from Zia Pueblo. This pueblo is thought to have been one of the Seven Golden Cities of Cíbola, which explorer Vásquez de Coronado sought. The red sun symbol was called a "Zia" and is shown on a field of yellow.... The red and yellow are the colors of Isabel of Castilla which the Spanish Conquistadors brought to the New World.... The flags of Spain, the Republic of Mexico, the Confederate States of America, and the United States of America have all flown over the "Land of Enchantment" during the long history of the state.

    —Office of the Secretary of State, New Mexico Blue Book, *2001–2002*

At some picturesque little railway station shining in the bright sun of the Southwestern desert country, the transcontinental traveler alights to pace the platform for a few minutes. His eye is attracted by the bright garb of the Indian woman who is offering bits of pottery for sale. A coin makes him possessor of an oddly-shaped jar or jug; when the puff of the train, a moment later, recalls him to his green plush seat, he carries with him in addition to the souvenir the impression that he has made the acquaintance of the Pueblo Indian in his native home. Hereafter he will feel a thrill of recognition when Indian matters are discussed.

    —Flora Warren Seymour, The Indians of the Pueblos, Little Blue Book No. 605, *Haldeman Julius Company, Girard, Kansas, 1924*

*D*espite the *New Mexico Blue Book* contention, a Zuni village and not Zia Pueblo was "thought to have been one of the Seven Golden Cities of Cibola, which explorer Vásquez de Coronado sought" in 1540. The medieval Latin European legend of seven fabulously rich cities dates from AD 1150, according to Roswell meteorologist and historian Cleve Hallenbeck (1987, 1; also Hammond 1979):

> In that year the Moors captured the city of Merida, in Spain, and—so runs the legend—seven bishops of the Church and their followers, fleeing *en masse* from the Moorish conquerors, boldly sailed away into the western ocean, seeking a legendary group of islands known as "The Blessed Isles," where they might re-establish themselves. After a long and stormy voyage, during which they more than once were swept out of their course, they came to a large and beautiful island, whereon they landed, burned their ships and founded seven settlements. They named the island Antilia. With the passage of time their settlements grew into seven great, rich, and beautiful cities that became known in Latin Europe as "The Cities of the Seven Bishops" or "The Seven Cities of Antilia." …After Columbus's discovery of the West Indies in 1492, it was believed by many people that one of the larger of those islands would prove to be Antilia. The name Antilles, now applied to the West Indies, is a reminder of that belief.

In Mexico, reports by Nuño de Guzmán in 1530 and Alvar Núñez Cabeza de Vaca in 1536 convinced the Spaniards that these seven cities lay in Indian lands to the north. The name Cibola, derived from an Indian word for buffalo, could have been a Comanche or other Plains term translated as referring "to the wealthy empire—another Mexico, another Peru—that Spaniards wanted to believe lay in the interior of North America" rather than to buffalo plains (Julyan 1998, 83).

In 1539 Estéban (Estevánico) de Dorantes, the black Moor slave in Cabeza de Vaca's party, accompanied Fray Marcos de Niza on his journey from Culiacán to within sight of a "city [that] is bigger than the city of Mexico," probably the Zuni village of Hawikku. Fray Marcos told the Indian "chiefs" accompanying him "how beautiful Cíbola appeared to me, [and] they told me that it was the least of the seven cities, and that Totonteac [Hopi] is much bigger and better than all the seven" (Hallenbeck 1987, 34, 19). The friar hastened back south without actually entering Cíbola because its inhabitants had earlier murdered Estéban, who journeyed ahead of the Franciscan's party and regularly sent back glowing word of his progress via Indian messengers.

The following year, Francisco Vásquez de Coronado headed a formal *entrada de conquista* that left Compostela on February 23 and reached Hawikku-Cíbola on July 7, 1540.

They stormed the pueblo and established headquarters there, naming it Granada. According to Coronado, all seven "cities" were in a radius of four leagues, some eighteen kilometers. Granada had "perhaps 200 houses, all surrounded by a wall"; another was "the same size as this," another "somewhat larger," and the remaining four "somewhat smaller." The disappointed Spaniards later heard of a great river to the east and populous "cities," which turned out to be Tiguex, the cluster of twelve Southern Tiwa pueblos along the Rio Grande near modern Bernalillo, where Coronado's army camped during the winter of 1540–41 (Riley 1975, 141). There and northward they found "other villages," which "are, for Indians, well worth seeing, especially one that is called Chia [Zia], another Uraba [Taos], and another Cicuique [Pecos]. [The last two] have many houses two stories high" (Winship 1896, 587; Hoebel 1979, 408).

Pottery was an art admired by Coronado and his men. Expedition chronicler Pedro de Castañeda praised Pueblo women for their "earthenware glazed with antimony and jars of extraordinary labor and workmanship, which were worth seeing." His praise was echoed in Hernán Gallegos's account of the 1581 Chamuscado-Rodríguez expedition: "These vessels are so excellent and delicate that the process of manufacture is worth watching; for they equal, and even surpass, the pottery made in Portugal" (Foote and Schackel 1986, 21). This lure is echoed in an 1882 *New York Tribune* clipping inserted into one of the scrapbooks kept by Colonel James Stevenson, who from 1879 led annual Smithsonian expeditions to the Southwest:

Ancient Indian pottery has been sought after through the past few years with great zeal. The custom of the average tourist, in seizing upon everything in the way of pottery that bears the semblance of age has made such a demand for 'prehistoric' wares that the ingenious mind of the native has led him to devise means of gratifying the aesthetic longings of his cultured brother. The method is simple. The Indian just manufactures it in proportion to the wants of the trade. (in Babcock 1990, 402–03)

Beginning around 1890 "and growing rapidly after 1910," what historian Richard H. Frost (1980, 5) calls "the romantic inflation of pueblo culture" transformed popular American attitudes toward the Pueblos, about whom previously there had been little "apart from a pervasive belief that [they] worshiped snakes and Montezuma, and were closely related to the Aztecs":

By the 1920s, in the popular mind the Pueblos were the most interesting of the American Indian tribes. Their positive qualities had grown larger than life. They were admired as ceremonialists and artists. Their pottery was sought by discriminating connoisseurs and curio-hunters. The beauty of their villages was interpreted in oil paintings displayed in prestigious eastern art galleries. Books and magazines sympathetically portrayed Pueblo life, and the style of their architecture inspired the remodeling of the capital city of New Mexico. The Pueblo Indian romance, a generation in the making, was fully ripe.

The Santa Fe Railway actively fostered this romance to increase passenger traffic.

Anthropologists as well as artists, writers, and photographers were enlisted in these Santa Fe/Harvey Great Southwest campaigns. Shortly before his sudden death in 1900, Charles A. Higgins, assistant general passenger agent in charge of advertising, accompanied George A. Dorsey, curator of anthropology at the Field Columbian Museum in Chicago, on "a memorable ten days' excursion into Hopiland." Dorsey (1903, 5; also Pardue 1996) recalls that afterward they boarded the east-bound train at Winslow, Arizona, on December 19, 1899, and "as we traversed for two days the broad stretch between Winslow and Chicago, our conversation, naturally, was of the Southwest, of its wonders, of the colors of its desert, of its atmosphere so pure that one can almost see into the beyond, of its ruins of ancient cities, of its Pueblos of to-day, conservative, proud, independent, mysterious." Higgins made Dorsey promise to prepare for him "an account of this land of which we were both so fond, explaining in popular manner the character of its peoples, and pointing out how they and their ruins might most easily be visited . . . [and it] should be accompanied by many photographs, which would present characteristic views, and by one or more maps whereupon might be seen the linguistic relationship of living peoples and the routes by which these peoples might be reached." In August 1901 at the Hopi Snake Dances, Higgins's successor, William Haskell Simpson, urged Dorsey to complete the project.

The initial printing of Dorsey's *Indians of the Southwest* in 1903 numbered 13,000 copies. Zia (Sia) is included in chapter six, "Lower Rio Grande Pueblos" (Cochiti, Santo Domingo, San Filipe [*sic*], Sandia, Santa Ana, Sia, Jemez, Isleta):

This is the smallest of all the Keresan pueblos, numbering about one hundred inhabitants. . . . Owing to the lack of water supply the people have never been successful at agriculture and are obliged to resort to other means for a livelihood. The women of the pueblo are famous potters and manufacture beautiful ware of white with red and brown decoration, which they dispose of to their more prosperous neighbors at Santa Ana and Jemez in exchange for agricultural products (73–74).

When his book first appeared, Dorsey was on partial leave of absence from the Field Columbian Museum, staying at the new Alvarado Hotel on the station platform in Albuquerque while working for the Fred Harvey Indian Department between January 1903 and April 1904. The Indian Department had been started in 1901 as a nonprofit organization.

After her father's death on February 9 of that year, when her brother Ford took over the family-owned business, Minnie Harvey Huckel "proposed the idea of establishing a museum at The Alvarado Hotel in Albuquerque [and] with the support of Ford Harvey … and John F. Huckel, her husband, plans were made to design and display ethnographic material in an elaborate craftsman-style museum" (Howard and Pardue 1996a, 9, 10). Two months before the Alvarado opened on May 11, 1902, the *Albuquerque Journal Democrat* of March 7 heralded the Indian Department's as "the most extensive ethnological museum in the country."

This fledgling endeavor was modeled after exhibitions and sales at world's fairs. German immigrant Herman Schweizer, known as "the Harvey anthropologist," was the main buyer and longtime "central force" in its operations. In a 1930 letter to writer Mary Austin, Schweizer relates:

Our place here was established thirty years ago on such a large scale, primarily as an advertising feature of the Santa Fe Railway, with a view of interesting the public in the Indians of the Southwest and their products, which purpose has admittedly been well served, and it has not only been of great benefit to the Santa Fe Railway, but to the Indians and all dealers in these products, as when we entered the field there was established values on anything, and a blanket or basket was worth only what anyone could get for it. The commercial side originally was a secondary consideration, as for commercial purposes alone the Railway Company would not have consented to devote such a large space for such a purpose. The major part of the Indian Building here was arranged in the form of exhibits, cozy corners, etc. to illustrate to people how these things can be utilized to best advantage. (Howard and Pardue 1996a, 12, 13, 15; also Howard 1996)

Pottery figured prominently in Indian Department enterprises throughout the Santa Fe/Harvey system from Chicago to California. As early as 1901 the Harvey Company bought from the already well-known Hopi-Tewa potter Nampeyo in Arizona for the department's new collection (Pardue and Howard 1996b, 171–72; also Kramer 1996). She is pictured twice in the introductory pottery section of Dorsey's *Indians of the Southwest:* in a 1900 photograph by Edward S. Curtis captioned "Nampeyo, of Hano, Decorating Pottery" and in an anonymous photograph (by Adam Clark Vroman) entitled "A Hopi Pottery Maker." The design from a pot Nampeyo made in 1904 and purchased by Fred Harvey Company architect Mary Jane Colter was used in several publications, including two covers on early booklets for the Indian and Mexican Building in Albuquerque. A "Notice" on the inside front cover of the twenty-fifth edition of *The Indian and Mexican Building, Albuquerque, N.M./Fred Harvey*, reads:

The California Limited, west bound, stops at Albuquerque one hour during which time passengers are invited to visit the Indian and Mexican Building and the Indian Museum. These buildings are adjacent to the platform and but a few yards from the train. At Albuquerque, a representative of Fred Harvey from the Indian and Mexican Building will accompany the train for several hours to show and explain to passengers ...specimens of Indian wrought silverware, Navaho blankets, ...etc. The stock is identical with that exhibited at Albuquerque, and may be purchased; the prices (plainly marked) are the same as charged there.

One of the Fred Harvey Indian Department's most reprinted publications, *American Indians: First Families of the Southwest*, was edited by its founder and head John F. Huckel. The cover of the first edition (ca. 1913) features a "Hopi Flute Boy," that of the second edition (1920), "A Cochiti Chief." The cover of the third edition (1926), a stylized, art deco olla maiden, was designed by Harvey Company artist Fred Geary and appeared on all subsequent editions. In cover image and contents *First Families* editions "exemplify the 'Pueblo-centrism' and the 'family values' of all domains of Santa Fe/Harvey discourse" (Babcock 1996, 208, 209; the three covers pictured in Howard and Pardue 1996a, 91).

In the 1930s the Santa Fe Railway and the Fred Harvey Company lobbied unsuccessfully to designate New Mexico as the Land of Pueblos. By the mid-1930s Tourist Bureau director Joseph A. Bursey succeeded in identifying the state as the Land of Enchantment. Still, in 1941, the year "Land of Enchantment" first appeared on license plates, the centerfold map in a New Mexico State Tourist Bureau booklet, *New Mexico "Land of Enchantment,"* identifies the Zia sun symbol as a "symmetrical design, now the trademark of things New Mexican, [which] is the symbol of the life-giving sun as conceived by the Indians of the Zia Pueblo. In red on a yellow background it forms the State flag of New Mexico."

That second state flag replaced the first one adopted in 1915 and originally designed to fly over the New Mexico Building at the San Diego Panama-California Exposition. In 1920 the New Mexico Chapter of the Daughters of the American Revolution began advocating for a new flag more "representative of New Mexico's unique character" and in 1923 sponsored an unsuccessful design competition. They finally appealed for help to Santa Fe district public health officer Dr. Harry P. Mera, whose avocational interest in archaeology led him to choose a sun design painted on a late 1800s or early 1900s Pueblo of Zia pot. The original pot design showed a face inside the sun's circle, but the DAR rejected it in favor of a plain center. Mera's wife Reba sewed a prototype for presentation to the state legislature, which adopted House Bill No. 164 on March 19, 1925 (Polese 1968, 32–33): "Said flag shall be the ancient Zia Sun Symbol of red in the center of a field of yellow. The colors shall be the red and yellow of old Spain."

Fifty-two years after the state flag's adoption, another Museum of New Mexico Zia pot was put to official government use. Paintings of Pueblo pots by Santa Fe artist Ford Ruth-

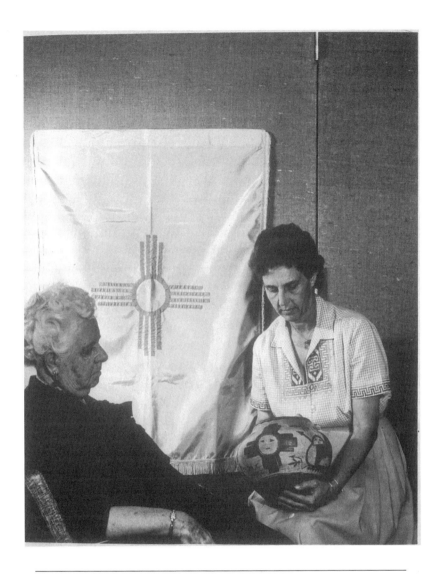

The second state flag, adopted on March 19, 1925. Mrs. Harry P. (Reba)
Mera, who sewed the prototype, looks at the inspirational Zia Pueblo pot
held by Betty Toulouse. (Museum of New Mexico Neg. No. 50131)

ling were subjects for a block of four thirteen-cent commemorative stamps issued by the
United States Postal Service on April 13, 1977. The museum and New Mexico Democratic
Governor Jerry Apodaca had "directly sponsored" the project. Each painting/stamp depicts
a different polychrome Pueblo pot fashioned by an unknown potter between 1800 and
1930: *Zia: Museum of New Mexico; San Ildefonso: Denver Art Museum; Hopi: Heard*
Museum Phoenix; and Acoma: School of American Research.

Official 1939 Road Map of New Mexico, *designed by Bradford-Robinson,*
Denver. The photograph shows famed San Ildefonso Pueblo potter Maria
Montoya Martinez and her husband Julian Martinez. The couple worked at
the San Diego Panama-California Exposition in 1915.

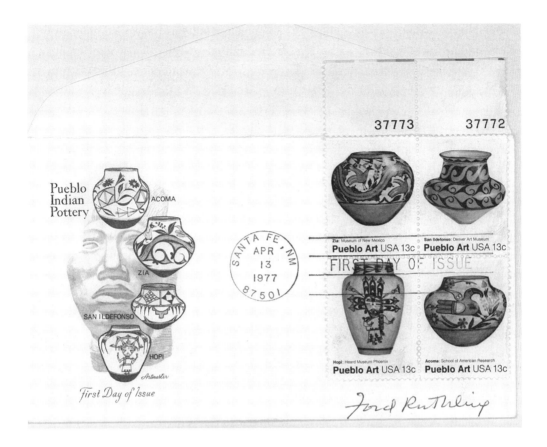

Pueblo Art postage stamps, First Day of Issue, Santa Fe, April 13, 1977.
According to the First Day of Issue Ceremony, Pueblo Indian Pottery Stamp
Program: "The designs of the Pueblo Pottery Stamps are based on
paintings by New Mexico artist Ford Ruthling, a student of Pueblo Indian
cultures.... Pots depicted on the stamps were made by unknown craftsmen
between 1880 and 1920, and each is now in the care of museum curators in
the Southwest: Zia, at the Museum of New Mexico in Santa Fe;
San Ildefonso, at the Denver Art Museum; Acoma, at the School of American
Research, Santa Fe; and Hopi, in the Heard Museum, Phoenix."

In his introduction to Francis H. Harlow's *Pueblo Art: Southwestern Indian Pottery*, a 1983 Somesuch Press miniature book with each of the four stamps affixed on pages throughout, Ruthling (in Harlow 1983, 9, 10; also Cameron 1977) recalls the issue's "success": "The local postmaster increased his gross profits by the sale of 135 million 13-cent stamps—which made that branch look great on the books in Washington." It "was entered into the world competition for stamp design and won the prize for best design and second most popular for 1977." He observes that "the value of historic Pueblo Indian pottery has soared beyond reason, and the audience of appreciators of it has broadened immensely."

Historian Joe S. Sando of Jemez Pueblo does not mention the Zia symbol's adoption on the state flag in his *Pueblo Nations: Eight Centuries of Pueblo Indian History*, but in his review of "Pueblo Economy" he (1992, 150) decries that "it sometimes seems as though everyone in New Mexico earns money from tourism except the Indians" because "native arts and crafts are sold throughout New Mexico and the Southwest, but the dealers who profit are mostly non-Indians." Two years later, in January 1994, Representative James Roger Madalena, a Democrat from Jemez Pueblo, introduced a bill in the New Mexico State Legislature to compensate Zia Pueblo $45 million for having used its sacred sun symbol on the state flag since 1925.

According to an Associated Press release printed in the *Albuquerque Journal* on January 28, 1994, Madalena, whose district includes Zia, "said the symbol is very sacred to the pueblo's 300 members ... [and this] marks [their] first attempt to right a wrong. 'It's long overdue,' he said." Their efforts were unsuccessful, and the following year, according to an *Albuquerque Journal* editorial of January 30, 1995: "Just when one might have been struck with the hypocrisy of a pueblo offering to 'sell' a sacred symbol, spokesmen said the dollar figure was merely to get the state's attention. 'We want the Legislature and the state to recognize this symbol rightfully belongs to the people of Zia,' said Peter Pino, tribal administrator, to the House Judiciary Committee." The editors note that "the ancient symbol, long in general use in New Mexico," was not contested until 1994, so "the state can't consider paying Pueblo of Zia for past or future use of the symbol on the state flag—and, given the assertion that the money was mentioned only as an attention-getter, perhaps that point is moot anyway." They recommend: "Zia should make clear just what it would like the state to do with regard to the Zia sun symbol, and then the Legislature can decide on a reasonable course of action."

A February 18, 2001, Associated Press release in both the *Albuquerque Journal* and the *Santa Fe New Mexican* reports that Zia tribal administrator Peter M. Pino (see Sando 1998, 287–91) again appeared before the New Mexico State Legislature and told the Appropriations and Finance Committee that "this issue has been a sore and hurt for the people of Zia for 76 years." Besides being the official state symbol, the Zia sun symbol "is widely used . . . by businesses and organizations, [and] Pino said the pueblo had found at least 96 private entities using the symbol." He and Zia Governor William Toribio assured lawmakers that there were no plans to sue and "no desire to stop the state from using this symbol," only a request "to approve a bill to require negotiations between the state and pueblo to determine how to compensate the pueblo for unauthorized use of the Zia symbol" and to pay "$50,000 for the Office of Indian Affairs to facilitate the proposed negotiations."

Pino "contrasted the state's years of silence and inaction to a request by Texas-based Southwest Airlines for permission to use the Zia symbol on an airliner. A religious elder said a prayer at a dedication ceremony last year for the plane. The company also made a donation to the pueblo for a college scholarship fund." The amount of the Southwest Airlines donation was not disclosed, but Pino urged: "Let us start talking. Let us find a solution like we found with Southwest." His ten-year-old granddaughter Sabrina Pino "also asked lawmakers to resolve the issue and said she represented the pueblo's future generations that could benefit from any compensation from the state."

On Flag Day, June 14, 2001, the North American Vexillological Association announced the results of a three-month, online survey judging United States and Canadian flags. New Mexico's Zia sun symbol flag narrowly defeated the Lone Star flag of Texas as North America's best. According to an Associated Press release in *The Santa Fe New Mexican* on June 16, 2001: "Following New Mexico in the top 10 were Texas, Quebec, Maryland, Alaska, Arizona, Puerto Rico, the District of Columbia, the Marshall Islands and South Carolina. The bottom 10 were New Hampshire, Idaho, Wisconsin, Kentucky, Minnesota, South Dakota, Kansas, Montana, Nebraska and [last] Georgia."

Everywhere in New Mexico You'll Find the Strange and Different

Just driving along through this clear air and bright sunshine, with an ever-changing scenic background, is a fascinating experience — but all along your route are strange and different things to stop and examine more carefully. On U. S. Highway 85, near the active town of Hot Springs, famous for its curative waters and the Carrie Tingley Hospital for Crippled Children, is the great Elephant Butte Dam and Lake, with boating, swimming and fishing to offer. Near Española, on U. S. Highway 285, are the ruined cliff dwellings of Puye, one of the most interesting spots in the State. North of U. S. Highway 54-66 between Santa Rosa and Tucumcari, is the big Conchas Dam, its construction supervised by Army Engineers. Other dams for irrigation projects are Alamogordo Dam near Fort Sumner, and Avalon and McMillan between Carlsbad and Artesia. Shiprock, towering desert landmark climbed but once, is near the town of Shiprock at the junction of U. S. Highways 550 and 666. In Southwestern New Mexico, near Silver City, once a gold and silver mining center, is the largest open-pit copper mine in the world. In this same section are Lordsburg and Deming, still redolent of the Old West, fine stepping points on U. S. 80. Near Roswell are the interesting Bottomless Lakes, and Bottomless Lakes State Park, with fine swimming facilities. East of Artesia and around the border town of Hobbs are the oil wells in what are predicted to be the giant oil fields of the future. The traveler entering New Mexico on U. S. Highway 60, 70 or 84 will find excellent accommodations in the thriving little city of Clovis, center of a fine dry-farming region. Southward on U. S. 70 is Portales, where irrigation is used to raise splendid crops. Everywhere in New Mexico you'll find good hotels, auto camp grounds and restaurants ready to accommodate you.

"Everywhere in New Mexico You'll Find the Strange and Different,"
New Mexico "Land of Enchantment," *State Tourist Bureau booklet, 1941.*

Part Three
Road: The Strange and Different

New Mexico! The first white men to set eyes upon its magnificent distances were valiant Spanish adventurers plodding weary leagues up from Mexico in search of the fabled seven Cities of Cibola and the Gran Quivira, seeking the new, the strange and the different. Since Coronado and De Vargas wrote so largely upon the first pages of American history, New Mexico has been the Land of Enchantment for the traveler. From the sixteenth century to modern today, New Mexico has lured men from afar off. The fascination is undimmed by time. You, too, will find it, share it, never forget it. Whether you must hurry through a week or two, or whether you can linger for a year or more, New Mexico will have something new for you each day.

—"Introduction," 2 Weeks in New Mexico "Land of Enchantment," New Mexico State Highway Department booklet, 1934, and from 1935 in New Mexico State Tourist Bureau editions

When he took office on January 1, 1935, Governor Clyde Tingley promised a "Greater New Mexico" and issued an invitation reminiscent of the one Mexican Governor Facundo Melgares offered to William Becknell in 1821: "To those who live outside New Mexico I want to extend an invitation to make the State their home, whether for one week, a month or twelve months in the year" (Tingley 1935). The governor immediately turned to roads and tourism for the twin keys to economic development, as he reiterated in December 1937 during his second term of office: "New roads will not only increase tourist travel to New Mexico but will greatly increase travel within the state ... [making] the state's great recreational areas more easily accessible both to tourists and our own residents" ("U.S. 66 Opened" 1937). Soon after taking office Tingley reorganized the Highway Department and Commission and set up a new unit, the New Mexico State Tourist Bureau, to initiate and coordinate advertising the state.

The New Mexico State Highway Commission had been established in 1917 to oversee the State Highway Department and later its publicity. The first issue of *New Mexico Highway Journal* (July 1923), originally an in-house organ, includes among the items about personnel, road construction, and other projects this notice:

> While automobile tourists seek the attractions of local scenery, there is another big element in drawing them. That is the condition of the roads. A state that keeps its roads in good order is going to get a great deal more vacation travel from now on than it ever had before. This will go far toward paying for keeping the highways in good condition (10).

Its first tourism article, Erna Fergusson's "Acoma, the City of the Sky," appeared in the second issue, dated October 1923 (see Zeman 2003). In July 1931 the *Highway Journal* merged with the State Game and Fish Department's in-house organ, *New Mexico Conservationist* (1927–31), to become *New Mexico: The Sunshine State's Recreational and Highway Magazine*, changed to *New Mexico: The State Magazine of National Interest* in November 1934. It became *New Mexico Magazine* in February 1938. Initially a free publication supported by advertising, it went on sale for fifteen cents a month, one dollar a year in 1933.

The magazine's first editor, Highway Department draftsman Ray W. Bennett, was replaced by "hunting-and-fishing enthusiast" Harry E. Shuart in 1931. The latter "introduced color, including a cover, *Navajo Shepherdess*, by famed painter Gerald Cassidy, an art column that was to last 31 years by Cassidy's wife Ina Sizer Cassidy, a *Poet's Page* and *Southwestern Bookshelf*." At the behest of newly installed Governor Tingley, *Albuquerque Tribune* reporter George M. (Fitz) Fitzpatrick, who had begun work at the paper in 1927 and wrote a column entitled "Off the Beaten New Mexico Path," became *New Mexico* editor in 1935 and kept the position for the next thirty-four years. He solicited manuscripts from "every published writer in the state" and "though he could afford only about $10 an article, …received contributions from such notables as painter Peter Hurd, Pulitzer Prize-winner Conrad Richter and Southwestern novelist Harvey Fergusson" (Hillerman 1974, 29; also Sinclair 1982).

The State Highway Department launched an official map program in 1925, but the first directed at tourists was the *1930 Road Map of New Mexico the Sunshine State*, drafted and illustrated by the department's chief draftsman Bertram C. Broome (Carroll 2001, 25, 26). That year the department also set up a Service Bureau to answer routine tourist requests for information. These efforts were complemented by the June 1933 inauguration "of a full-fledged highway patrol, carefully selected and trained, [whereby] New Mexico promises motor tourists and travelers within her borders not only scenery unsurpassed, historical settings and archaeological ruins of unique interest, fishing, hunting and recreation areas second to none, but excellent highways leading to all these regions, patrolled by a fine group of courteous, uniformed young men, alert to assist the stranded in emergency, to direct strangers, and to corral law breakers of every description, particularly violators of the highway code whenever and wherever encountered" (Bennett 1933, 7).

In 1937 the state's ports of entry became "ports of welcome" that served as "information bureaus" where motorists could receive "descriptive literature about the state" ("Ports of Welcome" 1937). The first fifty roadside Official Scenic Historic Markers were put up in 1937, and by 1941 there were over a hundred statewide. (In June 2002 there were 350 such roadside historic markers extant, and the program was administered by the State Cultural Properties Review Committee [Pike 2004; also Delgado 1990].)

By the time of the Second World War the state had secured the means for enchantment. Governor John E. Miles began his second term of office in January 1941 by cordially inviting "new readers of *New Mexico Magazine* who live outside the State . . . to visit New Mexico" and extending "to those who have vacationed here before . . . the hospitality for a return visit in 1941" (Miles 1941). His New Year "Greetings" recall and fulfill the intentions of the Territorial Bureau of Immigration:

> New Mexico has much that it can share with the rest of the world, and each year has seen a greater number of persons come to New Mexico to share these benefits —both as vacationists and as permanent residents.
>
> The census in 1940 showed New Mexico with the second highest percentage population gain in the Nation. We believe that strong, steady growth will continue. Our climate will continue to attract those who seek the sun and the health-giving air of the higher altitudes. Our magnificent scenic areas will continue to attract the vacationist, the hunter and fisherman, and the casual tourist. Our vast resources will continue to attract the pioneers—the rugged prospector and the wealthy investor seeking new fields of endeavor. Our towns and our rural areas will continue to attract those who seek a new start in a new land.

7
Land of Enchantment

Within the limits of Colorado, New Mexico, Arizona, and Southern California there are four centres of sublime and unparalleled scenic sublimity which stand alone and unrivalled in the world. Neither the Alps nor the Himalayas can offer any parallel to the phenomena of the mountain and desert systems of the Southwest.... Colorado, New Mexico, Arizona, and Southern California offer, all in all, a landscape panorama that for grandeur, charm of climate, and rich and varied resources is unrivalled. Imagination falters before the resources of this region and the inducements it offers as a locality in which to live surrounded by perpetual beauty. The air is all exhilaration; the deep blue skies are a miracle of color by day, and a miracle of shining firmament by night.... This entire Southwest can only be accurately defined as the Land of Enchantment.

—Lilian Whiting, 1. *"With Western Stars and Sunsets,"* The Land of Enchantment: From Pike's Peak to the Pacific, *1906*

The "Land of Enchantment" is adopted as the official nickname of New Mexico.

—*Section M, House Bill 13, "An Act Relating to State Symbols," signed by Governor Bill Richardson, April 6, 2003*

*N*ew Mexico became the Land of Enchantment by chance and by the design and diligence of two men: Albuquerque advertising executive Ward Hicks and freelance writer Joseph A. Bursey, who at one time worked for the Capitol Bureau of the *Albuquerque Tribune.* They consulted together about a program for publicizing the state even before Bursey became the first director of the New Mexico State Tourist Bureau in 1935.

Florida had started to use New Mexico's Sunshine State "slogan" when the two happened upon Lilian Whiting's 1906 travelogue *The Land of Enchantment: From Pike's Peak to the Pacific*. In an ad campaign launched on May 20, 1934, Hicks used only the first part of her title and apparently had little or no consideration for the book's text.

A journalist, essayist, poet, and travel writer, Lilian Whiting (1906, 3–4, 5) begins her book by chiding Americans ignorant of this Colorado-New-Mexico-Arizona-Southern-California "entire Southwest [which] can only be accurately defined as the Land of Enchantment":

> The good American of the Twentieth century by no means defers going to Paris until he dies, but anticipates the joys of Paradise by making a familiarity with the French capital one of the consolations that tend to the alleviation of his enforced terrestrial sojourn. All Europe, indeed, has become the pleasure-ground of American tourists, a large population of whom fail to realize that in our own country there are enchanted regions in which the traveller feels that he has been caught up in the starry immensities and heard the words not lawful for man to utter.

Whiting, who wrote seven other travel books (Boston, Florence, Italy, Paris, Athens, London, Canada), herself first journeyed to Europe from her Boston home in 1895 "and thereafter made eighteen pilgrimages abroad" (Terris 1982).

Like so many others of her day, Whiting had discovered her Southwest through the windows of Santa Fe Railway cars and enjoyed the Fred Harvey accommodations:

> There is one feature of this trans-Continental trip which is of the first importance to the tourist, and this is the line of artistic and beautiful hotels built after the old mission design, the architecture felicitously harmonizing with the landscape, —those Harvey hotels built in connection with the Santa Fé stations at principal points, as at Trinidad, Las Vegas, Albuquerque, and others, all christened with Spanish names,—the "Cardenas," the "Castañeda," the "Alvarado,"—all of which are conducted with a perfection of cuisine and service that is rarely equalled.... In connection with the Alvarado, at Albuquerque, are two buildings: one that offers a most interesting museum of Indian archaeological and ethnological collections, and the other showing native goods from Africa and the Pacific islands. Salesrooms connected with these enable the traveller to purchase any souvenir from a trifle, to the costly baskets, richly colored Navajo blankets, the strange symbolic pottery, or the objects of religious rites.

In 1905, twenty years before Major R. Hunter Clarkson announced the new Santa Fe/Harvey Indian Detours, she found that "a day's delay at Albuquerque enables the traveller to visit four interesting pueblos, —Santa Ana, Sandia, Zia, and Jemez, —in a day's stage ride between Jemez and Albuquerque" (1906, 195–96).

In Santa Fe Whiting encountered Colonel Max Frost, Republican leader, editor of *The* [Santa Fe] *New Mexican* (1889–1909) and secretary of the Bureau of Immigration (1889–1907). Among Frost's duties for the bureau was answering letters of inquiry: 1,010 for 1897–99, 2,200 for 1899–1900, over 6,000 for 1900–02, and 5,200 for 1904–06. In addition, "much of the secretary's time was consumed also by an increasing stream of visitors, each of whom seemed to have a special problem that required solving. In 1905 and 1906 as many as thirty persons appeared at the bureau office in Santa Fe each day" (Lang 1976, 199).

Whiting (1906, 225–26, 227) describes Frost as "a man who, though blind and para-lyzed, is simply a living encyclopaedia of historic and contemporary events…. He cannot move without assistance,—physically he is a wreck; yet he dictates columns of work daily; he is the most influential leader of the political party, and he is one of the makers of New Mexico. Every line of copy in his daily paper is read to him before it goes to press, and the vigorous editorial page is largely his work." He came to Santa Fe from Washington in 1876, "was urged to remain and become a citizen," and "became singularly identified with the general progress of the country." He serves as secretary of the Bureau of Immigration "with the most conspicuous ability":

> Under his electric touch and irresistible energy there is constantly prepared and sent out some of the finest transcriptions of the entire status of the country, in cli-mate, resources, and opportunities; in achievements already realized and in the potential developments of the future. Thousands of residents have been drawn to New Mexico through the data so ably set forth by Colonel Frost, the matter being, each year, revised to date. He knows, from personal observation and intimate con-tact, every part of the territory; he is personally acquainted with all the leading people; and no visitor in the territory can feel his trip in any sense complete with-out meeting Colonel Max Frost. If every state and territory in the Far West could command such efficient service in the literature of immigration as is rendered by Colonel Frost, there would be an appreciable increase of their settlers.

Despite Frost's "electric touch," Whiting (1906, 8) gives comparatively short shrift to New Mexico, which "has been more or less considered as one of the impossible and unciv-ilized localities, or has failed to establish any claim to being considered at all." Yet she does present the state as "the scene of surprises": "Traditionally supposed to be a coun-try that is as remote as possible from the accepted canons of polite society; that is also an arid waste whose temperature exceeds the limits of any well-regulated thermometer,—it reveals itself instead as a region whose temperature is most delightful, whose coloring of sky and atmosphere is often indescribably beautiful, and whose inhabitants include their fair proportion of those who represent the best culture and intelligence of our country" (182). Here, "the American civilization and high enlightenment has poured itself into this 'Land of the Sun King' [Montezuma],—the 'Land of the Turquoise Sky'" (194):

> It is no exaggeration to say that in many respects the archaeological interest of New Mexico, its atmosphere, its historic color, is as distinctive as that of Egypt or of Greece, Italy, or Spain. When, on December 15, 1905, the first long-distance telephone in Santa Fé established communication *viva voce* with Denver, while within a radius of fifty miles, ruins of prehistoric civilization fascinated the tourist, —surely the remote past and the latest developments of the present met and mingled after the fashion of "blue spirits and gray." (193)

Whiting's was not the only use of the phrase "land of enchantment" for New Mexico. In "A Number of Things," his April 8, 1911, *Saturday Evening Post* short story set in Socorro County, Eugene Manlove Rhodes calls it "a land of mighty mountains, far seen, gloriously tinted, misty opal, purple, blue and amethyst; a land of enchantment and mystery" (in Hutchinson 1975, 82). "Just back from the Snake Dance" at Hopi by car in August 1924, D. H. Lawrence exclaimed:

> Just a show! The Southwest is the great playground of the white American. The desert isn't good for anything else. But it does make a fine national playground. And the Indian, with his long hair and his bits of pottery and blankets and clumsy home-made trinkets, he's a wonderful live toy to play with. More fun than keeping rabbits, and just as harmless. Wonderful, really, hopping round with a snake in his mouth. Lots of fun! Oh, the wild west is lots of fun: the Land of Enchantment. Like being right inside the circus-ring: lots of sand, and painted savages jabbering, and snakes and all that. Come on, boys! Lots of fun! The great Southwest, the national circus-ground. Come on, boys; we've every bit as much right to it as anybody else. Lots of fun! (in Sagar 1982, 64)

Although such literary references may not have been familiar to Ward Hicks and Joseph A. Bursey, the Enchanted Empire of the Santa Fe/Harvey Indian Detours very likely was. In *Indian-detour*, a December 1927 Atchison, Topeka & Santa Fe Railway booklet, "The Enchanted Empire" is characterized thus:

> Words are futile things with which to picture the fascination of this vast, enchanted empire, unspoiled and full of startling contrasts, that we call the Southwest. It is a land of limitless panoramas and distances dwarfed by the clear, dry air; of flooding sunshine and intense color; of snow-capped peaks and twisting,

abysmal gorges; of sage and cedar and mountain forests; of lazy rivers and plung-
ing torrents; of broad mesas and rich, peaceful valleys. It is a land where the sunsets flame and the after-glow softens the harsh outlines of the wilderness into a
picture of unspeakable beauty; where the silence listens and the night stars glow
like headlights.

Bursey does not mention Whiting's book in his unpublished July 14, 1970, manuscript (Fray Angélico Chávez History Library, Museum of New Mexico, Santa Fe) "Birth of
a Slogan—THE LAND OF ENCHANTMENT":

Many people have asked me if it was original. The thought had never occurred to
me while it was under discussion, but if it had, I would have believed it to be original. Later we discovered that it had been used many places thousands of times.
But nothing came of it until, like Columbus discovering America, we did something about it.

Nevertheless, his Tourist Bureau secretary Bernice Duke recalls that "after Joe Bursey and
Ward Hicks learned that Florida was using the slogan of 'Sunshine State,' they luckily
stumbled across a book written in 1906 by Lilian Whiting...[and] the first part of the title
struck the men as being tailor made for New Mexico" (Dunleavy 1984, 64; also "Joseph
A. Bursey" 1961; Carrol W. Cagle in *Santa Fe New Mexican Pasatiempo*, March 24, 1968).
According to Bursey, Hicks had laid the groundwork for a New Mexico promotional program by forming "a state-wide organization composed of leading businessmen, newspaper
editors, chamber of commerce managers and individuals to push for [it ... while he], who
would profit finally from such an endeavor, stayed in the background."

On May 20, 1934, Hicks's Albuquerque agency, then Ward Hicks, Inc., later Ward
Hicks Advertising, under contract with the New Mexico State Highway Commission
launched a ten-week campaign intended "to bring tourists from the plains for holiday trips
in the cool highlands of the Sunshine State where blankets are needed every night" from
among the 810,000 readers of fourteen newspapers in Oklahoma City, Tulsa, Amarillo, Fort
Worth, Dallas, Houston, Austin, Waco, and San Antonio (Woodman 1934, 12, 13). The first
official use of the designation Land of Enchantment appears in quotation marks in the
three-column, ten-inch-deep advertisements: "Take a real Vacation this summer in cool
New Mexico 'Land of Enchantment'" and "7 National Forests call you to cool New Mexico 'Land of Enchantment.'" Text in the former reads:

Maybe you haven't had the vacations you needed in the last few years, so this year
take a REAL one! Come to New Mexico and bring the whole family to play out-of-
doors every day in brilliant sunshine and sleep under blankets every night. The

majestic mountains, rushing trout streams, and the fascinating historical interest of New Mexico are just an easy drive away, and you can find something new to see each day or just loaf and be lazy in some cool spot. Whether you camp out in the high country or take it easy in any of a hundred good hotels and ranches, you'll say this New Mexico vacation was the finest you ever had. Average minimum daily temperature for June, July and August at the U.S. Weather Bureau Station at the state capital over a 62 year period is just 55°!

Each ad includes a coupon which brought the inquirer free copies of the new 1934 highway map and the new 1934 edition (seventy pages) of the New Mexico State Highway Department's 1929 *Roads to Cibola: U.S. Scenic Highways of the Southwest . . . Official Tourist Guide of New Mexico.*

After he took office on January 1, 1935, Governor Clyde Tingley reorganized the Highway Department and established the New Mexico State Tourist Bureau to initiate and coordinate advertising for the state. During its first years of operation the bureau had the same three-person staff: director Joseph A. Bursey, appointed by Tingley in May, and Bursey's hires: secretary Bernice Duke and photographer Wyatt Davis. Initially, advertising work was contracted to Ward Hicks's Albuquerque agency. Almost all the Hicks design work was done by commercial artist Willard Harold Andrews, who had moved to Albuquerque from California in 1933 and "became a longtime principal at the highly acclaimed [agency] . . . known for his accurate and sensitive portrayal of Native Americans in a variety of media" (Carroll 2001, 26).

Andrews was responsible for designing the first three Tourist Bureau booklets published in its initial year of operation: a new edition of the Highway Department's 1934 *2 Weeks in New Mexico "Land of Enchantment"* (thirty-two pages, 50,000 copies), *"The First Americans": Indians of New Mexico* (thirty-six pages, 50,000 copies), and *Mission Churches of New Mexico* (forty pages, 25,000 copies). These were distributed within the state as well as sent to persons writing to inquire after seeing the bureau's first advertising campaign, carried by fifty-six newspapers in twelve states and fifteen national magazines with a total circulation of about twelve million in the summer and fall of 1935 (Bursey 1936b). Bursey (1936a, 19) directed bureau campaigns aimed not at those "already sold on the state [who] will come regardless, but . . . [those who] merely head west, with no fixed destination or itinerary, . . . open to conviction, eager to go somewhere and not difficult to persuade":

> The average tourist is highly gregarious, whether he will admit it or not. He wants to go where thousands have gone before him, and where thousands will come after he is gone. He wants to see the things which are already famous, and is relatively unconcerned with making discoveries for himself, or visiting natural wonders far off the beaten path.

2 Weeks in New Mexico "Land of Enchantment," *State Tourist Bureau booklet,*
1935. Designed by W. H. Andrews for Ward Hicks, Inc., its text is the same as that in
the first edition published by the New Mexico State Highway Department in 1934.

From the bureau's start, Bursey "formally adopted our new nickname" Land of Enchantment and began lobbying for its general acceptance. In his 1970 manuscript he recalls that
it "turned out to be some selling job":

It wasn't long until I could sympathize with the fellow who tried to change the name of Arkansas. It wasn't that people opposed the idea. They just didn't care. I wrote all the newspapers in the state, the chambers of commerce, the hotels, motels, restaurants, guest ranches, and all others who came in contact with tourists asking them to use the slogan on their menus, letterheads, and all pieces of literature. From the first I had complete cooperation from the Chambers of Commerce. The selling job was made more difficult because the publicity man for the Santa Fe Railroad [sic] was engaged in a similar move to have New Mexico change its nickname to THE LAND OF PUEBLOS. All their advertising and literature carried that slogan.

Although radio announcers began using Land of Enchantment on the air, Bursey did not consider the publicity sufficient until he got "an idea" from the New York license plates that carried notice of the 1939 New York World's Fair. He convinced Governor John E. Miles to "give me permission to place the new slogan on all our automobile plates" and, after also gaining permission from John McManus, warden of the state penitentiary where

he STRANGE and DIFFERENT in NEW MEXICO

18 *Ancient* INDIAN PUEBLOS

NOWHERE in North America does the Past extend into the Present as it does in the Indian Pueblos of New Mexico.

The recorded history of these people begins with Cabeza de Vaca in 1536, and his description of their villages led to the great expedition of Coronado in 1540. Some of these pueblos are still located today just where Coronado saw them. The ruins of others are still plain to see, and many others have been rebuilt near their original sites.

Ethnologists differ on the origin of these people, but the ruins of buried cities mark the homes of their forbears who lived in New Mexico thousands of years before the White Man first set eyes upon it.

RESERVATIONS

In addition to the lands of the pueblos, New Mexico holds four great Indian reservations.

1 SOUTHERN UTE
2 NAVAJO
3 JICARILLA APACHE
4 MESCALERO APACHE

1 Zuni, near point of Coronado's entry.
2 Acoma, the Sky City, with original Mission.
3 Laguna, on highway, with original Mission.
4 Isleta, on main highway, with original Mission.
5 Sandia, on highway just north of Albuquerque.
6 Santa Ana, with original Mission still in use.
7 Zia, with strange original Mission still in use.
8 San Felipe, with interesting re-built Mission.
9 Santo Domingo, with unusual re-built Mission.
10 Jemez, in the beautiful Jemez Mountain region.
11 Cochiti, between Albuquerque and Santa Fe.
12 Tesuque, with part of original Mission.
13 Nambe, of the Rio Grande group near Santa Fe.
14 San Ildefonso, famous for its black pottery.
15 Santa Clara, ranks with Ildefonso for pottery.
16 San Juan, named by Coronado in 1540.
17 Picuris, between Taos and Las Vegas.
18 Taos, with the largest communal dwellings.

Carlsbad Caverns NATIONAL PARK

9

[M]ORE than 150,000 visitors each year come to see the wonders this National Park that is [un]derground, which is considered [one] of the most beautiful and awe[ins]piring sights in the world. Park [Se]rvice Rangers conduct parties [over] good trails and stairways [thr]ough the most majestic rooms [in] the Caverns in a trip of four [ho]urs duration. Lunch is served [bel]ow the surface.

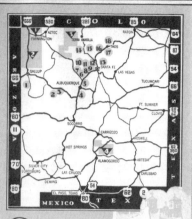

Oldest MISSION CHURCHES IN AMERICA

BETWEEN 1620 and 1630, one hundred and fifty years before the California Missions were begun, diligent friars were building a whole chain of churches in what is today New Mexico, and these Missions are the oldest in America north of the Rio Grande. In addition to those shown in the pueblo list opposite, there are the Mission of San Miguel at Santa Fe and the Mission of San Miguel at Socorro. Other interesting old churches, perhaps not original Missions, may be found at Taos, Santa Fe, Albuquerque, and such villages as Chimayo, Santa Cruz and Las Trampas. These ancient churches are monuments to a faith and courage seldom equalled and probably never surpassed.

Five of sixteen panels in the 1937 New Mexico State Tourist Bureau brochure
Welcome to the Land of Enchantment. *Designed by Willard Harold Andrews of Ward Hicks Advertising in Albuquerque.*

the plates were made, "the new [1941] licenses carried the proud slogan THE LAND OF ENCHANTMENT for the whole world to see." Bursey concludes: "After that the slogan sold itself with no further help from me."

In 1947 the Tourist Bureau, still under Bursey's direction, "filed with the Secretary of State for exclusive right to use the phrase [Land of Enchantment] as their trademark," according to the *Official New Mexico Blue Book, 1997–1998*, although, "oddly, the New Mexico Legislature has never adopted the phrase as the official nickname of the state." This was supposed to have been remedied by Section L ("'The Land of Enchantment' is adopted as the official nickname of New Mexico") of House Bill 633, "An Act Relating to Public Affairs; Adopting the State Nickname," signed on April 8, 1999. However, later that day House Bill 725, "An Act Relating to the State Question; Providing for an Official New Mexico State Question," was approved with a different Section L ("'Red or green?' is adopted as the official question of New Mexico"). Only the second bill signed by Governor Gary Johnson became law in 1999 (Steve Terrell in the *Santa Fe New Mexican*, August 14, 2001). It was not until Governor Bill Richardson signed House Bill 13, "An Act Relating to State Symbols," on April 6, 2003, that Section M ("'The Land of Enchantment' is adopted as the official nickname of New Mexico") became official state law.

8
Land of Sunshine

The Blood of Christ Mountains (Sangre de Cristo) never fail to thrill the beholder who watches the supernatural color changes which take place on their slopes at each sunset. The odd and unique houses of the [Santa Fe] Artist Colony are a perennial source of interest to newcomers as well as to old residents. Huge, gnarled, old trees border the running acequias. Flowers bloom and blow in each patio. Excellent hotels and numerous quaint shops border the old plaza which was once the end of the Santa Fe Trail and is today like the Café de la Paix in Paris—sit there long enough and everyone you know will pass by.

> —Roads to Cibola: What to See in New Mexico and How to Get There, *New Mexico Highway Commission booklet, July 1929*

In no other state of this union is the trend of life so clearly shaped by art as in New Mexico. Art has rescued this state from the commonplace and made it conscious of its own fine character. The arts have kept Santa Fe from becoming an "up-to-date burg" and made it unique and beautiful among the capitals of our country.... Santa Fe doesn't advertise for tourists or residents. They can't be kept away. Artists and writers constitute only a small percentage of the population, but their influence is wherever you look. Taos was a sordid little mud village when some of us first knew it. Now no one visits the Southwest without going to Taos. Its artists and writers are known throughout the world. The town is one of the jewels of New Mexico, and of this country....

Through its artists and writers, New Mexico has been made known to itself as well as to the outside world. It is capitalizing the charm of its historic landmarks, traditions, romantic episodes. The material for art and literature is limitless....

The conditions that bring forth great art are inherent in the soil, skies, wind, clouds, spaces of the great southwest. We who live in it have long felt the eternal character of these vast spaces, silent but vibrant with life and color—subtle, mysterious, elemental. Artists and writers are revealing this to the world.

> —From Edgar Lee Hewett's introduction to "Artists and Writers: A List of Prominent Artists and Writers of New Mexico," a special supplement to The Santa Fe New Mexican, June 26, 1940

While writing *The Land of Enchantment: From Pike's Peak to the Pacific*, Lilian Whiting (1906, 195) found that "New Mexico reminds one of Algiers. There is the same Oriental suggestion of intense coloring, of dazzling brilliancy of sky, of gleaming pearl, of floating clouds." Ninety years later, in *The Smithsonian Guides to Natural America: The Southwest, New Mexico and Arizona* (Page 1995, 25, 24), light is proclaimed the essence of "natural New Mexico," where "every vista in the state, every landform and ecosystem, whether it is unimaginable miles away or within the intimate confines of an adobe wall, is a creature of New Mexico's elusive, even angelic light":

> The most important natural area in New Mexico exists wherever one goes in the state. It is the sky overhead. For overhead is the great light show, the special quality people find in New Mexico that they cannot quite describe (the English language, perhaps the richest in the world in numbers of words, lacks fine distinctions about matters that are both meteorological and aesthetic). The sky and its sun are, in New Mexico, the soul-catchers.

D. H. Lawrence's description in "New Mexico," his essay for the May 1, 1931, *Survey Graphic* (in Sagar 1982, 96), is quoted: "The first moment I saw the brilliant, proud morning shine high up over the deserts of Santa Fe, something stood still in my soul, and I started to attend.... Never is the light more pure and overweening than there, arching with a royalty almost cruel over the hollow, uptilted world."

A hundred years before, Josiah Gregg (1954, 68) heralded the pure atmosphere of the prairies by explaining the actual three-mile distance between the wagon train and Round Mound, which seemed "but half a mile off—at most, three quarters":

> The optical illusions occasioned by the rarefied and transparent atmosphere of these elevated plains, are often truly remarkable, affording another exemplification of its purity. One would almost fancy himself looking through a spy-glass, for objects frequently appear at scarce one-fourth of their real distance—frequently

much magnified, and more especially elevated. I have often seen flocks of antelopes mistaken for droves of elks or wild horses, and when at a great distance, even for horsemen; whereby frequently alarms are occasioned. I have also known tufts of grass or weeds, or more buffalo bones scattered on the prairies, to stretch upward to the height of several feet, so as to present the appearance of so many human beings. Ravens in the same way are not unfrequently taken for Indians, as well as for buffalo.

The Smithsonian Guide (Page 1995, 24) deems such "purity" cosmogonic:

In New Mexico, on a proper day, every leaf of every creosote bush, every lavender wild-aster petal, every sunstruck rock face on a mountain miles off, stands out with a clarity that is existential. In such a light, the importance of a single rock, an individual flower, the existence of life itself, can strike one suddenly—fresh and poignant. What is distant seems near; what is near seems searingly real, insistent, poised. And with each change in the arc of the sun, especially at the beginning and end of its daily career, and with each passing cloud when they are present, the entire stage setting for the Creation is new, something never seen before.

When first she saw the "leopard land" around Santa Fe in December 1940, poet May Sarton (1976, 123–24, 125) found herself "unprepared in every way, unprepared for the air itself, seven thousand feet up, thin and dry so there is a bubble of physical excitement in one's chest; unprepared for the huge bare landscape that reminded me of Chinese paintings and of Northern Spain." She came from the East Coast to visit her art colonist friends Alice and Haniel Long: "I remember coming out in the early December dark and standing a moment under the immense sky, the hills lying at the horizon like great sleeping animals, and felt that tremor of something like fear which seizes one at the brink of major experience: out of the strangeness that opens a new layer in the subconscious, a homecoming—homecoming into a new world, an ancient world, the world of poetry for me."

Over a decade later, poet Winfield Townley Scott first came to Santa Fe from New England in the early 1950s. "The breadth and height of the land, its huge self and its huge sky, strike you like a blow.... Wind-blown, dry, half-barren, shining, the landscape vaulted about us as our friends drove us to Santa Fe from the station at Lamy," he writes in his 1957 essay "A Calender of Santa Fe" about that first year in the art colony (Scott 1976, 46, 48). On his first night in late August,

we had been driven, late afternoon, directly to our rented house on the Camino del Monte Sol and had not been into the center of the city—I stepped out onto the road and looked at a cluster of lights in the northwest. I assumed they were the lights of downtown Santa Fe. It was several days before I discovered they were the lights of Los Alamos, thirty-five miles away, and that the Jémez Mountains I looked at with a casual admiration out our west window were fifty miles away. This would be, back East, like standing in Providence and looking at Boston.

By October, Scott knew that "in this staggering spaciousness of earth and sky, light is the vital force, the nervous or majestic rhythm, the master painter."

Both May Sarton, who visited, and Winfield Townley Scott, who stayed, sought the company of artists and writers who had colonized first Taos and then Santa Fe (early e.g., Coke 1963; Weigle and Fiore 1982b). In July 1929 the New Mexico State Highway Commission recognized those art colonists in a thirty-two-page booklet "for Free Distribution," *Roads to Cibola: What to See in New Mexico and How to Get There:*

The cover design is an original woodcut done by [Santa Fe artist] Gustave Baumann, winner of international awards for his carvings. Mr. Baumann is one of the many famed artists who make their homes in New Mexico.

The double sketch in the middle of the book was made especially for ROADS TO CIBOLA by Will Shuster, painter, etcher, colorist and creator of a famous series of Indian heads now scattered in galleries and private homes all over America and growing in value and appreciation yearly. Mr. Shuster's home is in Santa Fe.

The poem is by Witter Bynner, poet, playwright, orientalist, some-time president of the American Poetry Association and one of the forerunners of the artist and writer emigration to New Mexico. Mr. Bynner's monumental work The Jade Mountain, translation of Chinese poetry on which he has been engaged fifteen years will be announced by his publishers shortly [*The Jade Mountain: A Chinese Anthology, Being Three Hundred Poems of T'ang Dynasty, 618–906*, Knopf, 1929]. His estate in Santa Fe is a veritable treasure trove of Indian and Oriental arts which he purposes to turn into a combined museum and garden of arts on his death for the use of coming generations of poets, painters and writers.

The photo layout at the back of the book was done by Willard F. Clark, a young artist from South America who now makes his home in New Mexico, and who directs a Santa Fe art gallery.

In his June 12 message, "A Word to Tourists," Governor Richard C. Dillon concludes: "If you are on a business trip you will find New Mexico a land of opportunities, where resources in agriculture, fruit growing, cotton, timber, livestock and minerals are practically untouched and awaiting development; also, a fascinating field for artists and writers." Inside the back cover, the New Mexico Highway Commission "(signed)" a testament to "The Total" that begins:

Roads to Cibola: What to See in New Mexico and How to Get There, *photo layout (Taos Pueblo, Pecos Ruins, In Northern New Mexico, Sanctuario of Miracles, Baking in Bee Hive Oven), New Mexico State Highway Commission, July 1929. "The photo layout at the back of the book was done by Willard F. Clark, a young artist from South America who now makes his home in New Mexico, and who directs a Santa Fe art gallery."*

In summing up in compressed form New Mexico's major attractions we find that the state is unique in presenting to view several tribes of Indians all of whom create an individual art and exhibit unique and original customs. Artists of international repute are found all over the state with two major art colonies housing large and well known groups, namely, the colonies of Taos and Santa Fe. A large group of writers whose names are household words also make New Mexico their home. It is probable that there are more of these two classes per capita in New Mexico than any other state. The greatest distinction which may be made, however, is that they are all producing workers and not dilettantes.

The "Blood of Christ Mountains (Sangre de Cristo)" are noted in conjunction with "the odd and unique houses of the [Santa Fe] Artist Colony [which] are a perennial source of interest to newcomers as well as to old residents." Among the original Santa Fe art colonists who lived in an "odd and unique" adobe studio on Camino del Monte Sol were poet Alice Corbin and her artist husband William Penhallow Henderson. During the 1920s the two attended Penitente Brotherhood Holy Week rituals in what is now known as Georgia O'Keeffe's Abiquiú, which "sits on a shelf below the Jemez mountains, facing, over the river valley below, the far distant slopes of the *Sangre de Cristo* range." There, after witnessing a Good Friday afternoon simulated crucifixion, Corbin (Henderson 1937, 14–15, 49) describes how

> the sun sinking at our backs had turned the cliffs across the valley into splendid cathedral shapes of rose and saffron beauty—a beauty that is touched here in this country with a sometimes terrible sense of eternity, loneliness, and futility. For all the gay laughter of youth on the hillside, the stark parable of the Crucifixion is close to the country's soul. It eats into the heart, this terror; and it is not difficult to imagine how the early Franciscans felt, as they gazed upon this terrible afternoon light on bare mesa and peak, and felt the thorns of this eternal loneliness pressing into their souls. Actual mortification of the flesh is perhaps less poignant.

The eastern spur of the Rocky Mountains from southern Colorado to Santa Fe is now called the Sangre de Cristo Mountains. In her 1927 novel *Death Comes for the Archbishop* Willa Cather (1999, 284–85) portrays a dying Jean Latour (Jean Baptiste Lamy) contemplating: "Yes, Sangre de Cristo; but no matter how scarlet the sunset, those red hills never became vermilion, but a more and more intense rose-carnelian; not the colour of living blood, the Bishop had often reflected, but the colour of the dried blood of saints and martyrs preserved in old churches in Rome, which liquefies upon occasion." Historian David Lavender (1980, 10) claims that "practically everyone knows [that] the phrase translates as 'Blood of Christ' and derives from the ruddy light that some sunsets spread across the western slopes—a widespread mountain phenomenon that the more matter-of-fact Swiss call, in their country, alpenglow."

Until the late nineteenth century the Sangre de Cristo Mountains were known as the Sierra Madre or "Mother Range" by Spanish-speakers and as the Rockies by English-speakers. Publicists for the Denver & Rio Grande Railway started using the name Sangre de Cristo, which appears in Lieutenant E. H. Ruffner's 1874–75 United States Army railroad route survey, as early as 1881. Their 1896 *Slopes of the Sangre de Cristo: A Book of Resources and Industry of Colorado* identifies it as "a title which the Spanish pioneers more than three hundred years ago gave to the entire Rocky Mountain range from Yucatan to British America." Art historian William Wroth (1983, 286, 287) claims that American journalists and popular writers in the 1890s "readily adopted" the railroad's name for the mountains because they "were fascinated with the penitential brotherhoods of the Hispanic mountain villages of New Mexico, Los Hermanos de Nuestro Padre Jesús Nazareno (popularly known as the Penitentes) . . . and reveled in creating for the benefit of readers in 'the States' an atmosphere of mystery and barbarism in describing the 'primitive' rituals of the Penitentes."

Both "the Blood of Christ Mountains (Sangre de Cristo) [which] never fail to thrill the beholder" and the "Artist Colony" so highly touted in the July 1929 Highway Commission *Roads to Cibola* are given scant mention in the 1935 New Mexico State Tourist Bureau brochure *2 Weeks in New Mexico "Land of Enchantment"* as attractions of "Old Santa Fe":

> Santa Fe! The City of Sacred Faith! The end of the Santa Fe Trail! The very name is redolent with history and romance. . . . Today in Santa Fe you may visit the Church of San Miguel, oldest Mission in America; the old Palace of the Governors, erected about 1610, before the Pilgrims landed, and seat of the Government of New Spain as well as Territorial New Mexico; where Lew Wallace wrote his immortal "Ben Hur" [1881], and where historical and archaeological relics are now collected for your interest. You may delight in the Art Museum, filled with specimens of the typical art of the Southwest, products of the art colonies of New Mexico, many of which are known throughout the world. In the shadow of the Sangre de Cristos you will come upon the magnificent building which houses the Rockefeller Museum of Anthropology.

The Taos Art Colony, founded by artists Bert G. Phillips and Ernest L. Blumenschein in 1898, receives more lavish praise:

> Probably no name so short for a spot so small is so well known throughout the world. Artist and writer alike have spread its fame, and today the blase world-traveler finds new thrills as he brushes past sheet-wrapped Indians in the tiny plaza, or gazes in amazement at the ancient terraced bulk of the pueblo itself. . . .

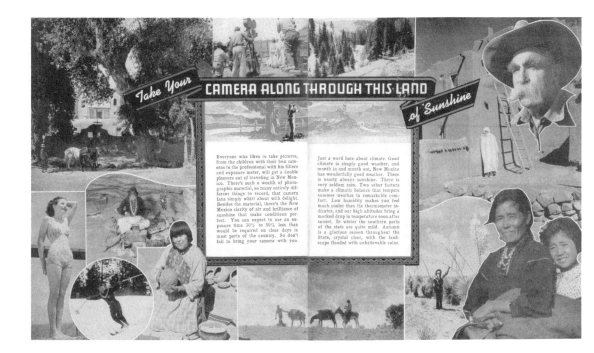

"Take Your Camera Along Through This Land of Sunshine," New Mexico
"Land of Enchantment," *State Tourist Bureau booklet, 1941.*

The Taos Art Colony has drawn from the world for its painters. Such noted men as Ernest Blumenschein, Bert Phillips, J[oseph] H. Sharp, Walter Ufer, Victor Higgins, Herbert Dunton, John Young-Hunter and Leo[n] Gaspard have found inspiration in the true Indian-types of Taos and in the austere beauty of this entrancing corner of New Mexico.

The charm of Taos is made up of the historical, the strange and unusual, and the quaint and different. You will always remember Taos.

During the Coronado Cuarto Centennial summer, on Wednesday, June 26, 1940, subscribers to *The Santa Fe New Mexican* and those who paid the fifteen-cent newsstand price were confronted with front-page headlines like: "GOP Awaits Platform: Wilkie Presses Fight"; "British Airmen Strike in German Territory: Politics Shake London"; and "U.S. Sends Cruiser South: Fleet Leaves Philippines on Mysterious Voyage." They also read that "Espanola Grows Double," from 314 in 1930 to 626, according to the 1940 Census. Another important notice was featured among these headlines:

BIG PAPER
The Artists and Writers edition of The New Mexican, containing much interesting information on the activities of the art colony, for which Santa Fe is famous, is herewith presented to subscribers.

The edition contains 46 pages.

The publishers wish to acknowledge the cooperation of Dr. Edgar L. Hewett, Mrs. Alice Corbin Henderson, Will Shuster and scores of others in its preparation.

"Artists and Writers: A List of Prominent Artists and Writers of New Mexico" was edited by Alison Dana and Margaret Lohlker. The supplement includes biographical sketches on, brief references to, photographs of, and/or samples of work by 148 artists and writers as well as articles on related topics and special advertising (Weigle and Fiore 1982a).

Dr. Edgar Lee Hewett, who wrote the introduction to the Artists and Writers edition, is pictured on the following page together with his biographical sketch, an article by him on "Art and Culture in Ancient America," an account of the School of American Research of the Archaeological Institute of America, which he directed (now School for Advanced Research, see Lewis and Hagan 2007), and a photograph of "Art Museum of New Mexico, Santa Fe." The biographical sketch concludes: "Hewett shuns the spectacular statements of the archaeological spellbinder and follows always the uncompromising course of the scientist, but to his study of facts and his report of investigations he brings the joy of the poet and the imagination of the artist." In 1940 the School of American Research, Museum of New Mexico, published Hewett's introduction and a selection of images from the June 26, 1940, *Santa Fe New Mexican* Artists and Writers edition as a booklet entitled *Representative Art and Artists of New Mexico*.

New Mexico artists and writers appeared regularly in *New Mexico Magazine*, which had started in July 1923 as *New Mexico Highway Journal*. In the July 1997 Commemorative Edition for its seventy-fifth year, Director of the Palace of the Governors Thomas E. Chávez (1997, 10–11) reflects on its "long, glorious past":

New Mexico Magazine, more than any other published outlet, is the vehicle wherein New Mexico's literary, historical, conservationist and artistic leaders have come together. Since its inception, virtually every major New Mexican writer and artist has contributed to its pages. The magazine's index is as complete a listing of these people as will be found anywhere.

The July 1997 "Special 75th Anniversary Issue" of *New Mexico Magazine* is one Editor-in-Chief Emily Drabanski (1997, 5, 44) presents as "filled with readers' favorite past stories from our state's top authors." In her editor's note to former editor Sheila Tryk's

"O'Keeffe's World" she writes that the piece "first appeared in the January 1973 issue of the magazine and was reprinted in May 1986 following artist Georgia O'Keeffe's death. The magazine is proud to republish it once again in this special issue, coinciding with the opening [on July 17] of the new O'Keeffe museum in Santa Fe." According to its first director, Peter H. Hassrick (1997, 9), the museum is "a gift from the private sector to the nation as a whole and, in particular, to the people of Santa Fe" from founders Anne and John Marion and The Burnett Foundation, who are "determined . . . [it] become another jewel in the crown of Santa Fe's wonderful family of museums."

> Certainly it is the Museum's mission to explore with some seriousness . . . the contribution O'Keeffe made to American art. It cannot be denied, however, that the public fascination with O'Keeffe also stems from a popularized version of the woman herself: her mystery, her personal strength and independence, her charisma—in fact, her whole story. . . . Her famous comment, "I should have kept a diary because they are going to get my life all wrong," suggests the difficulty of trying to summarize O'Keeffe's personal world for a public audience.

Historian Ferenc M. Szasz (2006, 89, 90) claims that "New Mexico's most celebrated native-born painter for the postwar era was probably San Patricio's Peter Hurd," while "the New Mexico artist who commandeered the widest attention in the postwar years, however, was Georgia O'Keeffe," who first visited New Mexico in 1917 and moved there permanently in 1949.

Ironically, until about 1975 O'Keeffe was probably more famous nationally than in her adopted state. Dressed in a long black gown, she would often be recognized shopping in Santa Fe, but her Hispanic neighbors in Abiquiu generally marked her out as an eccentric, best left alone. (In gratitude for this, she built a fifty-thousand-dollar gymnasium for the town.) The UNM Fine Arts Museum did not stage O'Keeffe's first in-state exhibit until 1975. Not until the Santa Fe Chamber Music Festival began to use O'Keeffe reprints as popular posters in the early 1970s did New Mexicans come to appreciate her talents. As late as 1975, a reporter observed that while O'Keeffe's fame was international, she was probably one of New Mexico's least-known residents.

If local residents ignored Georgia O'Keeffe, the national art critics did not. Except for her larger-than-life images of flowers—most of which were done before she moved to New Mexico—critics invariably linked her with the southwestern landscape. They delighted in her description of the Sangre de Cristo Mountains as "miles of grey elephants" or her assessment of New Mexico's light as "the faraway nearby." Her bleached cow skulls and her numerous renditions of Pedernal

Our Lady of Mount Pedernal: 20th Century Devotion to the Arts.
11⅝" x 8" oil on birch wood. © 1997 Elizabeth Kay, Cundiyo, New Mexico.
The text on the back of this Pythea Productions greeting card, all rights
reserved in 2000, reads: "The most powerful female figure in New Mexico's
art pantheon, Our Lady of Mount Pedernal [Georgia O'Keeffe] bestows
many benefits upon the art world. Her youthful art and image is sustained
by an elderly Archangel [Alfred Stieglitz], while a handsome young Angel
[Juan Hamilton] supports her creativity in old age. Like it or not, she
continues to entice almost everyone who comes in contact with her. Art
dealers, book publishers, interior designers, tourists, even real estate
developers petition her for blessings. She is especially called upon by
those trying to reconstruct their lives according to their own designs,
following Our Lady's inspirational words: 'I decided to start anew — to
strip away what I had been taught— to accept as true my own thinking.'
Her main attribute is her face, weathered by extreme exposure."
Used with permission of the artist.

Mountain ("It's *my* mountain") have confirmed that impression. Her *Black Cross, New Mexico* (1929), one of the first canvases she painted in the state, completed the identification. As a reporter noted in 1968, Georgia O'Keeffe had become the virtual symbol of the American Southwest. Founded after her death, the O'Keeffe Museum in Santa Fe attracts thousands of visitors annually.

A latter-day Montezuma and twentieth-century New Mexico icon (Merrill and Bradbury 1998; Lynes et al. 2004), Georgia O'Keeffe is absent from the June 26, 1940, Artists and Writers *Santa Fe New Mexican* supplement. Anschutz Collection curator George Schriever (1976, ii) wryly notes this lacuna in his preface to the 1976 republication of the School of American Research's 1940 *Representative Art and Artists of New Mexico:* "There must have been some reason for the omission ... particularly... of Georgia O'Keeffe who probably more than any other artist, has epitomized the Southwest in painting. Had Dr. Hewett been clairvoyant, he would have gone to any lengths to have insured that O'Keeffe would be represented." She is, however, paired with Shiprock in the introduction to the New Mexico section of *The Smithsonian Guides to Natural America: The Southwest, New Mexico and Arizona* (Page 1995, 25, painting 26–27): "In the undulating and intensely colored *Rust Red Hills (*1930*)*, Georgia O'Keeffe distills the essence of the New Mexico landscape."

9
The Colorful State

New Mexico is the anomaly of the Republic. It is a century older in European civilization than the rest, and several centuries older still in a happier semi-civilization of its own. It had its little walled cities of stone before Columbus had grandparents-to-be; and it has them yet. The most incredible pioneering the world has ever seen overran it with the zeal of a prairie-fire three hundred and fifty years ago; and the embers of that unparalleled blaze of exploration are not quite dead today.

—Charles F. Lummis, 1. "The Land of Poco Tiempo,"
The Land of Poco Tiempo, *1893*

It is difficult to think of a modern America in a village of the Pueblo Indians, while the inhabitants dance for rain. To be sure, a transcontinental train may thunder by, or an airplane soar overhead; but the prayers never stop, the dance goes on, and the fantastic juxtaposition seems to widen the gap between. Who could dream of the American Way in a mountain hamlet where the sound of the Penitente flute is heard above the thud of the scourges, and Spanish-American villagers perform medieval rites of redemption in Holy Week?

These are extremes of incongruity, but they are true. They diminish in the vicinity of the larger towns and cities and vanish altogether in some places; but their existence, strong or weak colors the contemporary scene....

> *Homogeneous, New Mexico is not.... Suddenly and without forewarning, from almost any point in the State, one may step from modern America into Old Spain, or into aboriginal Indian territory, within the space of a few miles, just as one passes from an almost tropic climate into an arctic one, due to the many abrupt transitions from plain to plateau, up mountains and down again.*
>
> —Workers of the Writers' Program of the Work Projects Administration in the State of New Mexico, compilers, "The State Today," *New Mexico: A Guide to the Colorful State*, American Guide Series, 1940

On May 5, 1952, when he finished the foreword to a reprint edition of Charles Fletcher Lummis's *The Land of Poco Tiempo*, Paul A. F. Walter claimed "the book is as up-to-date today as it was then." From its first publication in 1893 it "aroused the interest not only of the traveling public, but also of writers, painters, scientists...[who] took to heart in increasing numbers the slogan first sounded by Lummis, 'See America First!'" Walter (in Lummis 1966, ix) concludes: "Whenever I am asked, as I am occasionally: 'If I have time for only one book on the Southwest, which do you recommend?' I reply invariably: 'By all means read Lummis' *The Land of Poco Tiempo*!'" He (1916, 18–19) himself clearly had done so when he presented Chimayó as "A New Mexico Lourdes" in the January 1916 issue of the Museum of New Mexico's *El Palacio*:

Where [the Valley of the Santa Cruz] debouches from the second row of foothills, lies the Lourdes of the Southwest, Chimayo. Its famous chapel invariably elicits expressions of delight from the rare traveler who finds his way to this remote settlement. In outline it is an architectural, even though an unpolished, gem; its setting is so perfect that one gasps in admiration of its sheer beauty. Well attested are the miracles which even as late as yesterday, have been performed at this way-out-of-the-way wayside shrine, less than ten miles from the Denver & Rio Grande railway station.... A little distance down the road is the Penitente church, with a real campanile apart from the edifice. The valley is entirely rimmed by sandhills which in the setting sun shimmer in all colors and shapes much like the Grand Canyon. The settlement with its orchards and fields, fills the entire bowl bisected by the river, with its never failing supply of the purest water. The entire scene, even to the wayside crosses, is like a bit of ancient Spain or Italy transplanted to American soil.

Lummis first "saw" the Southwest on foot between September 12, 1884, and February 1, 1885, when he "tramped" 3,507 miles in 143 days from Cincinnati, Ohio, through New

Mexico to a new job as city editor for the *Los Angeles Times*, to which he sent weekly "dispatches" about his pilgrimage. In thus changing jobs he (1892b, 1, 2) disdained "railroads and Pullmans" in favor of "life—not life in the pathetic meaning of the poor health-seeker, …but life in the truer, broader, sweeter sense, the exhilarant joy of living outside the sorry fences of society." He also acknowledges: "I am an American and felt ashamed to know so little of my own country as I did, and as most Americans do."

Lummis's determination "to learn more of the country and its people than railroad travel could ever teach" was later echoed in "The Golden Key to Wonderland," his lead piece for the 1928 Santa Fe Railway/Fred Harvey Company Indian Detours booklet, *They Know New Mexico: Intimate Sketches by Western Writers*. In its foreword, publicist Roger

The Golden Key to Wonderland

"Sun, Silence, Adobe—New Mexico in three words." So I wrote in 1890, after six years' exploration of this "Land of Poco Tiempo." Plainly, these three imply more—Restfulness—Romance—Beauty—Mystery—Room and Peace.

Now that I have studied 36 years longer, let's say: "Sun—Silence—Adobe—Wonder—Finality—New Mexico in five words." For the Southwest (*all of which was once New Mexico*) is the very Land of Wonder among the lands of Earth; and in our own country, it is the Serene Elbow-Room the hand of Man can never spoil. Its oases shall swell and blossom, its little cities grow bigger; but its mighty day-wide reaches shall endure—unplowed and unabashed, unprettied and silent and free. It will always be a land where you can't make a noise "stick":

Charles F. Lummis. They Know New Mexico: Intimate Sketches by Western Writers, *Passenger Department, Atchison, Topeka & Santa Fe Railway (for Indian Detours) booklet, 1928.*

Birdseye calls New Mexico "still terra incognito to the majority of world travellers [because] its trails have become highways too recently for knowledge of the fascinating land they penetrate to spread abroad." Although Lummis feels "some pang at seeing his Unknown Land thrown open and easy to the multitude," yet it must be done:

> He winces, maybe, when a visiting convention of American Bankers elbows noisy into Pueblo home and temple alike; but so far from wishing to put a barbed fence around our Wonderlands, he would rather make it compulsory by Federal Statute that every American voter visit as many Lands as possible. Despite Babbitts and vandals, Americans *Need* to know the Southwest. It is "Good For What Ails Them"—part of which is smug, blank ignorance of their country. Over 35 years ago I invented the slogan "See America First!" I believe in it more profoundly than ever. Americans ought to see the Southwest, the most wonderful of all our Lands of Wonder.

Despite Lummis's claims to having "invented the slogan 'See America First!'" in the original introduction to his *Some Strange Corners of Our Country: The Wonderland of the Southwest* (1892a), his was a retroactive appropriation of the slogan "See Europe if you will, but See America First," created in the fall of 1905 by Salt Lake City Commercial Club secretary Fisher Sanford Harris to promote tourism in the intermountain West. Harris became executive secretary of the See America First League, launched at the first See America First Conference in January 1906. In 1905 Lummis called himself the originator of the idea and Harris's movement "laudable," but in 1912 he claimed to have "more than twenty years ago...originated the 'See America First' Crusade...[as] first to formulate the gospel and 'tell why,' and to do it on a large scale of publicity" (Schaffer 2001, 26–29, 32–33, 334).

Lummis was introduced to New Mexico by members of the Chaves family of San Mateo. His letters to the *Chillicothe Leader* in the Ohio town where he had been editor of the *Scioto Gazette* announce "Santa Fe at Last" in the final week of November 1884. The December 4 edition brings "A Historical Sketch of the Ancient Burg from the Days of the Medieval Tramp, Cabeza de Vaca, to That of the Tramp of the Period, Carlos Francisea Lummissii." There Lummis met speaker of the Territorial House of Representatives Amado Chaves and was "Wined and Dined Like a Lord," the first encounter in a lifelong friendship (Moneta 1985, 17, 18–19; also Simmons 1968; Thompson 2001). After leaving Santa Fe Lummis (1892b, 190) "tramped" to the Chaves family home in San Mateo, where "I formed my first acquaintance with those astounding fanatics, the Penitentes...ignorant perverters of a once godly brotherhood...formerly scattered all through New Mexico; but of late years [who] have died out save in the remoter hamlets like San Mateo.... We read with a shiver of the self-tortures of East Indian fakirs, most of us ignorant that in the oldest corner of our own enlightened nation as astounding barbarities are still practised by citizens and voters of the United States."

Lummis suffered a stroke and partial paralysis in late 1887; on February 5, 1888, he returned to New Mexico to recuperate as a guest of Amado Chaves. Near the Chaveses' San Mateo Ranch, on March 29 and 30, accompanied by Amado's brother Irineo and "a peon," both of whom carried cocked six-shooters, Lummis photographed several Penitente Brotherhood rites, including self-flagellants, cross-bearers, and a simulated crucifixion. He wrote an embellished account of his experiences in an illustrated article whose history he describes in his unpublished memoirs "As I Remember":

> But so unknown was the Brotherhood then, every magazine in the United States [some seventeen] returned the article I wrote about it. They deemed it a fake. It was only when John Brisben Walker ventured with his old time *Cosmopolitan* [Lummis 1889] that the matter saw the light for the first time. Since then the pictures of this medieval ceremony have figured in several of my books and the cult of the Penitentes is known the world over. (Fiske and Lummis 1975, 44–45; also Weigle 1976, 172)

Such "medieval ceremonies" were already known to New Mexico curiosity-seekers. The *Albuquerque Morning Journal* of Monday, April 14, 1884, carried a reporter's account of "Penitente Horrors: The Season's Festival in Full Blast at Los Griegos." That of Friday, April 23, 1886, announced "Penitentes' Day," when W. L. Trimble & Co. would run hacks to Los Griegos at noon, so city residents could view the "orgies" from the fourteenth century.

Medievalism developed in the late nineteenth century. At the Chicago World's Columbian Exposition of 1893, a painting depicting fifteenth-century Spanish flagellants was the most popular at the fair. Culture historian T. J. Jackson Lears (1994, 177, 168, 179) allows that "the painting's appeal no doubt involved titillation as much as spiritual aspiration," but sees it as part of the antimodernism of the time: "Among many late Victorians, there was widespread inquiry into what might be called a European folk mind, a realm of magic and myth preserved in popular tales and superstitions. Among a smaller number, there was a growing fascination with spiritual exercises and aspirations of Oriental, medieval, and Counter-Reformation mystics." For these, medieval mysticism was "otherworldly," appealing to "the longing for intense experience." Indeed, "on both sides of the Atlantic" there was a "fascination with medieval mentalities": "Often perceived as displaying childlike traits, the peasants, saints, and seers of the Middle Ages" were viewed as "an apotheosis of simplicity, a reassertion of moral will, an exaltation of vital energy, a revaluation of visionary experience."

Anachronism and medievalism are evident in "Old Spain in New Mexico," poet Alice Corbin's contribution to the 1928 Indian Detours booklet *They Know New Mexico*. She notes a "sense of arrested time in New Mexico," where "the illusion, and not only the illusion, but the actuality of a four dimensional vista, or of a cross section of time, is equally striking." In this fourth dimension, "every year during Lent, the Penitente Brotherhood (*Los Hermanos Penitentes* or *Los Hermanos de la Sangre de Cristo*), an unorthodox survival of the Third Order of Saint Francis, make religious pilgrimages and processions, including cross-bearing and flagellation—medieval symbols of atonement brought to this country by the first Spanish settlers and priests and common at that date throughout Europe."

Alice Corbin only worked as an editor on New Mexico's contribution to the WPA American Guide Series between February 1936 and July 1937, but her influence is evident in several of the book's opening essays, especially those heralding the anachronism,

Alice Corbin

Old Spain in New Mexico

The hills and mountains about Santa Fé and the valley above it, are piled up like waves arrested in mid-motion; and this sense of arrested time in New Mexico persists, and is only increased the longer one stays in Santa Fé. From the archaic stone-age world of the Indian pueblos, one passes into the medieval atmosphere of the Spanish villages. From these we descend gradually again to the half-pioneer modern world of the Santa Fé Plaza, where, as Carl Sandburg says, the "funeral faces" of automobiles stand where ponies stood at the hitching racks ten years ago. But it doesn't really matter whether one views this world from the back of a burro or cayuse, the arc of a covered wagon or the high-powered motor equivalent of the mule-driven stage coach. The illusion, and not only the illusion, but the actuality of a fourth

---

Alice Corbin (Henderson). They Know New Mexico: Intimate Sketches by Western Writers, *Passenger Department, Atchison, Topeka & Santa Fe Railway (for Indian Detours) booklet, 1928.*

primitivism, and medievalism of the state's non-"homogeneous" cultures. Seeing America, keeping at home Americans' money usually spent touring Europe, and enticing Europeans to this side of the Atlantic provided impetus for these guidebooks, launched in 1935 by the Federal Writers' Project (FWP) of the Work Projects Administration (WPA; after September 1, 1939, the Writers' Program of the Works Progress Administration). Intended to cover every section of every state, the series format was the result of debate among national FWP officials:

> [Director Henry G.] Alsberg and [associate director George] Cronyn favored a small encyclopedia for each state, which would contain essays on its history, education, agriculture, industry, and topography. [Tour editor Katherine] Kellock preferred a volume concentrating on tourist routes with a brief background of the state. Alsberg's view assumed that the staff would write primarily for *readers*; Kellock's, that their audience was *tourists*. The compromise was a guide beginning with a variety of essays followed by comprehensive tour descriptions. (Penkower 1977, 31, 32; also McDonald 1969)

As Alsberg wrote New Mexico FWP Director Ina Sizer Cassidy on January 17, 1936: "We are particularly interested in scenic or human interest subjects—traditions, folklore, oldest settlers, ghost stories—anything that can be visualized as a halo to illuminate some objects which travelers can gaze on with horror or delight or some other form of emotion" (Weigle 1985, xvi).

New Mexico's contribution to the American Guide Series was late. Selling for $2.50 and published by the New York firm of Hastings House in August 1940, it never reached New Mexico until September of that year, too late for most of the summertime Coronado Cuarto Centennial activities. The volume's sponsors—the University of New Mexico and the Coronado Cuarto Centennial Commission—and the state project workers were dismayed by the late publication date, the ugly blue-on-orange cover, and the subtitle *A Guide to the Colorful State* (Weigle 1985, xviii). As its final editor Charles Ethrige Minton wrote in a May 20, 1940, letter to national Writers' Program Director John D. Newsom: "The subtitle . . . was our own designation. There is no official State Name, and we found at least eight names that have been applied, such as 'Sunshine State,' 'Cactus State,' and so on, each worse than the other; so, because it is the most colorful of all the states in various ways, we decided on that subtitle, although we don't think it especially good" (Weigle 1989, 66).

The 496-page WPA New Mexico Guide contains three major divisions of text: (1) essays on state history, land, peoples, arts, and other aspects; (2) descriptive essays and information about Albuquerque, Santa Fe, and Taos; and (3) twenty-five automobile tours of "The Most Accessible Places" plus a calendar of annual events, a chronology, a bibliography, eight photograph sections, and an official 1940 state road map. Chimayó is along Tour 3A:

CHIMAYÓ, 9 *m.* [from Santa Cruz] (6,872 alt., 573 pop.), . . . was the eastern boundary of the Province of New Mexico from 1598 to 1695, the frontier place of banishment for offenders, which in those days meant punishment greater than prison. . . . Today, because of its sheltered position, it is the center of farming, fruit culture, and weaving. The road, winding through the village, is lined with lilac hedges and with adobe houses and patio walls that are covered in June with the yellow rose of Castile. In the fall when the shimmering gold of the cottonwoods contrasts with strings of scarlet chili that drape the houses, the harvesting of the crops is carried on, and the grain is threshed on primitive threshing floors with goats and horses tramping it out. During Lent processions of Penitentes, creeping up to the hilltop cross, scourge bare backs with yucca whips. Sometimes, in the spring of a dry year, can be seen a procession of men and women, the leader carrying an image of the Virgin or the Santo Niño (holy child) and all chanting prayers for rain as they walk across the dry fields. (Workers of WPA 1940, 297–98)

Two chapels are described as 1.3 miles down "a secondary dirt road" from Chimayó "over a small stream to a cluster of adobes." El Santuario de Chimayó is "a Christian sanctuary" that "was built as a thanks offering by Don Bernardo Abeyta in 1816, and is very well preserved." (Abeyta was a prominent figure in the Penitente Brotherhood [Steele and Rivera 1985, 16–19].) The second is "a privately owned square chapel about 50 feet from the Santuario . . . [where] the custodian here will respond to the ringing of a bell, which hangs in the campanile, and sell layettes of value, blessed by Santo Niño, to expectant mothers" (Workers of WPA 1940, 298–99).

According to artist Elizabeth Kay (1987, 47–48, 2–3), then a Chimayó resident, after Abeyta's death in 1856 one of his neighbors, Blas Severiano Medina, "was stricken with severe rheumatism" and "received a revelation instructing him to pray for healing to the Santo Niño de Atocha." After recovery, he made a pilgrimage to the Niño's shrine in Fresnillo, Mexico, and brought back a statue of the Holy Child of Atocha. "He returned with it to El Potrero on February 15, 1857, and the people were so delighted by the *santo* that they gave land for the construction [completed in 1858] of a private chapel . . . about two hundred yards northwest of Abeyta's Santuario." The chapel remained in the Medina family: "Until their deaths in 1985, Ramon and Saranita Medina owned the chapel and ran a small store next door. A rather touching characteristic of the little store was a supply of baby shoes that Saranita gave at no charge to those who wanted to make a votive offering to El Santo Niño de Atocha."

El Santuario did not stay in the Abeyta family. Bernardo Abeyta's daughter Carmen Abeyta de Cháves assumed care of the chapel after his death on November 21, 1856, and her daughter María de los Angeles Cháves inherited it. In the late 1920s pilgrimages and the family's means declined. They began selling the structure and its furnishings, including a statue of Santiago on horseback. Alice Corbin Henderson (1938, 123) remembers how artist Gustave Baumann "had discovered that the beautiful old church and its furnishings were being sold piecemeal; the small Santiago on horseback was in the hands of one curio-dealer, and the historic carved doors were being bargained for by another." *The Santa Fe New Mexican* editor E. Dana Johnson was alerted, and the paper carried a spread on the situation.

The WPA New Mexico Guide (1940, 299) encapsulates a version of what happened next: "The Santuario was in possession of the Abeyta family until the fall of 1929, when Mary Austin . . . obtained from an anonymous donor $6,000 with which the Society for the Preservation and Restoration of New Mexico Churches purchased the property and transferred it to the Roman Catholic Church." That Society had largely overlapping membership with the Spanish Colonial Arts Society, which actually made the purchase and transfer on October 15, 1929. Austin and artist Frank Applegate were among the key founding members of the latter organization in 1925 (Weigle 1996a). Austin (1932, 214, 215) claims to have been the first to use the term *Spanish Colonial* and credits Johnson with popularizing it at her insistence so that "Spanish Colonial Art became a recognized subject of interested comment in the Press." She was lecturing at Yale University when Applegate wrote her about the Santuario's plight. In her obituary for him she recalls how in New Haven "I was able to find a Catholic benefactor who made possible the purchase of the building and its content, to be held in trust by the Church for worship and as a religious museum, intact, and no alterations to be made in it without our consent."

El Santuario again received considerable press in March 1992, when the Department of Tourism, the state's latter-day Tourist Bureau, advertised in a dozen national magazines, including *Travel & Leisure*, *Holiday*, and *National Geographic Traveler* (see Weigle 1994, 216–20). The full-page, full-color ad is topped by a Mark Nohl photograph of the Santuario entrance. The caption underneath proclaims: "An open gate awaits those who come for the healing earth found in El Santuario de Chimayó." The text reads:

Every Easter, the faithful make their pilgrimage to Chimayó.

Before dawn, pilgrims will begin arriving by the thousands. They will come on foot from hundreds of miles around, some chanting, some praying, and others bearing crosses. For centuries the faithful have come to this, the "Lourdes of America," to partake of the *tierra bendita* or blessed earth, which is said to heal the sick.

As you roam the town in search of its famed Ortega weavings or wonder at the crutches of the healed that line the walls of the shrine, you'll learn that Chimayó is more than a place to pray and give thanks. It is a place to heal the soul.

El Santuario de Chimayó. It's just one of the many wonders of New Mexico, and it's waiting for you.

the *Chapel*
of the SANTUARIO

The Santuario de Chimayo is one of the best known shrines in the Southwest and draws its pilgrims from Colorado to Chihuahua, Mexico. It is no unusual sight to see from a dozen to fifty travelers, footsore and weary, wending their way to this little church.

The Santuario was erected in 1816 by Don Bernardo Abeyta as a monument of appreciation for the health and prosperity of his family and himself. The church was privately owned for many generations but is now the property of the Catholic Diocese of New Mexico.

A modest building, the Santuario is constructed of adobe, with walls out of plumb, and bearing the marks of the inexpert but faithful native masons who built it.

"The Chapel of the Santuario," Mission Churches of New Mexico, *State Tourist Bureau booklet, 1935. One of five "Old Churches" pictured and described along with ten "Old Missions" and three "Mission Ruins," the Santuario at Chimayó is presented last.*

The March 21, 1992, *Albuquerque Journal* carried a front-page banner headline: "Chimayó Ad Outrages Pilgrims: Archdiocese Questions Exploitation of Event." Reporters interviewed Nancy Everist, advertising and marketing manager for the Department of Tourism, who explained, "It's a culturally authentic thing, and that's what people are interested in seeing." However, Nambé resident, writer, and *santero* Orlando Romero protested: "Is there nothing sacred anymore? ...This is totally tacky, outrageous. To a great many people, the pilgrimage is a very sacred ritual, and for the tourism department to make it an attraction for people to come and gawk at is very offensive to me." Romero and others planned to circulate a petition among pilgrims during Holy Week for later transmission to the Department of Tourism. It reads in part: "The pilgrimage is not a tourist attraction and its advertisement as such demeans and exploits a religious experience as a method of attracting tourists. Its advertisement is inappropriate, insensitive and should never occur again."

According to the March 24, 1992, *Albuquerque Journal*, Marsha Adams, deputy cabinet secretary for the Department of Tourism, was "shocked" at the outcry. She admitted an "oversight" in not consulting the Archdiocese of Santa Fe or "Hispanic Catholics who work in the Department of Tourism." Reverend Richard Olona, chancellor for the Archdiocese of Santa Fe,

> said the potential for tourists to invade an essential part of Hispanic Catholic culture outweighs the potential benefits of tourism.... "We don't need to have something very close to faith and culture exploited in any means," he continued. "I know the Department of Tourism wasn't trying to do that, but they should have contacted us. They shoot themselves in the foot when they do something like this." [He] noted that many places and events connected to religion—including the Vatican—are tourist attractions. The difference is many who make the pilgrimage to Chimayó don't want the attention of tourists, he said.

When he returned from state business to Mexico, Secretary of Tourism Michael Cerletti addressed a letter to *The Santa Fe New Mexican* on April 2. The paper reported on April 7, 1992, that he "expressed regret for 'whatever pain or misunderstanding this ad may have caused anyone.'" He stressed that all callers to date were "inquiring about Chimayo and New Mexico in general. . . . Not one has asked about the pilgrimage." Nevertheless, *Time* magazine of April 13, 1992, carries among its "Business Notes" on page fifty-three a small photograph of the ad and two paragraphs entitled "Hey, Look at the Pilgrims!": "Worshipers are signing a petition condemning the ads . . . [and] in another manifestation of their protest, pilgrims say they will bar tourists from photographing their procession."

Chimayó is both Lourdes (Marian apparitions in 1858), which it predates by some forty years, and Venice, where a bustling "pilgrimage 'trade'" in international religious tourist traffic had developed by the late fifteenth-century (Turner and Turner 1978, 6). First mentioned in 1714 documents and definitely established as Tzimayó by the 1740s, its initial Hispanic settlement was called Plaza del Cerro. According to the 1971 New Mexico Historic Preservation Plan (in Larcombe 1983, 172–73), the area was known for its "fine crops of fruit and chili in addition to the staple corn and frijoles, and the weaving of blankets and other wool textiles":

> Between 1813 and 1816 the Santuario de Nuestro Señor de Esquipulas was built just down the road from the plaza, bringing in many pilgrims and greatly augmenting the economic standing of the plaza. Another chapel near the Santuario, built in the 1860's, further stimulated business and other activity. Also, by this time the San Luis Valley in Colorado had been settled, and Chimayó had a good trade with towns there, exchanging fruit and chili for wheat and potatoes. Before the new Santa Fe-Taos highway was built in 1917, following the Rio Grande Canyon, travel from Santa Fe to Taos used the Chimayó-Las Truchas-Peñasco route whenever weather permitted, making Chimayó a stop on a major road.

After World War I this main artery became a byway. In the June 1931 *New Mexico Highway Journal* Elizabeth Willis DeHuff (1931, 39), another writer who "knew" New Mexico for the 1928 Indian Detours booklet, promises those who venture along it that they will find "The Santuario at Chimayó" still tended by a "pariente" of the Abeyta/Cháves family, and be rewarded with a glimpse of the coveted Middle Ages:

> As one stands drinking in the peaceful setting, deeply stirred with feelings inherited from mediaeval ancestors dreaming mystically in pastoral pursuits, there comes hastening around the wall of the church yard an elderly man with drooping gray mustache, waving a large key and exclaiming "**llave!**" With the graciousness of his ancestors, he bids one **"Buenos dias!"** . . . and although you may not understand his Spanish, he will continue occasionally to address polite remarks to you in that language, for he speaks no English. To him, the sacred spot, now a well, is not a show-place; so unless you know of the well beforehand, he will not take you into that room, where many candle-holders of various sorts and kinds and of all ages stand as symbols of the devout prayers of his people.

10

Carlsbad Caverns, the Eighth Wonder

Carlsbad Caverns National Park is open throughout the year. Although surface temperatures vary widely according to the seasons, the temperature in the caverns remains stationary at 56°, summer and winter. Therefore, clothes of ordinary weight, plus a light sweater or other wrap, are needed for the trip through the caverns at all times of the year. No special clothes are needed, since trails and stairways are followed the entire distance. Low heeled shoes, however, are advisable. The trip through the Caverns requires about five hours, allowing one-half hour for lunch, and few, if any, places in the world will so richly reward the traveler in so short a time. Near the Caverns is the attractive little city of Carlsbad, where good hotels and camps offer splendid accommodations, and where a free bathing beach on a lake freshened by mineral springs provides special refreshment in summer. Carlsbad derives its name from these mineral springs.

—*"Carlsbad and the Caverns," 2 Weeks in New Mexico "Land of Enchantment," New Mexico State Tourist Bureau booklet, 1935*

Comments following the Department of Energy Community Day 1992 tour of the Waste Isolation Pilot Plant southeast of Carlsbad: "I'm really interested in the whole idea of getting way deep underground."—Michael Knott of Santa Fe; "I didn't realize it was feasible or possible to take as many precautions as they're taking. I feel really comfortable with this place."—Michael Woods of Panhandle, Texas; "I expected it to be high-tech, but I didn't expect it to be this high-tech."—Wilson Martin of Las Cruces; "I wanted to confirm that what I'd read about this place was accurate, and it is. I just regret there have been so many delays."—Martin's wife

Jackie; "It is an illusion that one can reach conclusions about or be satisfied with the safety just by visiting the site; you cannot see safety."—Lokesh Chaturvedi (who did not take the tour), Environmental Evaluation Group, New Mexico.

> —Chuck McCutcheon, "Hundreds of Visitors Plunge into Underground WIPP Tours," Albuquerque Journal, *May 3, 1992*

*B*efore Carlsbad became involved in the commerce of the nearby caverns and a century later their artificial underground neighbor, the nuclear Waste Isolation Pilot Plant, it had entered the booming, nineteenth-century commerce of health. Soon after 1888 when it was named for brothers Charles Bishop and John Arthur Eddy, ranchers and railroad promoters, the town later called Carlsbad was heralded as "the Pearl of the Pecos" (Julyan 1998, 64). Missouri journalist and historian Walter B. Stevens visited in 1892 and found: "The streets of Eddy are full of people who have come to the Pecos to prolong life. This is a climate so dry that to die means to dry up, not to decay" (in Jones 1967, 115). Its growing reputation for waters from a spring northwest of town that had the same mineral content as waters in that "famous European spa known to Germans as Karlsbad . . . , now in Czechoslovakia [Czech Republic] and renamed Karlovy Vary by the Czechs, . . . founded in 1349 by Karl IV and named for him" (Julyan 1998, 63) spurred voters in 1899 to change their town's name to the Americanized Carlsbad and thereby capitalize on both health and tourism. However, it was Bat Cave, twenty-five miles southwest in the foothills of the Guadalupe Mountains, that proved the very much bigger attraction.

As editor Luther Perry announced in the September 15, 1922, *Carlsbad Current-Argus* after accompanying the first scheduled sightseeing party into the cavern on September 10: "Carlsbad has one of the wonders of the world at her very doorstep but does not realize it" (Nymeyer and Halliday 1991, 41). That realization was not long in coming. Just over a year later, President Calvin Coolidge proclaimed Carlsbad Cave National Monument on October 25, 1923.

In March 1923 Mineral Examiner Robert A. Holley from the United States General Land Office in Santa Fe had been charged with the task of surveying the cavern to determine whether it warranted such status. In April he explored from the natural entrance to the Jumping Off Place at the far end of the Big Room. The frequently cited first sentence of his May 8 report reads: "I enter upon this task with a feeling of temerity as I am wholly conscious of the feebleness of my efforts to convey in words the deep conflicting emotions, the feelings of fear and awe, and the desire for an inspired understanding of the Divine Creator's work which presents to the human eye such a complex aggregate of natural wonders in such a limited space." Holley recommended "the construction of steps, stairways and walks, as well as the establishment of a good lighting system, . . . not only to relieve the actual fatigue attached to the journey, but to eliminate the actual danger that exists under present conditions [in] this cave [which] is of such wonderful character as to be worthy to be established as a National Monument" (Nymeyer and Halliday 1991, 65, 67).

A further impetus came when prominent El Paso attorney Richard L. Burges attended a water users' meeting that summer. Chamber of Commerce President W. F. McIlwain, who became the first custodian (superintendent) of Carlsbad Cave National Monument between 1923 and 1927, urged participants to visit "Carlsbad Mammoth Cave," which greatly impressed Burges. Thinking Holley was a geologist, he wrote to the U.S. Geological Survey for a copy of the report. Holley was unknown to them, but staff geologist Willis T. Lee, stationed in Albuquerque since 1903, was planning a trip to inspect an irrigation ditch north of Carlsbad and would also visit the cave. In September Lee added his enthusiastic endorsement for national monument status to Holley's.

Carlsbad area locals, especially Mescalero Apaches, long knew of Bat Cave. Supposedly cowboys were the first whites to enter it in the 1880s. Around 1900, though, guano miner boss Abijah ("Bige") Long and cowboy, then guano miner Jim White

entered the cave, first separately, then together. Both were long connected with the cavern. Both spawned ghostwritten books about their early days with the underground wonders, which do not mention the other. They worked together, then evidently had a bitter falling-out. Directly or indirectly, both claimed to be the cavern's discoverer; it is unlikely that either was.

Nevertheless, White is the one commemorated on a bronze plaque in the lobby of the Carlsbad Caverns National Park Visitor Center: "Beginning in 1901, Jim White made the first known /extensive explorations of the Carlsbad Caverns. /He was chiefly responsible for bringing the attention /of the public, scientific groups and the federal /government to the importance and significance/of the caverns" (Nymeyer and Halliday 1991, 14, 46).

For a time Jim White was Long's foreman in the new guano mining operations, continuing that occupation for some twenty years largely in order to pursue his passion for cave exploration and development. The company drilled shafts directly into Bat Cave, and for years cavern visitors, two at a time, had to be slowly lowered the 170 feet via guano bucket and pulley-hoist. By 1915 White had started work on rudimentary trails into the scenic part of the cavern, but few ventured the arduous road from Carlsbad and the malodorous descent to the underground wonders.

The catalyst for cavern publicity came from Carlsbad photographer Ray V. Davis, whom Jim White first led beyond the large natural entrance, down Devil's Den, and as far as King's Palace in 1914. Davis pioneered successful means to photograph underground and exhibited his pictures in town. Interest in his photographs together with White and his wife Fannie's accommodations at the mining operations on top prompted Davis and other

"Of Course You'll See Carlsbad Caverns National Park,"
New Mexico "Land of Enchantment," *State Tourist Bureau booklet, 1941. Note the*
semiformal cave-touring attire.

Carlsbad businessmen to organize thirteen locals to join the "first scheduled sight-seeing party to visit Carlsbad Cavern" on September 10, 1922 (Nymeyer and Halliday 1991, 41). Although White refused money for lowering them into the cave and acting as guide, he did accept a dollar from each for their supper, breakfast, and bunks the night before.

The following year Jim White led and Ray Davis photographed for Robert Holley's fate-

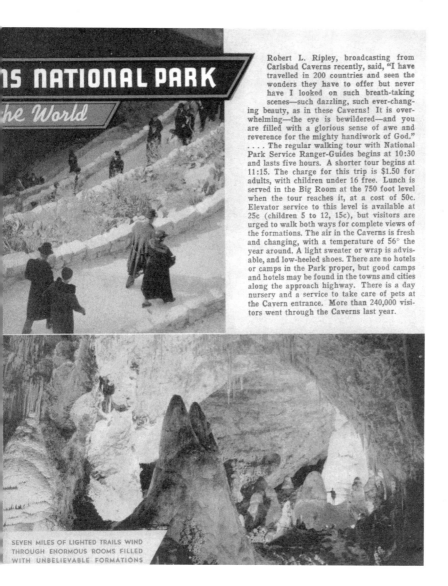

Robert L. Ripley, broadcasting from Carlsbad Caverns recently, said, "I have travelled in 200 countries and seen the wonders they have to offer but never have I looked on such breath-taking scenes—such dazzling, such ever-changing beauty, as in these Caverns! It is overwhelming—the eye is bewildered—and you are filled with a glorious sense of awe and reverence for the mighty handiwork of God." . . . . The regular walking tour with National Park Service Ranger-Guides begins at 10:30 and lasts five hours. A shorter tour begins at 11:15. The charge for this trip is $1.50 for adults, with children under 16 free. Lunch is served in the Big Room at the 750 foot level when the tour reaches it, at a cost of 50c. Elevator service to this level is available at 25c (children 5 to 12, 15c), but visitors are urged to walk both ways for complete views of the formations. The air in the Caverns is fresh and changing, with a temperature of 56° the year around. A light sweater or wrap is advisable, and low-heeled shoes. There are no hotels or camps in the Park proper, but good camps and hotels may be found in the towns and cities along the approach highway. There is a day nursery and a service to take care of pets at the Cavern entrance. More than 240,000 visitors went through the Caverns last year.

SEVEN MILES OF LIGHTED TRAILS WIND THROUGH ENORMOUS ROOMS FILLED WITH UNBELIEVABLE FORMATIONS

ful April 1923 survey. Three weeks after Coolidge's proclamation the *New York Times* of Sunday, November 18, 1923, carried a double-page rotogravure spread of seven underground photographs by Ray V. Davis. They were billed as "First Photographs of the Carlsbad Cave, Recently Discovered in New Mexico, Officially Declared Among the Largest and Most Beautiful in the World, and Now Perpetuated by the President as a National Park [*sic*]." The *Carlsbad Current-Argus* declared that "this will perhaps mean the greatest newspaper advertising that the caves could ever receive" (Nymeyer and Halliday 1991, 111, 67).

The greatest magazine advertising at the time came from two *National Geographic* articles by Willis T. Lee: "A Visit to Carlsbad Cavern, New Mexico" (January 1924) and "New Discoveries in Carlsbad Cavern" (September 1925)—the first illustrated with eighteen

Jim White, "Chief Guide and Discoverer of the Carlsbad Caverns,"
in booklet by Blanche C. Grant, Cavern Guide Book: Carlsbad Caverns, Carlsbad,
N.M. *(Topeka, Kansas: Crane & Company, 1928). Grant begins "Jim White's Story*
of His Discovery of the Cavern" thus: "A tall lank youth of eighteen, a cowboy, was
building a drift fence to hold cattle back on the slopes of the Guadalupe mountains in
southeastern New Mexico and came upon the eighth wonder of the world—the Carls-
bad Caverns. James Larkin White knew nothing about world wonders in those winter
days of 1900. He just knew he had found a mighty hole in the mountainside and its
dark recesses beckoned to him."

copyrighted Davis photographs, the second with twenty photographs by Davis, Lee, and
National Geographic staff photographer Jacob Gayer. Attorney Richard Burges had been
unsuccessful in persuading the National Geographic Society to sponsor an expedition to
the unknown cavern, but Lee showed promotional flair, following up the acceptance of his
January 1924 article with another request:

He knew the Society was interested in archaeology, so he wrote to one of Carlsbad's amateur archaeologists, Carl Livingston, telling him to "Procure for me the skull of an ancient man." Livingston, by chance, had a friend who had one decorating his piano. Livingston sent it to Lee, who took it to the National Geographic Society. The results were immediate: the Society provided $16,000 to Lee for the "National Geographic Expedition." (Crane 2000, 16)

Carlsbad lawyer, rancher, writer, and one-time banker Carl B. Livingston (Bursey 1932), in whose house Lee and his family stayed, claims the geologist aspired "to delve into the archaeological wonders of the mountains, and incidentally to make himself famous." Lee's twenty-one-year-old daughter Elizabeth and nineteen-year-old son Dana actively participated; Livingston, Jim and Fannie White, and Ray Davis were among the locals employed by the expedition. According to Livingston (1934, 11), Dr. Lee cannily kept his work secret:

> We were down there in the Cave behind closed doors *making* — the 8th Wonder of the World. The Colossus of Rhodes was made of bronze; the Great Pyramids of Cheops of hewn stone; the Hanging Gardens of Babylon of brick; and now this 8th Wonder was being made of "baloney!" ...In working up the geneology of the Cavern on its coat of arms certainly should be emblazoned the great bull — for the 8th Wonder was built of a skyscraper of "baloney" as high as the Empire State Building. That is exactly what it took to make the world realize the real truth of the greatness of the Carlsbad Cavern.

On July 16, 1924, the expedition opened their "baloney" cavern to some 150 invited guests, including New Mexico Governor Arthur T. Hannett, Texas Governor Patrick Morris Neff, and forty journalists. Dr. Lee guided them through:

> "See this remarkable passage that leads to a still more remarkable chamber?" Those addressed would open their eyes wide in astonishment.... "Such was discovered by me less than 30 days ago!" But the old-timers were not there to relate what they had discovered 30 years ago.

White spent the day "in the background, ...operating the hoist ..., lowering and raising the bucket with its human freight, little dreaming of the fame that was about to become his." Afterward the entourage gathered for a barbecue at Washington's Ranch on the Black River, where White and a large crowd of locals were denied admittance. When the official speeches were through, two uninvited Carlsbad residents contrived to have White, "still dressed in his work clothes," introduced as "JIM WHITE, THE DISCOVERER AND THE FIRST EXPLORER OF THE CARLSBAD CAVERN." According to Livingston, while they were making these claims, "Dr. Lee's face turned all the colors from ultra-violet to infra-red," while "those forty newspaper men and women ate it up" (Livingston 1934, 43, 12, 45, 46).

Jim White's Own Story: The Discovery and History of Carlsbad Caverns, by James Larkin White, "The Cave's Original Discoverer and Explorer," was ghostwritten in 1930 by Frank Ernest Nicholson, a journalist "who identified himself as a member of 'the cave explorers club of France,' author, speleologist, and 'explorer of caves on five continents.'" He had led a much-ballyhooed, unsuccessful exploring expedition into the cavern in February 1930. Funding was cut on March 15, and, "suddenly impoverished," Nicholson "cranked out the famous booklet *Jim White's Own Story* (to pay a board bill, according to tradition). Throughout America it spread the legend of the compelling drama of a humble cowpuncher [and] soon the public forgot the man who wrote this most famous of cave tales and turned to Jim White as the idol—the Hero of Carlsbad Cavern" (Nymeyer and Halliday 1991, 136–37, 142, 147).

From 1928 through the spring of 1929 White served as chief ranger of the Carlsbad Cave National Monument. Taos artist and writer Blanche C. Grant (1928, 28–29) lauded him in her *Cavern Guide Book:*

> No one knows as much about the caves as does Jim White. . . . Still young, tall, wiry and sharp of feature, Jim White keeps his kindly gray eyes keen for any new find in his beloved caves as well as watching carefully all those who go down into the darkness under his guidance. "I take care of the sick ones, the old ones and the kids," he said the other day, as he walked away from the cave entrance to the land of his pride—the Land of the Great Fantastic, the Eighth Wonder of the World.

White resigned in 1929 due to poor health and "drinking sprees." He wanted to be named chief explorer for the National Park Service, which instead in 1930 offered him concession rights next to the underground Lunch Room, where he signed copies of his life story. Tourists crowded his stand, "plying him with questions about his early days in the cavern and snapping his picture beneath the old guano bucket hanging in an alcove above him" (Nymeyer and Halliday 1991, 44, 45). Increasingly withdrawn, Jim White died on April 28, 1946, penniless except for the proceeds from his booklet.

The Cavern Supply Company operated the underground Lunch Room, which began food service on May 16, 1928. Ray V. Davis and Carlsbad businessmen Bert Leck, Frank Kindel, and Harry McKim had started the company in 1927 under a concessioner contract with the National Park Service. They built the lunch counter 750 feet down inside and a large stone headquarters to sell food and souvenirs near the main entrance. In 1929 Davis relinquished his interest in the company and the rights to his photographs before moving to Canyon, Texas, for three years. He returned to Carlsbad in 1932 and opened another photographic studio until retirement in 1951. Ray V. Davis Days were declared in the City of Carlsbad on September 16, 1970, and at the cavern on October 25, 1973, the fiftieth anniversary of Carlsbad Cave National Monument.

On May 16, 1927, Colonel (an honorary title) Thomas R. Boles became superintendent of Carlsbad Cave National Monument and held that post until 1946. The *Carlsbad Current-Argus* of March 9, 1928, reported that Arthur E. Demaray of the National Park Service announced that Boles had been chosen "to make Carlsbad's cavern the greatest showplace in the world." Indeed, the press soon began to call him "Mr. Carlsbad Caverns" and even "The King of the Underworld" (Nymeyer and Halliday 1991, 114). Celebrities who visited during his administration included aviator Amelia Earhart on September 11, 1928; cowboy humorist Will Rogers on May 10, 1931 (Wheeler 1949); and Robert Ripley, who broadcast a "Believe It or Not" program from the Big Room in the fall of 1939. Hollywood and movie newsreel crews shot footage in the cave. There were frequent conferences with governors from New Mexico, Arizona, and Texas and other public officials in attendance, meetings of local fraternal groups like the Masons and Elks, and weddings, the first such ceremony held at the Rock of Ages on June 23, 1927. The first bat flight presentation was in September 1929 (Crane 2000, 11). In 1933 Boles arranged "a pioneer light and sound show": an underground presentation of Franz Joseph Haydn's oratorio *The Creation* with a cast of 175 and an audience of 371 (Nymeyer and Halliday 1991, 116).

What finally cost Superintendent Boles his job was the Rock of Ages ceremony he initiated as part of the ranger-led tours. Horace M. Albright (1985, 325–26), director of the National Park Service from January 1929 to August 1933, recalls that tour groups were invited to sit around the base of the monumental Rock of Ages stalagmite,

> looking back at the great room they had just seen. The guide or a ranger would then give a short statement about the park, and suddenly all the lights would be extinguished and the cavern would be in complete darkness. A few moments later, from a point a half-mile back on the trail, the first verse of "Rock of Ages" would be sung by rangers or a quartet from the town of Carlsbad or a group from a church choir or even a lone singer. As the singers advanced along the trail, lights were turned on behind them, with more lights turned on at the end of each verse. And when the last verse was sung near the great stalagmite, the cavern room was fully lighted. It was an emotional experience that brought tears to the eyes of many visitors.

In 1944 Newton B. Drury, National Park Service director from August 1940 to March 1951, ordered Boles to stop "the practice of the hymn singing and lights going on and off," but the superintendent, "who believed the ceremony added greatly to the visitors' park experience, did not comply with the Director's order." Two years later, "Drury finally got exasperated and transferred Boles to Hot Springs National Park, despite outcries from New Mexico congressmen."

When President Herbert Hoover proclaimed Carlsbad Caverns National Park on May 14, 1930, it meant the cavern had outstripped the Grand Canyon by going from national monument to national park status in seven rather than eleven years. A March 1927 Santa Fe Railway booklet heralded the caverns as "Like a Grand Canyon Underground": "There is only one Grand Canyon ... Bridge of the Rainbow ... Painted Desert ... Petrified Forest.... To these attractions, comparable only in that they seem to float in color against the deep blue of the sky, the Santa Fe Southwest now adds a subterranean marvel—the Carlsbad Caverns of New Mexico" (in Weigle 1997, 172). In *Piñon Country*, his contribution to the American Folkways Series edited by Erskine Caldwell, poet and author Haniel Long (1941, 218, 219) contrasts the tourist experience at each:

> The Carlsbad Caverns are an event of inward and outward living in a different way from the Grand Canyon. Other visitors to the Canyon at the time you are there can hardly matter to you.... There is a great hush, and a great air of decorum, as though an important personage had just died. As a young man said, you see the Canyon in a top hat.
>
> This loneliness and formality and sense of being cut off from the comforts of your kind help make the Canyon a deep experience. The Cavern can be as deep an experience, but you do not continue on your way thinking only of the fantasia of substance under the surface of the earth. You have in mind also the people you went underground with, for they give you as much cause for thought as the stalactites and stalagmites. Going through the Cavern is a folk festival. You must be at the Cavern at a set time, and become part of a group of hundreds of people; and with this party, under the eye of the rangers, take a walk of six subterranean miles. In the course of descending, ascending, hurrying, pausing, sauntering, sidling, you stop for a forty-five-minute luncheon at a cafeteria in an enormous and well-lighted chamber. If you aren't acquainted with a dozen or so people by now, it will happen here, or else what a pity.

Historian Hal K. Rothman (1998, 159, 160) claims that Carlsbad Caverns was "the first area to force itself into the national park category with automobile visitation" and "served as a prototype of the new parks that automobile travelers demanded." Its "publicity reflected science and romanticism" and was "tuned to the increasing emphasis on convenience in modern America instead of the older, more reverential notions of the meaning of nature." Rothman quotes a July 1939 *Popular Mechanics* article, "Greatest Show Under the Earth": "Nature, the greatest showman of them all, outdid herself on Carlsbad Caverns

Both The Caverns And White's City

Here are two entrances that no visitor ever forgets. One leads to the world-famous Carlsbad Caverns and the other to every overnight accommodation that the traveler could hope for.

White City is the largest tourist court within 100 miles of Carlsbad Caverns. It is owned and operated by Charles L. White, who is also mayor and chief of police. There is a restaurant and service station among other conveniences.

You'll enjoy doing "just as you please" at White City where there's an interesting museum you'll always remember.

White's City advertisement at the bottom of page 87, Picturesque Southwest: Travelers' Guide to Southwestern Attractions, *vol. 1, no. 1, 1937. This 120-page, 35-cent, oversized "magazine" was published by the Southwestern Publishing Co., El Paso, Texas.*

...but it remained for modern science to make it accessible and convert it into the most dramatic natural phenomenon in the world."

By 1927 visitors in automobiles could find services much closer to the cave than the town of Carlsbad at White's City. Its founder, Charles Lee (Charlie L. or Charley Lee) White, no relation to Jim White, had come to southeastern New Mexico from Kentucky in

1909. He opened a mercantile company in Loving in 1914 and there "soon installed the first handoperated gasoline pump in the town."

> In 1926 he and his family were on an outing to see the much talked about bat cave when he was struck with the idea of acquiring the land at the mouth of the canyon leading to the caverns. Not even waiting to visit the caves, he rushed to Carlsbad, the county seat, to file homestead papers. So with lots of foresight and very little money, and plenty of "Savy" he built the "White's Cavern Camp" which consisted of a home, 13 units for visitors and a filling station. In the years to come he added a garage, café, grocery store, drug store and museum. (in Weigle and White 1988, 87–88; also Ripp 1984; Bryant 1985)

Carlsbad's newest cave, the United States Department of Energy's Waste Isolation Pilot Project (WIPP), is twenty-six miles southeast of town. That cavern's guano, transuranic waste, is said on a 1995 "WIPP Fact Sheet" obtained at the Carlsbad DOE Visitor Center in March 1995 to be "heavier than uranium, which is the heaviest naturally occurring element . . . [mostly consisting of] contaminated laboratory gloves, tools, dried sludges, and other material from laboratory or production facilities." The DOE claims that "as early as the 1950s, the National Academy of Sciences recommended disposal of radioactive waste in geological formations, such as deep salt beds." Southeastern New Mexico was tested in the 1970s, construction authorized by Congress in 1979, and the first underground excavation begun in 1982.

In its fight to gain clearance for storing the first "defense-generated radioactive waste," the DOE opened a Visitor Center in Carlsbad: "a full-color, multi-dimensional, hands-on experience, as unique as the WIPP facility itself." Before the 2,150-foot-deep repository was operational, the DOE sometimes gave tours of the billion-dollar facility to assure the public of the plant's safety. A Santa Fe native and Clovis resident's letter to *The Santa Fe New Mexican* of May 24, 1992, attests to the success of that year's Community Day tour, which

> was conducted professionally, and the safety of the tourist was of the utmost concern. The tour guides were knowledgeable and answered every question with intellect and without bias. I have been a closet supporter of the WIPP Project for several years. Now I consider myself to be an open supporter and proponent of nuclear waste storage in southeast New Mexico. The efforts by the Department of Energy to ensure the safety of the region are, in my opinion, more than ample to meet the requirements.

The DOE's efforts were lampooned the following August, when the National Park Service provoked considerable public outcry with its decision to close the underground lunch-

The WIPP Waste Handling Building is shown with flowers, yucca, mesquite, sage, and scrub oak.

Waste Isolation Pilot Project – WIPP, *inside back cover of undated brochure*
produced by Westinghouse Electric Corporation for the United States
Department of Energy at the Waste Isolation Pilot Project in Carlsbad,
New Mexico, under contract number DE-AC04-86AL31950. Obtained by the
author at the United States Department of Energy Waste Isolation Pilot
Project Visitor Center, Carlsbad, March 1995.

---

room at Carlsbad Caverns because it "isn't needed these days when high-speed elevators can whisk visitors from the depths of the caverns to the surface in a minute" (*Albuquerque Journal*, August 20, 1993; also editorial, August 21, 1993). A John Trever cartoon in the *Albuquerque Journal* of August 26, 1993, shows a uniformed DOE guard at the gate beneath a sign reading "WIPP UNDERGROUND N-WASTE REPOSITORY [with freshly painted addition] and LUNCHROOM" telling a tourist couple and child who are in their car that "with time on our hands and Carlsbad Caverns closing their cafeteria, we thought we'd take up the slack."

The fight to keep the lunchroom open proved successful the following year; the unsuccessful fight to delay WIPP lasted another five years. The tractor-trailer hauling the first three containers of low-level nuclear waste did not leave Los Alamos National Laboratory until just before 8:00 p.m. on March 25, 1999, for its 260-mile trip.

As the truck rumbled away from the place where the atomic age had been conceived 54 years earlier, jubilant Los Alamos workers lined the road to greet it....

But when the truck reached the outskirts of Santa Fe, about 15 miles south, the primary onlookers became environmental activists who had fought for years against the prospect of ever witnessing such a sight. One tried to block the vehicle's path with his car before New Mexico state police interceded; others waved signs and beat Tibetan shaman drums in protest.... The truck continued south, a state police escort and television crews in tow. Finally, at around 4 a.m., nearly 500 weary but excited bystanders cheered as the caravan pulled up to a cluster of stark white buildings rising out of the barren expanse of scrub oak, coyote trails, and mesquite upholstering the southern New Mexico desert. The truck had arrived to deposit its cargo at the world's first permanent deep underground burial site for nuclear materials. (McCutcheon 2002, 15)

In 2001, as the two-year anniversary of this first truckload approached, there was mounting concern over the future of Nevada's proposed Yucca Mountain facility for burying high-level nuclear waste. If it does not open, "everyone from local nuclear activists to Attorney General Patricia Madrid worry that WIPP, open and functioning, may become the federal government's second choice," according to *Santa Fe Reporter* staff writer Winifred Walsh (March 7–13, 2001). Should this transpire, the new battle would be waged in and between the key cities of Santa Fe and Carlsbad, the former antagonistic, the latter supportive. Tourism figures into these contentions:

Look on a map of New Mexico and it becomes apparent why there is a difference in perspective between the residents of Santa Fe and Carlsbad. Santa Fe is in the northern, denser part of the state. Despite a relatively small population of 67,000, it's considered a major city because it's the state capital, visited by thousands of tourists each year for skiing, cultural events and the arts. Carlsbad, with a population of nearly 25,000, is in one of the most isolated sections of the state. Artesia, about 40 miles away and equally as small, is the closest city. The nearest large city is El Paso, Texas, a two-and-a-half hour drive away. Carlsbad Caverns and the Pecos River bring a number of tourists to the city, but they usually do not stay long. Carlsbad's economy has historically relied on potash mining, Santa Fe's on tourism.

11
The Volcano State

Located southwest of the town of Shiprock, New Mexico is a unique towering, bird-like volcanic rock formation that can be seen for miles in all directions. Shiprock, as this mighty sand-colored column was named by Anglo settlers, is known to the Navajo as "Tse Bitai," or rock with wings. The peak is 7,178 feet above sea level, and is at the center of three volcanic pressure ridges that pushed the rock skyward millenniums ago.... Fast Facts. There are no facilities, but you may enjoy the view from the rest area and picnic tables near the volcanic pressure ridge that extends south of the peak.

—Discover Navajo: The Official Navajo Nation Tour Guide, *Navajo Tourism, 2000*

The Navajo Nation cordially welcomes you to visit one of the most unique landmarks—The Four Corners. This is the only place in the United States where four states come together at one place: Arizona, New Mexico, Utah, and Colorado. Here a person can stand in all four states at one time.

The Four Corners Monument, located at an elevation of 5,000 feet above sea level, makes for a perfect year round visit....

There are many [other] attractions such as Monument Valley, Canyon de Chelly, Little Colorado River Gorge, Rainbow Bridge, Grand Falls, Betatkin, and Window Rock. These are the "Seven Wonders of the Navajo Nation." The tribe is noted for its tapestry rug weaving, silver crafts and basketry.

—*From the six-panel* Four Corners Monument Navajo Tribal Park *brochure obtained there in May 2001*

7he cover of the January 2001 issue of *New Mexico Magazine* features Paul Bonnichsen's photograph of a snow-covered Shiprock. Inside, his full-page photograph of the same view without snow and with the summit shrouded in clouds is captioned: "Perhaps New Mexico's most famous form, Ship Rock Peak, near the Four Corners area, is all that remains of a large volcano. The Navajo Nation considers the formation sacred." The two are part of "Land of Volcanoes," in which New Mexico Museum of Natural History and Science Research Curator of Volcanology/Space Science Larry S. Crumpler (2001, 61) asks: "What is geologically exceptional about New Mexico?" Each of the Four Corners states has a "geologic specialty"—Arizona the Grand Canyon State, Utah the Dinosaur State, and Colorado the Rocky Mountain State. He proposes that New Mexico become the Volcano State:

> In the same way that uniqueness and diversity is New Mexico's specialty in culture and art, diversity of volcanic landforms is its geologic specialty. Like a bird sanctuary where bird-watchers may see many different species in one small area, New Mexico is a "volcano sanctuary" to volcanologists. The fact is, this is one of the best places on the continent to see the landforms associated with volcanoes.

During the twentieth century Shiprock became New Mexico's Mount Olympus. A Harvey Caplin photograph of it, which originally appeared in the July 1956 issue of *New Mexico Magazine*, was chosen for the four-cent stamp issued on January 6, 1962, to commemorate the golden anniversary of New Mexico statehood ("Statehood Stamp" 1962; Tissot 1997, with stamp photo 71). A muted color photograph by George H. H. Hurley, showing Shiprock at dawn or dusk, adorns the 1995 cover of *The Smithsonian Guides to Natural America: The Southwest (New Mexico, Arizona)*. Inside, a two-page spread of the full photograph showing sky, clouds, and outlying lava dikes precedes the two-page introduction to Part One: New Mexico. The caption reads: "Shiprock soars 1,100 feet from the surrounding desert. The Navajo's sacred 'Rock with Wings' is an ancient volcanic remnant" (Page 1995, 24; also Baars 1995, 217).

The *Official 1940 Road Map of New Mexico* commemorating the Coronado Cuarto Centennial, 1540–1940, features a painting by Tesuque artist Wilfred Stedman showing Shiprock with hogan, sheep, and Navajo herders in the foreground. In the 1940 WPA New Mexico Guide, the Shiprock formation is on Tour 6B, along NM 164, which "branches right from US 66, 0 *m.* at a point 17.8 miles west of Bluewater and parallels the Atchison, Topeka & Santa Fe Railway for a short distance":

From 56 *m.* SHIPROCK (L), an igneous cliff formation, resembles a giant ship,

Commemorative "First of State" postage stamp issued on January 6, 1962,
to mark fifty years of statehood. Shiprock photo by Harvey Caplin, 1956.

full sail on a calm sea. The Navaho call it *tae-bidahi* (the winged rock). This rock
that towers 1,400 feet above the surrounding country has served both Indian and
white man as a landmark. There are many legends connected with it, and the
Navaho explain its origin thus: Long ago when they were besieged by Utes, and
almost overcome by them, the medicine men held a ceremony, making medicine
all day and night. As the second night came on, and all the besieged people were
praying and chanting, the rocky ground on which they stood rose in the air, its
crags formed wings, and it sailed away, leaving the enemy behind. All night it
sailed and until sundown of the next day, when it settled in the midst of this great
open plain, where it has since remained, a sentinel and a sacred mountain. (Workers of WPA 1940, 333, 341)

New Mexico: A New Guide to the Colorful State does not mention this UFO, claiming
simply: "As the traveler heads south from the town of Shiprock, the monolithic formation
called Shiprock (because of its resemblance to a sailing craft with wind-filled sheets)
looms to the west." Instructions are given as to how to follow "about three miles of twisting dirt track" to get to the base. "A climb around the base affords many fine views of the
hogback, the monolith itself, and the barren canyons, walled by red rock, to the west. As
with all such rock monuments in Navajo country, it is forbidden to climb the Shiprock
because of its religious significance" (Chilton et al. 1984, 585, 586).

Journalist Toby Smith (in *Albuquerque Journal Magazine*, March 15, 1988) notes the
two deaths and one climbing accident that "caused the director of the Navajo tribe's Parks
and Recreation Department to issue, on May 12, 1971, a proclamation prohibiting anyone
from climbing Shiprock, as well as other Navajo rock formations":

Two climbers have died on Shiprock. A plaque, midway up the rock formation, honors the first: Bernard Topp, a 27-year-old soldier from Minnesota, who died in 1957. Eight years later, Robert Schroeder, a 20-year-old student from Wyoming, fell and died. In the spring of 1970, a daring rescue saved the life of a Californian who had fallen on his way down the rock.... Navajos maintain that Shiprock is sacred; to climb it is to profane it. Added to that notion is the Navajos' fear of death and its aftermath. A death on Shiprock, Navajos believe, brings evil spirits to a holy place.

Smith interviewed Gallup attorney and rock climber Bob Rosebrough, "who has tried almost single-handedly to persuade the Navajos to reconsider the ban and permit climbers to lawfully enjoy Shiprock."

Records of unsuccessful attempts to scale the formation date from the 1930s. A 1936 Colorado climbing group "got about halfway up when one member fell." Not seriously injured, his mishap was recounted in "an article in *The Saturday Evening Post* extolling Shiprock's unconquerability." Rosebrough calls the first successful ascent by four Sierra Club of California members in October 1939 "a climb far ahead of its time." The next successful climb was in 1952 and more frequently since until, he told Smith, "it became a 'classic' climb, like El Capitan [in Yosemite National Park, California]. Every American climber and mountaineer had to have it." Smith reports that "those who placed their names in the register that lies inside an old Army ammunition can at the summit of Shiprock include some of the greats of American climbing: David Brower (he was among that first successful party), Royal Robbins, Harvey Carter, Chuck Pratt and Fred Beckey" (Smith in *Albuquerque Journal Magazine*, March 15, 1988; also Ungnade 1972, 170–75; Kosik 1996, 244).

In "Touring the Four Corners," a special section of *The Farmington Daily Times* of April 28, 1999, visitors are reminded that: "Many Navajos consider the rock a sacred spot. Two families claim grazing rights to the road and land around Shiprock, and their wishes should be respected." The Navajo story about Shiprock is that "here, long ago, ...the mythic hero Monster Slayer battled two giant flying creatures that were eating the Navajo people." In contemporary times, "parts of the films 'Natural Born Killers' [1994] and 'Pontiac Moon' [1994] were shot here." There is a picture of a balloon floating past Shiprock in the annual Shiprock Balloon Rally, an invitation-only event that began in 1990. In 1996 it took place on February 24 and 25, when, according to journalist Betsy Model (in the *Santa Fe New Mexican*, March 21, 1996): "Almost all the pilots had participated in years past. Many of them cite the mystical feeling they have as they approach the formation of Shiprock as drawing them back."

Official 1940 Road Map of New Mexico, *designed by Bradford-Robinson, Denver.*
Painting by artist Wilfred Stedman.

The *Daily Times* staff also report that "a trip to [the town of] Shiprock is like a trip to a foreign country half an hour from downtown Farmington—and you don't need a passport." It might seem little different; "yet the Navajo language and values are still practiced on a daily basis in home life, government, education, medicine and justice." Since "it is a polite society where respectful guests are welcome," visitors are reminded "that it is good taste to ask before taking photos of homes or people." Places for eating local specialties like Navajo tacos or mutton stew and fry bread and shopping are noted, as is the annual Northern Navajo Fair at the end of September and the first week in October.

In the early twentieth century, Shiprock was home to weavers of rugs called yei that incorporated sandpainting designs. Sandpaintings (Navajo '*iikááh*, meaning 'place where the gods come and go') are "essential parts of curing ceremonies whose purpose is to attract the Holy People so that they will help with the complex curing process." Considered "the exact pictorial representation of supernaturals," these "stylized designs created during the ceremonies are strictly prescribed and...always destroyed at the end of the ritual." Anthropologist Nancy J. Parezo (1983, 1, 2) traces the commercialization and secularization process through which "Navajo sandpaintings changed from an exclusively ephemeral sacred form to a permanent decorative art" made by laymen "for sale in the international market as luxury items in the form of fine art, decorative art, and souvenirs ...[and] not bought or used by the Navajo."

In the 1880s a very few weavers began to use sandpainting designs in their work, which is not otherwise "religious." The first known yei and yeibichai rugs, the former with simplified figures of the Holy People and the latter a linear row of human dancers impersonating masked gods, date from 1885, but do not reappear until the turn of the century.

> Yei and yeibichai rugs have been incorrectly called prayer rugs or ceremonial rugs . . . , but they are strictly secular, commercial items, although the symbolism they contain may sometimes be considered sacred by the Navajo. . . . The idea that these were traditional prayer rugs was probably the fabrication of a trader who was attempting to increase their value and hence increase sales, for it was evident that Anglo customers would pay more for a rug or object which is felt to be religious or symbolic. Clearly, the Anglo customers who bought the rugs in the early twentieth century considered them to be religious in nature, and this characterization along with their rarity and intrinsic interest contributed greatly to their popularity.

After World War I, Shiprock trader Will Evans popularized yei rugs in "a regional style... [with] brightly colored figures on a white background" and "continued to price the rugs exceptionally high [to make] the buyer feel that he was purchasing something precious" (Parezo 1983, 42, 44).

The town of Shiprock is on Tour 9 in the 1940 WPA New Mexico Guide:

SHIPROCK, 15.4 *m.* [from the state line south of Cortez, Colorado] (4,903 alt., 2,131 pop.), named for an imposing rock mass (R), was the headquarters for the Northern Navaho Indian Agency from 1903 till the subagencies were all consolidated at Window Rock, Arizona, in 1938. It is now a Navaho district office. The Rattlesnake Oil Fields (R) near Shiprock contain some of the highest grade oil in the United States but the flow is limited and the lack of marketing facilities further reduces their value. From these and two other fields on their reservation the Navaho receive annually a total of about $50,000 in royalties. There is an annual Navaho Fair held here early in October with sports and exhibits of arts and crafts. (Workers of WPA 1940, 363; also Wilson with Dennison 1995, 54; Linford 2000, 263–65)

Rattlesnake Field was first drilled in 1924 and had eighty-three oil wells by 1946, but production, which ceased altogether in 1966, was limited due to difficulties in extracting and handling the unusually light petroleum (Baars 1995, 157).

The Navajo Tribal Council had recognized the importance of coal in 1943 but derived little revenue from it until 1963, when Utah International, Inc., opened a strip-mining operation on 31,400 acres of Navajo land near Fruitland between Shiprock and Farmington to provide fuel for the developing Four Corners Power Plant (Baars 1995, 172). In "San Juan's Black Gold," journalist John L. Parker (1964, 12, 15) describes completion of the initial phase of "construction of a $62 million coal-fire generating plant, newest and largest in [the Arizona Public Service Company's] complex of power plants serving ten of Arizona's fourteen counties," and the first outside that state. "From the top of the tall boilers at this new generating plant you are within sight of half a dozen Navajo *hogans*. Grazing sheep and goats are a common sight nearby as the herders ride up to look over the operation."

One of the highlights of this big project [is] a 1,275-acre cooling pond alongside the plant. One hundred feet deep in places, with an average depth of 29 feet, the pond is a man-made lake containing 39,000 acre feet of water, making it among the largest privately developed artificial lakes in the West.... This lake has been turned over to the Navajo Tribe for recreation purposes. Catfish and trout have been planted. The local Navajo recreation committee has built boat-launching ramps, parking lot facilities and picnic areas at the lakeside. Named Morgan Lake, it is rapidly becoming the most popular resort and fishing center in the area.

Shiprock, "famous landmark of pioneer travelers since the days of the *conquistadores*," is "twenty miles distant." Near it "can be seen the uranium-vanadium metals processing plant of the Vanadium Corporation, and the helium extraction plant of the Bureau of Mines."

In 1977 the Four Corners Power Plant and Navajo Mine were "the world's largest such operation...[serving] the electrical needs of El Paso, Tucson, Phoenix, Albuquerque and Los Angeles" (Baars 1995, 172). In the 1984 New Mexico Guide, it is on Tour 2, which runs the length of U.S. 64 from Clayton, past Round Mound, to Shiprock and Four Corners:

> At 417 miles, N.M. 489 goes south to Fruitland and Kirtland and the Four Corners Power Plant. Fruitland is an Anglo farming community with neat homes and graceful willow trees. It was settled in 1877 by a group of Mormons. The Four Corners Power Plant is an enormous electricity-generating unit on the south side of Morgan Lake. The adjacent Navajo Mine is the largest open-pit coal mine in the United States. Tours are given on a regular schedule. In keeping with the grand scale of these operations, it is said that the smoke from the Four Corners Plant was the only manmade phenomenon visible with the naked eye to the astronauts on the moon. (Chilton et al. 1984, 316)

The 1997 *Southwest USA: The Rough Guide* deems this region "notorious": "After this coal-fired generating station opened in the 1960s, it was said to be the single greatest source of pollution in the United States, emitting more noxious gases than either New York City or Los Angeles. Regulations have tightened since then, but...there's no incentive for outsiders to linger" (Ward 1997, 75). Nevertheless, reassuring tours touting the plant's safeguards are still conducted, according to the *Farmington, New Mexico, 2001 Area Guide*, published in Albuquerque by the Starlight Media Group. Among those with Farmington as "a terrific starting point" are "Industrial Tours" of the San Juan Generating Station, Navajo Mine, San Juan Mine, La Plata Mine, and Four Corners Power Plant, "at the turn-off just over 11 miles west on Hwy 64," where visitors may arrange to "view major operating components of this two-million kilowatt coal-fired power plant and its state-of-the-art environmental control equipment."

The 1997 Rough Guide writers are no more complimentary to the original Four Corners attraction:

> The **Four Corners Monument Navajo Tribal Park** (summer daily 7am-7pm, winter daily 8am-5pm; $1.50), reached by a short spur road half a mile northeast of US-160, is the only place in the United States where four states meet at a single point. However exciting you may find the concept, the reality is bleak and dull. A steady stream of visitors mooch around the pivotal brass plaque, ponderously contorting a limb into each state for demeaning photographs. Navajo stalls on all sides sell crafts, T-shirts and fry-bread. (Ward 1997, 62)

Four Corners marker, ca. 1948. Navajo artist Jimmy Toddy (Beatien Yazz,
Little No-Shirt) stands with Sallie Wagner, then Mrs. William Lippincott and with
her husband owner of the Wide Ruins, Arizona, trading post.
(Museum of New Mexico Neg. No. 003160)

The thirty-eighth (Colorado, August 1, 1876), forty-fifth (Utah, January 4, 1896), forty-seventh (New Mexico, January 6, 1912), and forty-eighth (Arizona, February 14, 1912) states meet at the coordinates of 37° north latitude and 32° west longitude. Appointed by Congress to determine Colorado's southern boundary in 1867, surveyor and astronomer Ehud H. Darling set a terminal monument at what would become Four Corners the following year. In 1875, U.S. Surveyor and Astronomer Chandler Robbins "erected a substantial stone monument" as an "initial point" for surveying the New Mexico-Arizona boundary. It

Four Corners Monument Navajo Park,
photo by the author, May 21, 2001

was intact in 1878 and 1885, but in 1899 U.S. Surveyors Hubert D. Page and James M. Lentz found "that the stone had been disturbed and broken [so] marked and set a new stone at the original Robbins location." Howard Carpenter, who surveyed the northern Arizona boundary, found it intact in 1901. In 1931 U.S. Surveyor Everett H. Kimmell "identified the Page and Lentz stone, and a marked stone deposit, finding the larger stone again broken . . . [and] constructed the concrete monument now marking the Corner of the Four States" (Ellis 1983, 68, 69). In 1962 the U.S. Department of the Interior built a concrete slab around Kimmell's monument.

The New Mexico State Highway Department's *New Mexico: The Sunshine State Official Road Map 1935* is the first to mark "the only point in the United States common to four state corners." During the 1940s those who ventured eight miles along a "twisting, high-centered trail" where "you cross and recross from New Mexico into Arizona as you guide on a sad little telephone line" found a monument that "is a very modest 30-inch block of concrete." In her June 1949 *New Mexico Magazine* "Trip of the Month," journalist Betty Woods (1950, 43, 44) reports: "At its base someone built a circle of stones and cut it into four pieces like a pie. An initial in each of the four sections signifies its state." Nearby are the ruins of a stone building "put up, occupied and abandoned by a trader less than thirty years ago" because "not enough Navajos came to trade [nor] enough hardy tourists

...to see." This had housed Wilken and Whitecraft's Four Corners Trading Post, set up around 1910 and abandoned by 1941 (Linford 2000, 211). Woods indicates visitors might encounter a Navajo woman who has her sheep corralled in the ruins, but most likely it will be deserted, a place of "legend and loneliness" that is "a birthplace of whirlwinds."

The Navajo tribe established the Four Corners Monument in 1964, by which time a paved road connected the site with already paved highways. In her January 1968 "Trip of the Month," Betty Woods (1973, 63) describes a new marker, "an unusual and very permanent 'sand painting' done in sandstone, cement and turquoise instead of sand. While most Navajo sand paintings are allowed to last only from dawn to dusk, this one is made to last for centuries": "On it you read the inscription HERE MEET IN PEACE, UNDER GOD, FOUR STATES.... Within the corner of each state's boundary lies that state's Great Seal."

During the early 1980s the Teec Nos Pos Navajo Chapter nearby in Arizona began collecting a dollar per carload from Four Corners visitors and in 1986 proposed that the U.S. Department of the Interior and the four states level the surroundings to "create a new 40-foot square open area with small display areas and flagpoles at each corner, shops, museum and campground" (Sherry Robinson in *Albuquerque Journal*, December 28, 1986). This and more was in place in 2000, when *Discover Navajo: The Official Navajo Nation Visitor Guide* indicates: "Four Corners Navajo Tribal Park has a visitor center, a demonstration center, Navajo arts and crafts booths, picnic tables and portable restrooms.... Be sure to bring a camera—no where else in America can you stand in four states simultaneously!"

On July 12, 2000, Four Corners Monument Navajo Tribal Park observed the 125th anniversary of the coordinates' 1875 marking. A brief reenactment included Navajo Nation President Kelsey Begaye, Ute Mountain Ute Vice Chairman Selwyn Whiteskunk, Four Corners Heritage Council Executive Cleal Bradford, and others. James Gorman, the monument's park manager, estimated "the peak of the morning crowd at 1,200 visitors." Also in attendance were the U.S. Postal Service senior district managers for the four states and postmasters from Shiprock; Teec Nos Pos, Arizona; Montezuma Creek, Utah; and Towaoc, Colorado. Despite a long line at the Visitors Center, most "hard-core, stamp-crazy philatelists to the casual vacationer who just happened by ...said the wait was worth it [because] Wednesday's festivities marked the first time in U.S. history a citizen could collect four postmarks from four states at the same location on the same date" (Larry Di Giovanni in *The Farmington Daily Times*, July 13, 2000).

In 1968 the Navajo Tribal Council issued a map, *Welcome to Exciting Navajoland*, to mark the end of "our century of progress" since returning from the agony of the Long Walk and the Fort Sumner, New Mexico, incarceration, 1862–1868:

Lines on a map show only its roads and boundaries. Navajoland is much more than that; it's a sovereign nation. Navajoland is the Navajo people, from industrious workmen and busy secretaries to youngsters tending sheep along the highways. Along with sawmills and electronic assembly plants, ours is a life of trading posts and scenic beauty. A land of time enough and room enough.

Having celebrated our century of progress in 1968, we move forward into a century of achievement. The way of the Navajo will preserve this 16 million acres of splendid geography for all to see and enjoy.

The Navajo people bid you welcome.

Color photographs of Monument Valley, Rainbow Bridge, and Shiprock (captioned: "Shiprock, in northeastern Navajoland is a volcanic plug, but time and the elements have shaped it to resemble an old windjammer under full sail") are included as part of "the scenic Splendor of Navajoland." Each is also depicted on the map, which marks "Four Corners" with only a cross.

In 2000 Navajo Tourism in the Navajo Nation Office of Economic Development published *Discover Navajo: The Official Navajo Nation Visitor Guide*, "graphically designed, edited and printed by The Prewitt Company, a Navajo-owned firm." Four Corners Monument is fifteenth and Shiprock seventeenth among the thirty-six sights in a Navajoland that echoes that of 1968 and suggests fulfillment of the "century of progress" Tribal Council's vision for "a century of achievement":

Diné Bikéyah, or Navajoland, is larger than 10 of the 50 states in America. This vast land is unique because the people here have achieved something quite rare: the ability of an indigenous people to blend both traditional and modern ways of life. The Navajo Nation truly is a nation within a nation.

In years past, Navajoland often appeared to be little more than a desolate section of the Southwest, but it was only a matter of time before the Navajo Nation became known as a wealthy nation in a world of its own.

12
2001—Route 66,
Essence of Enchantment

New Mexico is an amazing place, especially for explorers. Whether you're a newly arrived visitor, a native or someone coming back for another dose of the state's magic, there's always something new to discover here.

This year [2001] we join the rest of the nation in celebrating the 75th anniversary of one of the great modern pathways to discovery—Route 66. This paved thoroughfare has joined the ranks of other extremely important historic pathways to New Mexico, including El Camino Real and the Santa Fe Trail.

But Route 66 for the first time enabled more travelers than ever to venture into New Mexico. . . . The road opened up new opportunities for New Mexicans and allowed other Americans to discover the beauty and treasures of the Land of Enchantment with less difficulty.

—*Governor Gary E. Johnson, "A Note from the Governor,"* 2001 New Mexico Vacation Guide, *Department of Tourism, 2000*

A little over a century after the Santa Fe Trail opened in 1821 and almost fifty years following the Atchison, Topeka and Santa Fe Railroad surmounting Raton Pass in 1878, Father of Route 66 Cyrus (Cy) Stevens Avery delivered the keynote speech at the first meeting of the National U.S. 66 Highway Association in Tulsa on February 4, 1927. He "recommended that [the new road] be called The Main Street of America, a name that was to appear on brochures, maps, postcards, and in travel guidebooks for the next half-century" (Scott and Kelly 1988, 17; also Scott 2000). By the time of its being decommissioned in 1984, however, Route 66 was better known as the Mother Road, John Steinbeck's designation for it in his 1939 novel *The Grapes of Wrath*. Whether as Main Street of America or the Mother Road, it was Route 66 that inherited Josiah Gregg's Commerce of the Prairies and the Great Southwest of the Santa Fe Railway and the Fred Harvey Company.

Launched in 1926, the inaugural year of the Santa Fe/Harvey Indian Detours, Highway 66 between Chicago and Los Angeles was largely the result of work by oil producer and Oklahoma State Highway Commissioner Cyrus Avery. A leader in the American Association of State Highway Officials, Avery helped that organization petition Secretary of Agriculture Howard M. Gore in 1924 "to underwrite immediately the selection and designation of a comprehensive system of through interstate routes and to devise a comprehensive and uniform scheme for designating such routes in such a manner as to give them a conspicuous place among highways of the country as roads of interstate and national significance." He served as consulting highway specialist to the twenty-one-member board appointed by Gore and managed to engineer a middle course for what became Route 66, between the northern Santa Fe Trail and the southern Butterfield Stage Line. It "roughly corresponded to the old Gold Road from Fort Smith, Arkansas—a route that happened to come directly through Avery's hometown of Tulsa and the state capital, Oklahoma City" (Wallis 1990, 7).

A shorter U.S. 66 across New Mexico opened in November 1937. Surfaced from the Texas line to the Arizona line, it brought "a saving in mileage of approximately 98 miles, and a time-saving in crossing the state of approximately four hours" ("U.S. 66 Opened" 1937; also Schneider 1991; Usner 2001). According to *New Mexico's Historic Route 66*, an undated eight-panel folded brochure written by Michael E. Pitel of the New Mexico Department of Tourism for the Diamond Jubilee in 2001:

> The earliest route was a circuitous, 501-mile wash-board journey in 1926. Westbound motorists encountered Glenrio, then Tucumcari. Past Santa Rosa, they turned north, then at Romero (later Romeroville), west. In Santa Fe they turned southwest, passing through Albuquerque to Los Lunas. There they turned northwest to Correo, then west to Grants and Gallup.
>
> They found the route 126 miles shorter in 1938. Instead of turning northwest past Santa Rosa, they continued west through Buford (later Moriarty) and Albuquerque, all the way to Correo.
>
> As these motorists traveled through New Mexico, they encountered live rattlesnakes, teepees and turquoise jewelry, sagebrush and tumbleweeds, hogans and Harvey Houses, real Indians, blue skies and unending sunshine. Some of them traveled no further. In New Mexico, some of them realized they had come home.

The first guidebook to Route 66 was self-published by editor and author Jack D. Rittenhouse in 1946. After he and his wife Charlotte "got together all the WPA Guidebooks for the Route 66 states for some background ... and gathered some rough data about the road," in March of that year he alone "took off from L.A. and headed east toward Chicago on Route 66 ... driving my 1939 American Bantam, manufactured by the American Bantam Car Co. of Butler, Pennsylvania" (Wallis 1990, 17, 19). In the preface to the facsimile of the 1946 first edition, Rittenhouse (1989) notes that he "was not the first writer to see a possible postwar boom in western travel," since "in 1866, Edward H. Hall wrote his guidebook 'The Great West' because he believed the end of the Civil War would 'swell the tide of immigration setting into the Eldorado of the West.'" During the March 1946 round trip "to double-check my facts" he also

had to inspect the scenery, so I drove from dawn to dusk at 35 miles an hour. There were no tape recorders then, so I scrawled notes on a big yellow pad on the seat beside me. Each night I dug out my portable manual typewriter and typed my notes.

I made some errors in language. I became so enthused over New Mexico that in one place the text refers to the Gulf of NEW Mexico. And, like many new authors, I wrote about the Rio Grande River, using the redundant wording that is permitted once but not twice to a writer. It was my first book. I was just past thirty-three years old.

We printed 3,000 copies and sold them for a dollar each, doing business by mail to bookshops, newsstands, cafes, and tourist courts (no one then called them motels) along US 66. And I learned the hard way that a self-publishing author usually has a fool for a distributor. I never reached my full market.

Reviewers ignored the little book, but Duncan Hines, who was best known for his restaurant guide, wrote me a nice letter praising the book because it would help people actually see the countryside, not just zip through it. Now [Albuquerque, 1988], as with the old US 66 signs, that first edition has soared in price as a collector's prize.

President Dwight D. Eisenhower appointed a President's Advisory Committee on a National Highway Program. Its report led to the Federal Aid Highway Act of 1956 with guidelines for a national interstate highway system. According to author Michael Wallis (1990, 26):

Finally, the last stretch of U.S. Highway 66 was bypassed in 1984, near Williams, Arizona, when a final strip of Route 66 was replaced by a section of Interstate 40. There was a ceremony and speeches and a lot of news coverage.

Front cover and centerfold New Mexico map,
Drive US 66: Shortest, Fastest Year-'round Best Across the Scenic West,
an undated (post-1937), twelve-page "folder published for free distribution
by the National Highway 66 Association," designed by Willard Andrews,
Ward Hicks Advertising, Albuquerque.

The bypassing of Route 66 had actually taken not one but five different interstates—Interstate 55 from Chicago to St. Louis; Interstate 44 from St. Louis to Oklahoma City; Interstate 40 from Oklahoma City to Barstow, California; Interstate 15 from Barstow to San Bernardino; and Interstate 10 from San Bernardino to Santa Monica. As one of the old highway's aficionados put it, the opening of the interstates made it possible to drive all the way from Chicago to the Pacific without stopping. The government called that progress.

Thank God, not everyone agreed.

U.S. 66 was officially decommissioned on June 27, 1985.

Cy Avery's Route 66 in time became the setting for what author and journalist Phil Patton (1986, 230–31, 232, 233) calls "sentimental journeys" that reveal "the history of our changing notions of the road as the way to the heart of America":

At first, 66 was a road for the pioneer auto tourists in search of American wonders. Later, for the Okies, it was a route for playing out once more the hope of prosperity down the road, of the realization of the American dream, thwarted on their home territory but alive, surely, further west, in California. For the students of America, journalists, novelists, and photographers, who followed the migration, it was a way to see what was really happening in the America of the thirties. By the fifties, it had become a road on which to see the dark and curious sides of America with an alienated eye, or again, a road to California—whose promise was still prosperity, but now compounded of blonds, surfing, and beach houses—in a Corvette. "Get your kicks on 66," the phrase from Bobby Troup's [1946] song had it; the width of that sentiment's appeal was indicated by the fact that musicians as diverse as Nelson Riddle and the Rolling Stones recorded the song. In the seventies 66 was a locus for collectors of the camp imagery of the roadside past: the teepee motels, diners, Indian Cities, and giant dinosaurs. Sixty-six stood for the whole complex of backroads culture.

For the first automobile tourists, though, "it was a way to see America, the real country, populated by 'real Americans,' …and see America, the proponents of the highway seemed to mean, as if you were the first to see it: regain the sense of discovery of the first explorers and pioneers."

By the time of the Diamond Jubilee of Route 66 in 2001, both the Santa Fe Trail and Route 66 were part of the Scenic and Historic Byways Program begun in 1991 and administered by the New Mexico State Highway and Transportation Department. Santa Fe Trail National Scenic Byway covers 480 miles of the state:

> Mention the Santa Fe Trail and the mind's eye quickly brings forth the image of America on the move, from a young, backwater country to a great nation.
>
> The rumble of freight wagons, the shout of the bullwhacker, the snap of the whip, and the bellow of oxen are all trail sounds that evoke the pioneer spirit….
>
> Today we can still find remnants of the trail. They await us at scores of sites, great and small, across five of the United States. They can be followed from one historic landmark to another. They can be commemorated colorfully with living history presentations like those of Arrow Rock, Fort Larned, Bent's Old Fort, and Fort Union. They can be recalled vividly in books. With each encounter we get in touch with ourselves. This is why the Santa Fe Trail is our national treasure. (Arellanes n.d., 31)

Route 66 Historic Trail includes "all former US 66 alignments—mile marker 373.5 (Texas border) to mile marker 0 (Arizona border) excluding those portions overlaid by I-25 & I-40":

> If one post-World War II definition of freedom was being able to get in your car, turn on the ignition and go anywhere you wanted to, then Route 66 offered an asphalt of independence from the wind-buffeted shores of Lake Michigan in Chicago to the balmy beaches of the Pacific in Santa Monica.
>
> Hundreds of businesses played a part in this 2,448-mile road show. For the scores of communities it once served, it was the Main Street of America. Although it began in 1926, old '66 is remembered for the way it fueled America in the '40s and '50s.

After World War II, the entire country seemed to be heading west, fueled by tens of thousands of ex-GIs who longed for a look at what America held in store for them. Paved since 1937, that shimmering highway beckoned. (Arellanes n.d., 21)

The February 1989 "special issue" of *New Mexico Magazine* was its first devoted to U.S. 66: "Route 66: Paved with Memories." In her "Editor's Note" Emily Drabanski writes that "we hope you get a few kicks as we travel along Route 66 this month." In her "Editor's Note" for the February 2001 Route 66 Diamond Jubilee "Special Collectors' Issue" she recalls: The 1989 "issue disappeared almost overnight. Since then, interest in reviving and preserving Historic Route 66 has grown tremendously." She introduces contributor Elmo Baca as one who, "through his many preservation initiatives, has become intimately familiar with efforts to preserve historic landmarks along Historic Route 66."

In "Saving the Mother Road," State Historic Preservation Officer Baca (2001, 32, 33–34) delineates "A Border-to-Border Challenge":

New Mexico and Route 66 preservationists are racing against time, the elements, and modern sensibilities of shopping, convenience and comfort to save what's left. In particular, vintage gas stations, motor courts, "tourist traps," and classic neon signs are rapidly disappearing or looking forlorn.

Ironically, the "ruins" of Route 66 also possess intangible romantic and poetic qualities that attract many adventurers (especially Europeans). Sometimes the faded paint and pockmarked face of an Indian chief or sombrero or bucking bronco on a sign or facade speaks more directly and intimately with us than the ubiquitous golden arches. Even the great Pegasus of Mobil Oil fame has flown away. To rehabilitate and preserve or allow to decay and ruin is a potent question and challenge now facing the New Mexico Route 66 community. Too often we have no choice.

Baca claims the movement "has matured dynamically since President Lyndon B. Johnson signed the National Historic Preservation Act in 1966," expanding "beyond archaeology and architecture" to include "protecting pristine 'viewsheds' and cultural landscapes."

Historic preservation in the digital age is much more concerned with contextual frameworks than ever before. Today we speak about the importance of preserving lifestyles and "lifeways." For Route 66, it means that the experience of driving on a narrow, two-lane road without shoulders (in defiance of modern highway safety standards) is quintessential. Many would also argue that certain diners and their menus offering mouthwatering and cholesterol-loaded roadway fare should be designated historic landmarks.

Following the summertime Diamond Jubilee celebrations, in the fall of 2001 New Mexico, like the rest of the country, was challenged by the events of September 11. Secretary of Tourism Janet L. Green headed a department with a mission, as stated in the *New Mexico Blue Book 2001–2002*, "to market New Mexico as an enchanting visitor destination to the world." In November she announced a new advertising campaign called "Essence of Enchantment."

Created by the Albuquerque advertising agency Rick Johnson & Co., Essence of Enchantment targeted "people seeking spiritual well-being." Like Lilian Whiting before her, Green claimed that the state "is uniquely positioned to capitalize on the human need for well-being, for self-improvement and the need to satisfy a spiritual hunger." The "59 percent of the U.S. population that feels the need to satisfy a spiritual hunger . . . have increased the sales of self-improvement books by 45 percent in the past two years and the sales of books on spirituality by 50 percent in one year." This population tends to "travel for pleasure at a 36 percent higher rate than the average consumer." Rick Johnson & Co. research indicated that "the purpose of a vacation has changed over the past 20 years": "In the 1980s, people focused on looks and materialism. In the 1990s, they were interested in getting away from stress. Now they're looking for self-improvement and spiritual well-being—a trend that has intensified in the wake of the Sept. 11 terrorist attacks" (*Santa Fe New Mexican*, November 13, 2001).

Almost a century before, in her *The Land of Enchantment: From Pike's Peak to the Pacific*, Lilian Whiting (1906, 5) called on poetry to proclaim: "'Yet all experience is an arch wherethro' /Gleams that untravell'd world,' exclaims Tennyson's Ulysses, and the wanderer under Western stars that hang, like blazing clusters of radiant light, midway in the air, cannot but feel that all these new experiences open to him vistas of untold significance and undreamed-of inspiration." Enhanced communication between worlds is its hallmark: "'It may be we shall touch the Happy Isles,' is the haunting refrain of his thoughts when, through the luminous air, he gazes into the golden glory of sunsets whose splendor is forever impressed on his memory."

Whiting is included as "perhaps the most popular among all the New Thought writers" in author, editor, and publisher B. O. (Benjamin Orange) Flower's *Progressive Men, Women, and Movements of the Past Twenty-Five Years*. He (1914, 179–80; also Tumber 2002, 57–65) claims that "her series of 'World Beautiful' books, three volumes, and 'The Life Radiant,' 'The Outlook Beautiful,' 'The Joy That No Man Taketh from You,' 'Life Transfigured,' 'From Dream to Vision of Life,' and her volume of poems, 'From Dreamland Sent,' have probably done more to popularize the broad New Thought principles and the wholesome optimism of Emerson, Browning, and other masters of nineteenth century metaphysical thought than the works of any other writer": "Miss Whiting, though by church affiliation an Episcopalian, is as intellectually hospitable as is the most liberal Unitarian, and after the death of her intimate friend, Kate Field, she had remarkable psychical experiences which resulted in making her a pronounced spiritualist or a believer in the power of spirits to return, under certain conditions, and communicate with mortals." Flower counts Whiting's study of Elizabeth Barrett Browning, her "'Boston Days,' 'Paris the Beautiful,' 'Italy the Magic Land,' 'The Florence of Landor,' 'The Land of Enchantment,' and 'Athens the Violet-Crowned' . . . among the most charming popular biographical and descriptive writings of the present day."

Essence of Enchantment echoes Whiting's popular spiritualist Land of Enchantment. During a December 2001 interview (Sue Major Holmes in *Albuquerque Journal North*, December 24, 2001; also Rosalie Rayburn in *Albuquerque Journal Business Outlook*, November 19, 2001; Krza 2002), Secretary of Tourism Janet Green notes that it was already in the planning stage before 9-11 but expresses hope that "the new campaign will put New Mexico in the forefront of meeting the needs of a skittish nation when things rebound." She claims that "the state is not trying to define spirituality, but rather is trying to capture the feeling through history, vistas, historic trails, myths and legends." Ads "will show not only a beautiful photo, but also 'the content that goes along with that.'" Using "a phrase tourism officials found successful in past campaigns: 'Put Yourself in a State of Enchantment,'" they "let people imagine themselves in New Mexico. For example, words over a photograph of ancestral pueblo ruins read: 'These ruins are more than a doorway to the past; they're a monument to mankind's enduring spirit.' In smaller print: 'As evidenced by the ancient civilization of the Anasazi, New Mexico is a land rich in imagery, spirituality and mystery. The myths and legends that spring from its very soil inspire those willing to listen.'"

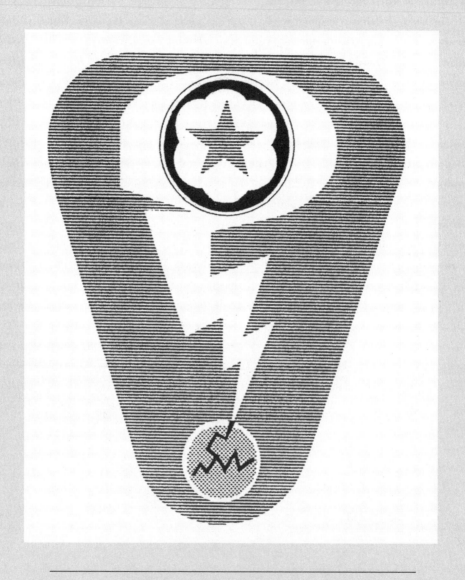

Manhattan Project military personnel patch, inside back cover, Trinity Site
July 16, 1945, *U.S. Government Printing Office booklet, 2000.*

Part Four
Air: The Science State

A variety of fascinating juxtapositions exist in New Mexico with ancient archae-ological treasures sitting in close proximity to some of the world's most modern facilities.

Los Alamos National Laboratory, birthplace of the atomic bomb and an international think tank for science in general, is situated next to the ancient Bandelier Cliff Dwellings in the wooded canyons of the Jémez Mountains. In Albuquerque, the highly technological Sandia National Laboratories sits across the Río Grande from the primitive rock art found at Petroglyph National Mon-ument on the West Mesa and down the road from Sandía Man Cave, where evi-dence of some of the first human beings on Earth was found.

The Mimbres culture depicted wildlife on rocks and pots in the southern New Mexico desert near Trinity Site, where the world's first nuclear bomb was detonated in 1945. Nearby, the Very Large Array radio telescope, the largest of its kind in the world, uses state-of-the-art technology near Socorro to probe deep space. It provided a key backdrop for the sci-fi thriller Contact.

The International Space Hall of Fame with its OMNIMAX theater at the Space Center in Alamogordo stands just a few miles away from Three Rivers Petroglyph National Recreation Site, where ancient Indian artists carved images from their daily lives onto rocks.

—"Introduction: Arts and Science," 2001 New Mexico Vacation Guide, *New Mex-ico Department of Tourism, 2000*

7he February 1999 *New Mexico Magazine*, identified on the cover as a "Special Space Issue: Roswell incident, Native cosmology, Astronomy, Science fiction, Rocketry pioneers, Space artists, Science timeline, Into the future, High-tech spin-offs," announces that "as we approach the Millennium, the Land of Enchantment also has gained a reputation for its advances in science and technology." A map of "points significant to science's history and future" shows twelve "Science hot spots" in the state: 1. Sun Dagger, Chaco Canyon; 2. Very Large Array Radio Telescope; 3. Langmuir Laboratory for Atmospheric Research (vicinity Socorro); 4. Santa Rita (vicinity Silver City); 5. National Solar Observatory, Sunspot (vicinity Alamogordo); 6. White Sands Missile Range; 7. Trinity Site; 8. Goddard Rocket Flights Mescalero Ranch (vicinity Roswell); 9. Roswell Incident; 10. Los Alamos National Laboratory, Bradbury Science Museum; 11. Sandia National Laboratories, National Atomic Museum (Albuquerque); 12. Santa Fe Institute. The International Space Hall of Fame in Alamogordo is shown on the map but not included among the twelve in the text (England 1999a, 36, 37).

Another such point is announced in the December 2001 *New Mexico Magazine:* new entry signs on U.S. 84 and U.S. 60 reading VILLAGE OF FT. SUMNER /HOME OF REAR ADMIRAL /WILLIAM S. 'DEAK' PARSONS /THE ATOMIC ADMIRAL. While a navy captain, Parsons served as head of ordnance and associate director for the Manhattan Project at Los Alamos. He assembled and armed the bomb aboard the *Enola Gay* on its flight to Hiroshima. According to historian Al Christman (2001, 73, 75), "Deak Parsons' nuclear odyssey began in Fort Sumner with boyhood electrical experiments and intricate erector-set constructions," and "the Navy's foremost nuclear expert" now "takes his place among the colorful array of Native Americans, explorers, sheepherders, cowboys, railroad builders, soldiers, outlaws and homemakers of Fort Sumner's historic past."

13
The Space State

Every year thousands of people "Discover Columbus."

Columbus is a high desert community and its clear, dry, warm weather with low humidity and no pollution draws many visitors. The "Land of Enchantment" sun shines on Columbus nearly 355 days a year.

Located 32 miles south of I-10 at Deming and three miles north of the U.S./Mexico border, the village was designated a National Historic Site in 1975.

Columbus—the site of Gen. Francisco "Pancho" Villa's infamous 1916 raid, has played an important role in the history of our country....

The attractions of Columbus are numerous: the charm of the village and its talented, energetic residents; a thriving community theater group; the beautiful sunsets; the stark beauty of the landscape, broken by outlines of the Tres Hermanas and Florida Mountains in the distance; the successful blending of Anglo and Hispanic cultures; and one of the nicest state parks in New Mexico.

The quaint Mexican border town of Las Palomas, is just three miles south of Columbus and for those with a taste for big city attractions, it's just a short one-hour drive to El Paso, Texas, 60 miles to the east.

—Columbus, New Mexico, A Surprise in an Historic Setting: Visitors Guide, *unidentified Department of Tourism-labeled booklet, n.d.*

Roswell is a unique community that blends old time family fun with futuristic, out of this world excitement.

Roswell has become famous for a reported alien U.F.O. crash in the desert near the city in 1947. Referred to as the Roswell Incident, it provokes arguments and investigations even today. Residents of Roswell have adopted the alien visitors as our most famous tourists. Roswell is home to the International U.F.O. Museum and Research Center, which houses accounts of the Incident and other U.F.O. information. Within the city of Roswell you will see many different representations of our aliens, and never more than during our annual U.F.O. Festival held in July. During the week-long festivities we host alien parades, costume contests, fashion shows, and even Roswell—The Musical, *which runs throughout the summer.*

But Roswell is much more than aliens. At the Roswell Museum and Art Center, we are fortunate to have works by internationally renowned artists such as Peter Hurd, Henriette Wyeth and Georgia O'Keefe [sic]. Roswell also has a symphony Orchestra that performs regularly, the Historical Center for Southeastern New Mexico and the Robert Goddard Planetarium.

For outdoor family adventures, Roswell offers Spring River Park and Zoo right in the heart of town. Nearby Bitter Lakes National Wildlife Refuge and Bottomless Lakes State Park provide several different outdoor recreation opportunities from fishing to bird watching to simply enjoying the beautiful landscape of New Mexico.

Unlike our most famous tourists, you won't have to travel across the universe to visit our city. However, I am certain whatever distance you travel, you will find the City of Roswell "a down to earth place to visit . . . an out of this world place to experience."

—Mayor Bill B. Owen, letter in Roswell, *vol. 79, no. 1, n.d. (available 2001), Roswell Chamber of Commerce booklet*

7he first seven miles of Atchison, Topeka and Santa Fe Railroad track had been laid out of Topeka, Kansas, by April 26, 1869, when founder Colonel Cyrus K. Holliday proclaimed his vision of "the broad Pacific, and on its breast are the ships of the Santa Fe riding in from the Orient" (Bryant 1974, 2). Holliday's Orientalism was unexpectedly realized in 1880 on the station platform at Galisteo Junction (later Lamy). The Santa Fe's main line had opened operations between Las Vegas, New Mexico, and the junction on February 9, 1880, with a branch line eighteen miles north to Santa Fe in service on February 16, 1880.

Five weeks later, on the evening of March 26, "soon after the arrival of the train from Santa Fe, as the operator ... and two or three friends were taking a short walk before retiring for the night," they were, according to the *Santa Fe Weekly New Mexican* of March 29, 1880, "startled by voices evidently coming from above them ... [and] astonished to see a large balloon coming from the west."

> The construction of the balloon was entirely different to anything of the kind ever seen by any of the party, being in the shape of a fish, and at one time was so low that fanciful characters on the outside of the car, which appeared to be very elegant, were plainly seen.
>
> The air machine appeared to be entirely under the control of the occupants, and appeared to be guided by a large fanlike apparatus....
>
> The balloon was monstrous in size, and the car, as near as could be judged, contained eight or ten persons. Another peculiar feature of the air machine was that the occupants could evidently sail at any height they chose, as soon after passing the Junction, it assumed a great height and moved off very rapidly toward the east.

Before leaving, the balloon's apparently merry passengers, who made music and spoke an unknown tongue, jettisoned "a few articles," although "owing to the imperfect light the only thing which was found was a magnificent flower, with a slip of exceedingly fine silk-like paper, on which were some characters resembling those on Japanese tea chests." A "later report" the next morning noted a cup "of very peculiar workmanship, entirely different to anything used in this country," had been found and retained by the Galisteo Junction operator. Both "can be seen by any one who desires to see them." However, at 9:00 p.m. on March 27, the *New Mexican* reported:

> This evening a collector of curiosities passed through this place and on being shown the magnificent flower and cup dropped from the balloon which passed over this place last night, offered such a sum of money for them that it could not be refused and he became the possessor of them. He gives it as his opinion that the balloon must have come from Asia, and thinks it possible it came from Jeddo [Edo, ie, Tokyo].

Several days later the *Weekly New Mexican* published an account headlined: "Solved at Last: The Explanation of the Baloon [*sic*] Mystery which has been perplexing Galisteo." The "collector of curiosities" had been "excavating for ancient curiosities" at the Old Pecos Church when a party of tourists arrived. They were shown the Galisteo objects and a "wealthy young Chinaman" among them shouted joyfully when he saw the writings. According to historian Robert J. Tórrez (2004, 113, 114):

> He explained that for some years, China had held "great interest" on the subject of aerial navigation. Large investments had produced experimental aircraft shortly before he had left Peking, and "strong hopes were expressed that victory had at last crowned these efforts." The visitor opined that the "mysterious aerial phantom" was in fact "the first of a regular line of communication between the Celestial Empire and America."
>
> The young man further explained that when he left China, he had been engaged to marry a young lady from a very wealthy family. His fiancée, who had a sister who lived in New York, was apparently aboard the balloon. Knowing he was in this part of the country, she must have written the note, placed it in the cup, and dropped it overboard, hoping, as it did, that the message would find its way to him. The visitor from China was reportedly last seen boarding the train and headed to New York, confident his fiancée would be awaiting him when he arrived.

The Santa Fe track was completed to Albuquerque in April 1880 and to Pinta, Arizona, in July 1881. Its progress helped spur the organizers of the first Territorial Fair in October 1881. Unsuccessful balloon ascensions were attempted at the 1882 and 1889 fairs. The first successful ascension during the fair was in 1907, when Joseph Blondin brought a hydrogen balloon from New York and "flying solo, he drifted 18 miles up the valley past Alameda where he was shot at eight times by superstitious farmers, who, luckily, were poor marksmen." Secretary of the Fair Roy A. Stamm bought the balloon, retained Blondin as pilot, and in the 1909 fair sold rides in the tethered vehicle for one dollar apiece. "Later in the fair," according to historian Marc Simmons (1982, 323), Stamm and Blondin "made a free flight that carried them 11,000 feet over the crest of the Manzanos to a landing in the Estancia Valley . . . [thereby beginning] Albuquerque's long infatuation with ballooning," which culminated with the establishment of its annual Balloon Fiesta in 1972.

Stamm had an airplane brought in for the next year's Territorial Fair, but it could not take off in Albuquerque's altitude so remained parked on the ground for visitors to view. In 1911 fair commissioners "contracted with famous stunt pilot Charles F. Walsh to make three flights of fifteen minutes each in his single propeller Curtis biplane, . . . shipped in by railway express [and] assembled at the fairgrounds." On the last flight Walsh took Roy Stamm's younger brother Raymond "on a 3-mile circuit from the fairgrounds . . . [and thereby] set a world's record—the first time a passenger had been lifted and carried from 5,000 feet above sea level." According to Simmons (1982, 324):

On one of his earlier fair flights, Walsh had circled over the baseball diamond while a game was in progress, dropping small sacks of flour on the players. Intended as a playful gesture, the Albuquerque press took note of the more ominous implications: "It demonstrated clearly the practicability of the use of the biplane as a implement of war, since it would be possible to drop bombs on an army or battleship with deadly effect."

Five years later the United States Army established Columbus Army Air Field, its first operational military airbase in the United States at Camp Furlong, and used eight observation biplanes to assist "the world's first motorized cavalry ... a fleet of four-wheel-drive Nash and Jeffry automobiles" in its pursuit of Mexican General Francisco (Pancho) Villa, a legendary horseman, and his mounted forces, who had raided the town on the night of March 9, 1916 (Young 1984, 100). General John J. (Black Jack) Pershing led the unsuccessful punitive expedition: "All of the vehicles and the airplanes soon perished in the desert and were never recovered. Decades later, adventurers trying to retrace the U.S. Army's invasion route found concrete bridges over ravines, rusted heaps of jerry cans that transported gasoline, but little else" (Braddy 1965, 33–34).

"The first grease rack" sign, Pancho Villa State Park, Columbus,
photo by the author, April 12, 2005.

FIRST MILITARY AIRBASE
Just across the highway from this point the United States Army established in 1916 its first operational airbase in the United States. It used several cloth-coated biplanes in its unsuccessful punitive expedition against Mexican General Fran-cisco (Pancho) Villa after his forces raided this area

"First Military Airbase" sign, Pancho Villa State Park, Columbus, photo by the author, April 12, 2005.

Villa's was the last hostile action by foreign troops in the continental United States, and Pancho Villa State Park in Columbus is "the only public park in the U.S. ever named for a foreign invader" (Young 1984, 99). Approved by the New Mexico State Legislature in 1959, when it opened in 1961 the park offset some of the impact on Columbus of losing El Paso & Southwestern train service that year. The park "and later the paving of the highway (SR 11) southward to Nuevo Casas Grandes and Juarez on the route to the city of Chihuahua, revived its faltering economy [and] Columbus is now a major port of entry as well as a tourist attraction" (Young 1984, 103).

Columbus is in the history essay in Part I of the 1940 WPA New Mexico Guide, but it is not included among Part III's automobile tours of the state's "Most Accessible Places." By contrast, Roswell, where another army air field would be established in 1941, receives lavish praise along Tour 7b, which runs 307.6 miles from Santa Fe to the Texas line through Carlsbad, Loving, and Malaga:

ROSWELL, 193.9 *m.* (3,600 alt., 13,443 pop.), in less than seventy years has grown from a barren plains trading post to one of the most modern and attractive cities in the State with miles of wide, paved streets shaded by fine old cottonwoods

and willows, and attractive homes, gardens, and public buildings. Its many industries include a flour mill, cotton gins, creameries, and meat-packing plants. It has
an airport, a railroad, bus lines, a radio station (KGFL), the fully accredited New
Mexico Military Institute (*see below*), tennis courts, and a golf course (*fees 25¢ and
50¢*). Its population, which is 90 per cent Anglo-American, 9 per cent Spanish
and Mexican stock, and 1 per cent foreign born, observes several festivals including San Juan's Day, June 24; Eastern New Mexico Old Timers' Reunion and Dinner, September 15; Mexican Independence Day, September 16; and the Eastern
New Mexico State Fair and Roswell Rodeo, which runs for a week, beginning
about October 7. The State Fair is the most popular with the townspeople and usually attracts 50,000 visitors. Many wear costumes common when Roswell was a
lone store on a cattle trail in the wilderness, and all gather around the chuck
wagon; but instead of "sow belly and beans," eat barbecue meat, buns, pickles,
and drink black coffee....

The New Mexico Military Institute is 1 mile north of the center of town.
The central campus consists of 75 acres of level mesa land situated on a hill overlooking the main part of Roswell and shaded by numerous trees. The total value
of buildings, furniture, and fixtures approximates $1,500,000.... In the J. Ross
Thomas Memorial Building, are large murals by Peter Hurd, depicting incidents
and scenes in the early history of Roswell. These can be seen by visitors at any
time during the day. In the classroom of Captain Starr are five paintings by the
same artist, illustrating *The Last of the Mohicans*. (Workers of WPA 1940, 347–48)

The Roswell Army Air Field site was acquired in 1941 for use as a Military Flying
Training Center and Bombardier School. Six years later, a front-page headline in the
Roswell Daily Record of Tuesday, July 8, 1947, announced: "RAAF Captures Flying Saucer
on Ranch in Roswell Region/ No Details of Flying Disk Are Revealed." The accompanying
article was written by Lieutenant Walter Haut, the base Public Relations Officer, under
orders from commanding officer Colonel William H. Blanchard.

By 1990 Haut conceived the idea for what would become the International UFO
Museum and Research Center in Roswell. He joined with Glenn Dennis, the mortician on
duty at Ballard Funeral Home the night of July 7 who received a call from the base inquiring about embalming and an hour later saw debris in open ambulances at the base infir-
mary, and Roswell realtor, businessman, and developer Max Littell. They incorporated on
September 27, 1991, opened in October with a display in the Sunwest Bank Building,
moved to a Main Street storefront and opened on October 24, 1992, and finally opened a
facility in the former Plains Theater at 114 N. Main on January 2, 1997. The IUFOMRC
won the Tourism Association of New Mexico's award for "Top Tourist Destination of New
Mexico" in December 1996. Attendance was reported to be 69,000 in 1996, 192,100 in

"*Roswell and the Ruidoso Country,*" 2 Weeks in New Mexico
"Land of Enchantment," *State Tourist Bureau booklet, 1935.*

1997, and above 180,000 in 1998 and in 1999 (Rene Romo in *Albuquerque Journal*, July 23, 2000).

Citing the publication of Whitley Strieber's *Majestic* (1990), Kevin D. Randle and Donald R. Schmitt's *UFO Crash at Roswell* (1991), and Stanton T. Friedman and Don Berliner's *Crash at Corona: The U.S. Military Retrieval and Cover-up of a UFO* (1992), as well as television coverage of the Roswell Incident on shows like "Unsolved Mysteries," NBC's "A Closer Look," and CNN's "Larry King Live" in July 1991, historian William E. Gibbs (1993, 145–46) claims that "what had been a mysterious incident of the 1940s turned into a media phenomenon of the early 1990s," and "city officials scurried to capitalize on this newfound publicity." By July 1996 *Forbes Magazine* reported that "P. T. Barnum is alive and apparently living in Roswell, N.M.":

> City hotel room tax revenues have risen 36% over four years. Hotel operators say up to one-fifth of their business comes from UFO seekers. By some estimates the UFO craze pumps more than $5 million a year into this community of 50,000, which badly needs the money, median household income here being 27% below the national average. UFO mania probably lowers the still high jobless rate—7%—by a full point. (Barrett 1996)

Roswell's first annual UFO Festival, UFO Encounter '95, was held on July 1 and 2, 1995. Chief organizer Stan Crosby, husband of Deon Crosby, then director of the International UFO Museum and Research Center, arranged the trade show, parades, contests, crash site tours, lectures, and entertainment. UFO Encounter '97 received multimillion-dollar publicity when it made the cover of *Time* magazine on June 23, 1997: "The Roswell Files: This month is the 50th anniversary of a weird crash in New Mexico. Now the site is a Graceland for *X-Files* fans and UFO lovers. What *really* happened out there?" Crosby is quoted in "Roswell or Bust: A town discovers manna crashing from heaven and becomes the capital of America's alien nation" (Handy 1997, 67):

> An informal survey suggests that Roswellians themselves are generally less inspired by the whole thing than amused, although some—Christian Fundamentalists in particular—are offended by the city's growing embrace of its unique legacy. "There's kind of a love-hate relationship with this thing," says Stan Crosby, a self-described oil-and-gas man who is the chief organizer of Roswell UFO Encounter '97.... "It's not like we have the prettiest beach," admits Crosby, "or the Carlsbad Caverns. But you know, we've got to go with what we've got. And it sure brings them in." He is already thinking three years hence, when the theme will be Roswell UFO Encounters: On to the Millennium.

Handy (1997, 62) introduces the city (population 49,000) as "the birthplace of Demi Moore" and "home to the nation's largest mozzarella plant," whose "citizens are still struggling to come to grips with the strange events that put the city on the national map and made its name a national buzz word connoting both otherworldliness and governmental perfidy." Some tell Bill Pope, interim CEO of the Roswell Chamber of Commerce: "Gosh, I don't like this. I don't want to be known as the kook capital." This "civic distinction" was "long ignored by most Roswellians—Moore, for one, says she never heard of it while growing up—until a recent surge of national interest in extraterrestrial phenomena, both 'real' and fictive, convinced locals that rather than be ashamed of their heritage, they might instead make some money from UFO-related tourism."

Such enterprise is evident in journalist Toby Smith's account of the media's July 1, 1997, bus tour to "the alleged crash site which, it turns out, is one of at least four suspected crash sites. But this is the one Roswell supports ... about thirty miles from town."

> The Corn family, owners of the land, has lived in the area since 1879. Way, way back, Martin Van Buren Corn [see Weigle 1985, 153–55] raised horses and one of those animals was sold to noted lawman Pat Garrett. Billy the Kid, New Mexico's best known historical figure, then stole the horse from Garrett during The Kid's murderous breakout from the Lincoln County Jail in 1880. The Corns purchased this particular parcel—twenty-four square miles—in 1976. About six years ago, the Corns kept noticing strangers driving about, not in grime-caked pickups with gunracks, but in gleaming Chryslers with out-of-state plates. When Miller "Hub" Corn asked what they wanted, he learned that his land likely lay where a flying saucer crash-landed in July 1947. Since then, the Corns, who will tell you that ranching is not an easy way to make a living, will also tell you that they have bear-hugged UFOs. The family charges fifteen dollars per person to enter. "I could be a real hard-butt and lock the gate," says Hub, "but people will still get in."

At the site, down the path from "two huge stone obelisks, which Hub Corn had erected a few weeks before," they found "a boulder, the base of which is decorated with bouquets of flowers," and onto which is carved: "We Don't Know Who They Were /We Don't Know Why They Came /We Only Know /They Changed Our View /Of the Universe /This Universal Sacred Site /Is Dedicated July 1997 /To the Beings /Who Met Their Destiny /Near Roswell, N.M. July 1947" (Smith 2000, 50–51).

Journalist Dawn Stover (1997, 82) begins her June 1997 *Popular Science* story on "50 Years After Roswell" at the Roswell Airport, which "is being eyed as a potential site for an all-night rock concert expected to draw as many as 150,000 people to this town of 50,000 on July 5" as part of Roswell UFO Encounter '97, "planned for July 1 through July 6 [which] will also include a UFO conference, a film festival, an alien costume contest, a 'Crash and Burn Extravaganza' spaceship-building contest, laser shows at the local planetarium, and 'Alien Chase' foot races." Stover also describes visits to the International UFO Museum and Research Center, downtown Roswell; Hub Corn's Ranch, thirty miles north of Roswell; Ragsdale's Campsite, fifty miles west of Roswell; and the Debris Site, seventy-five miles northwest of Roswell. She (1997, 88) ends at City Hall, downtown Roswell:

Roswell, *front panel of undated (1990s), six-panel Roswell Convention and Visitors Bureau brochure. The second front panel lists "Local Accommodations"; the third, "Other Attractions," including the Robert H. Goddard Planetarium, Roswell Museum and Art Center, Historical Center for Southeast New Mexico, Roswell Symphony Orchestra, and Roswell Community Little Theatre. The three reverse panels are devoted to "The Roswell UFO Encounter."*

The office of Roswell Mayor Thomas E. Jennings is decorated with stuffed aliens and UFO T-shirts. Hanging from the ceiling lamp is a small flying saucer.

"We're developing another industry in Roswell," Jennings told me prior to our departure, "and it's called tourism." He estimates that some 25 percent of

Roswell's motel bookings are for people visiting the museums and crash sites. The town has even created a new slogan to attract overnight guests: "Crash in Roswell."

To many businesspeople in town, it really doesn't matter what happened here 50 years ago. "It fell into our lap," says Jennings, "and we're trying to capitalize on it."

After the 1997 festival, Jennings, who was mayor from 1994 to 1998, tried to register "Roswell, New Mexico," as a global trademark so "every time [it] is used in a movie or book, the city would be entitled to royalties." According to an Associated Press release (in *Santa Fe New Mexican*, December 14, 1997):

"Before the crash, Roswell was just another dusty town in southern New Mexico," Jennings said. "But now we have worldwide name recognition, and we think the town should capitalize on this phenomenon."

An agent from a Los Angeles-based licensing company, NRP Productions, posed the idea in October. The agent, Neil Russell, said his company would pay the $100,000 registration fees to globally license the city's name and seal in exchange for a third of the profits.

Claiming that "we don't want to be greedy, but we do want to ensure accuracy in the usage of Roswell products," Jennings concludes: "Shoot, everybody is making a profit off of aliens right now but us."

Roswell boasts two "points significant to science's history and future" on the map of "Science hot spots" in the February 1999 "Special Space Issue" of *New Mexico Magazine:* No. 9 Roswell Incident and No. 8 Goddard Rocket Flights Mescalero Ranch. Text for the latter reads: "In 1930, rocket pioneer Robert H. Goddard needed a bigger place to test his rockets than Massachusetts, where he had done his initial research. He settled on the Mescalero Ranch northeast of Roswell, and built his support facilities and launch pads in the Eden Valley 10 miles from the ranch. On Dec. 30 of 1930, he launched the first in the Roswell series" (England 1999a, 37, 38). According to Toby Smith (2000, 31):

Omitting the name Robert Goddard from a list of Roswell's UFO personalities is a bit like leaving Tang off an inventory of outer space beverages. And yet such an oversight typically happens to Goddard. After all, as the father of modern rocketry, Robert Hutchings Goddard had nothing to do with flying saucers; he died two years before the Roswell incident. Lord knows what he would have made of "(Jim) Beam Me Up" on the side of shot glasses marketed in Roswell, or "Probe This" on the front of sweatshirts for sale in the city.

Goddard did, however, understand that space travel could be possible, and he labored to make it as acceptable as bus travel. Which helps to explain why so many people have faith in things extraterrestrial, and why those same people are cocksure a UFO could make scheduled stops throughout the universe. What's more, Goddard worked to set the mold for the American astronaut, who became a holy man of popular culture.

The birthplace of New Mexico's astronaut Harrison H. (Jack) Schmitt, "the only scientist to walk on the Moon," is No. 4 on the map of "Science hot spots." Designated "lost in space," Santa Rita "sprung up in a copper-rich area. Indeed, it was called 'Santa Rita del Cobre,' or copper, by its founder. In 1910, a large copper company began open-pit mining, gradually digging away the land until the village was isolated on an island in the center. Finally, it was abandoned and the site is now one of the largest open-pit mines in the country" (England 1999a, 37). In 1976 Schmitt helped start the Society of Persons Born in Space:

> Membership in this society is restricted to people born in the old Santa Rita Hospital when it was located on a piece of ground which is no longer there. Those born in that hospital in the good old days came into the world at a spot which is now a few hundred feet in the air in the North Pit of Kennecott's Chino Mine. Therefore, the originators of the Society claim "that we were born in space."
>
> The Society came into being in 1976 at a banquet in Salt Lake City honoring the Apollo 17 lunar mission. Jack Schmitt, Apollo 17 Lunar Module Pilot, and Gilbert Moore, General Manager of Thiokol's Astro-Met Plant, Wasatch Division, were reminiscing about the good old days in New Mexico and discovered that both were born a few years apart in the Santa Rita Hospital. One thing lead to another, and the Society was formed with Schmitt as Chief Astronaut and Moore as Program Director. (Jones 1985, 131)

Both Goddard and Schmitt have been inducted into the International Space Hall of Fame, "a giant golden cube nestled at the base of the Sacramento Mountains" in Alamogordo. "As the facility expanded along with its mission, the name became the Space Center [now the New Mexico Museum of Space History], of which the hall is a part. The museum displays artifacts of the Space Age, including the suit of space chimp HAM (and his grave), an Apollo Guidance Unit, the Coke and Pepsi Space cans, a fake Moon hemisphere used by CBS News to explain the Moon landings, a lunar sample return container, and a glove worn by [Neil] Armstrong on the Moon, among other things" (England 1999b, 66). According to Executive Director Gregory P. Kennedy's introduction to the 1989 Space Center booklet guide, *The International Space Hall of Fame:*

Within this museum, we tell the story of mankind's conquest of space. What makes this museum unique is our international perspective. Our visitors can learn about Chinese, European, and Indian launch vehicles and spacecraft. We have exhibits on both the American and Soviet manned space programs. And, we continue to grow.

The International Space Hall of Fame opened on October 5, 1976. Since then, more than a million people have visited, and the current attendance is about 110,000 people each year. Alamogordo was selected as the site for the state-operated facility because the Tularosa Basin is truly the cradle of the space age. America's modern space program can trace its roots to White Sands Proving Grounds (today, White Sands Missile Range), and much of the early space biology and aeromedical research which led to manned space flight occurred at nearby Holloman Air Force Base.

14
The Atomic State

Driving across southern New Mexico, the traveler nearing the attractive town of Alamogordo catches sight of what seems to be an immense field of snow, stretching away to the mountains. This strange sight, so unbelievable in summer, proves to be the Great White Sands, a National Monument and one of Nature's strangest phenomena—even in New Mexico, land of the strange and unusual. The White Sands are 100% pure gypsum, undoubtedly destined for a great recreational future, but at present a thirty-mile desert white as snow. The scant vegetation at the edges disappears as the interior is neared, leaving an area as devoid of life as the Sahara itself. Even the field mouse wears a coat as white as ermine on the White Sands, but rainfall produces strange lakes, sometimes crimson red. It is a land of mystery and thrills.

As if to prove her greatest contrasts, Nature has also provided near Alamogordo a summer playground of unsurpassed greenery and beauty, high in the heart of the Lincoln National Forest in the Sacramento Mountains. Here is the highest golf course in the world, where your poorest drive is already 9000 feet above sea level at its start. Hotels and furnished cottages are available at Cloudcroft and in winter the pines echo the shouts of the snow enthusiasts, the squeak of skis and the rush of tobaggans.

Near Alamogordo are immense lumbering operations, and to the northeast, dividing the beautiful Lincoln National Forest into two parts, lies the Mescalero Apache Reservation, where descendants of Victorio and his notorious successor, Geronimo, pursue their peaceful lives and strange customs under government guidance.

—*"Alamogordo and the White Sands,"* 2 Weeks in New Mexico "Land of Enchantment," *New Mexico State Tourist Bureau booklet, 1935*

In deciding whether to visit ground zero at Trinity Site, the following information may prove helpful.

Radiation levels in the fenced, ground zero area are low. On an average the levels are only 10 times greater than the region's natural background radiation. A one-hour visit to the inner fenced area will result in a whole body exposure of one-half to one milliroentgen (mrem).

To put this in perspective, a U.S. adult receives an average of 90 milliroentgens every year from natural and medical sources. For instance, the Department of Energy says we receive between 35 and 50 milliroentgens every year from the sun and from 20 to 35 milliroentgens every year from our food. Living in a brick house adds 50 milliroentgens of exposure every year compared to living in a frame house. Finally, flying coast to coast in a jet airliner gives an exposure of between three and five milliroentgens on each trip.

Although radiation levels are low, some feel any extra exposure should be avoided. The decision is yours. It should be noted that small children and pregnant women are potentially more at risk than the rest of the population and are generally considered groups who should only receive exposure in conjunction with medical diagnosis and treatment. Again, the choice is yours.

At ground zero, Trinitite, the green glassy substance found in the area, is still radioactive and must not be picked up.

—Trinity Site, 1945–1995, *White Sands Missile Range Public Affairs Office booklet, 1995*

*I*n 1928 author Eugene Manlove Rhodes, then living in Alamogordo, chided boosters of northern New Mexico by telling readers of the Santa Fe Railway/Fred Harvey Company Indian Detours booklet *They Know New Mexico: Intimate Sketches by Western Writers*: "Thanks to art and automobiles, Santa Fé, Taos, Acoma, and Zuñi are known in the land; but Southern New Mexico is still unpainted and unknown." An "unexpected result" of the "labors" of "painters, historians, and archaeologists crowded in the north" adds "a new mistake to an old one": "It has long been held that New York is America; it is now taught that Santa Fé is New Mexico." He claims: "Santa Fé, herself so long neglected, is firmly incredulous of beauty, interest, or charm to southward; deports herself stepsisterly, as toward another Cinderella. Yet some of us have never understood why longitude is not counted from the Meridian of Mesilla." In this "Cinderella country" Rhodes identifies "our great 'show places' [as] Carlsbad Caverns, Ruidoso, Cloudcroft, the White Sands, Elephant Butte Dam and Palomas Hot Springs [Sierra County, vicinity of Hot Springs, which is today Truth or Consequences]."

Rhodes moved to California in 1931 and died there on June 27, 1934. At his directive, "his body was returned to Rhodes Canyon, overlooking the great country that he had loved." The "mountain wagon [that] carried his body from Tularosa up the twisting, rocky road through the pass that still bears his name" was followed by "Bob Martin, Hiram Yoast, and forty-odd others who had known him and who had peopled his writings." There, "a wooden marker was placed. As Eddy Orcutt put it in his 'Memorial to Gene Rhodes,' published in the *Saturday Evening Post* [August 20, 1938] a few years later, 'Gene had asked that there be no ceremony at the grave, but the yuccas were in bloom'" (Charles 1953, 13). The 1940 WPA New Mexico Guide gives directions to Rhodes's grave:

> Right from Tularosa on NM 52, a graded dirt road, which runs through a valley of gypsum and lava beds and crosses Rhodes Pass in the San Andrés Mountains, to a barbed wire fence (R) at 46.7 *m*. Right (*on foot*) under this fence; then R. 100 *yds.*, and L. (West) 35 *yards*, to the GRAVE OF EUGENE MANLOVE RHODES (1869–1934) beloved New Mexican author. Plain wooden boards are set in the ground about 10 feet wide and 15 feet long. A tall piñon, with a small juniper rooted at its feet, leans over to shade the spot. (Workers of WPA 1940, 372)

Later, "a great red boulder, a ton or more in weight was taken from the site of Gene's old corral and transported to his grave to receive a bronze plaque designed by William Penhallow Henderson. His epitaph reads/ *'Eugene Manlove Rhodes, /Paso Por Aqui''* (Charles 1959).

The New Mexico State Legislature, "realizing that it was beyond the ability of Rhodes' family and friends to maintain his grave," in 1951 "passed a measure making the New Mexico State University custodian of Gene's burial place," and "the college each year sends a representative on the annual pilgrimage to the grave." In June 1959, the twenty-fifth anniversary of Rhodes's death, the Alamogordo Chamber of Commerce sponsored a special pilgrimage to his grave, "which will be attended not only by old timers from throughout New Mexico, but also will draw his Rhodes fans from far distances." Because the "grave is within the secret area of the White Sands Proving Ground not far from where the first atomic bomb was exploded, governmental permission must be given to enter the area" (Charles 1959).

Rhodes died the year after President Herbert Hoover proclaimed 142,987 acres of gypsum dune fields as White Sands National Monument on January 18, 1933, two days before Franklin D. Roosevelt took office. New Mexico's U.S. Senator Bronson M. Cutting telegraphed congratulations to "White Sands' Father" (Schneider-Hector 1993, 119), Alamogordo insurance agency owner Tom Charles, who had come to Otero County from Kansas in 1907. Concerned about the county's failing business fortunes during the 1920s, Charles corresponded with state and federal officials to alert them to the situation. He and his second wife, Bula, "also began writing a series of travel articles for publications like

The text within the booklet image reads:

The Great White Sands near Alamogordo and Tularosa

Chimney Rock near Pine Lodge Southern New Mexico

Cottages in the Pines Lincoln National Forest

Golf above the clouds at Cloudcroft

Indian Village on Mescalero Reservation

COME to the Land of Sunshine in Southern New Mexico by motor or train. Winter or summer, it is the wonderland of the Southwest. Retaining all the picturesque features of the Old West with its traditions of Billy the Kid, Geronimo and Chief Victorio, Southern New Mexico blends with this background of history the industry and enterprise of the modern pioneer. In this land of magnificent distances settlers from the East and North have built their homes, reared great engineering works and reclaimed the fertile soil. An Inland Empire in the making may be seen in a tour of the New Mexico Southwest at any season of the year. The warm hospitality of the pioneers has been retained and the visitor will find a hearty welcome in every town and city in this section.
In this land of sunshine—on the all-year route from coast to coast—there is a wealth of attractions for tourists and for those who are seeking a new home where opportunities abound and life always is worth while.
The wonderful all-year climate of this section offers much to the tourist, the home-builder and the health-seeker. Scenic beauties and masterpieces of nature that are classed among the wonders of the world await the sightseer on every hand, while the sportsman and lover of outdoor life has abundant opportunity for enjoying his favorite pastime, whether it is golf, which he may play here above the clouds, fishing in the lakes and mountain streams, or big-game hunting in the vast virgin forests.
The Lincoln National Forest, playground of the Southwest, with its scenic attractions and splendid facilities for summer outings, calls irresistibly to the traveler. This great recreational area embraces

Southern New Mexico Invites You, *inside front cover, Southern New Mexico Association, On the All-Year Motor Route, undated (late 1920s) booklet. "The purpose of this booklet is to extend to you a cordial invitation to visit Southern New Mexico, whether your purpose is to view the wonders and scenic beauties of this section, to enjoy an outing of a few days or months, or to investigate the opportunities and advantages that are offered to the home-builder and the health-seeker." Members of the Southern New Mexico Association are the commercial clubs of Alamogordo, Capitan, Carrizozo, and Cloudcroft and the chambers of commerce of Artesia, Carlsbad, Deming, Hatch, Hot Springs, Las Cruces, Lordsburg, Roswell, Silver City, and Tularosa.*

the *New Mexico Highway Journal* ..., extolling not the hardships of Otero County but its blessings, most prominently the Lincoln National Forest, the Mescalero reservation, and the White Sands" (Welsh 1995, 28).

At first Charles lobbied for a national park in the region. He allied himself with Tularosa Basin rancher Albert Bacon Fall, who with Thomas B. Catron served as New Mexico's first U.S. senators of statehood. According to historian Michael Welsh (1995, 19–20):

> As a senator (1912–1920), and then as the ill-fated Secretary of the Interior under President Warren G. Harding (1921–1923), Fall managed to expand his holdings at Three Rivers by a factor of ten (over one million acres of leased and purchased land). One aspect of his career that has drawn the ire of historians was his repeated efforts from 1912–1922 to take Mescalero land for a national park, with the dimensions shifting several times (finally including a small 640-acre section of White Sands).

Tom Charles supported Fall's "All-Year National Park," but after 1923, when he "picked up where Fall left off," came to believe, "as did many of his time, that the white sands alone could support a two-pronged economic rationale: part of it could serve as a scenic 'playground' for tourists, while the rest would remain a natural resource for gypsum miners." By 1929 he was lobbying for national monument rather than park status. Charles served as the monument's first custodian from 1933 until 1939, when he left to begin the White Sands Service Company and "as concessionaire . . . took people on bus and auto tours into the dunes until 1943, when he became ill and died" (Houk and Collier 1994, 54, 55).

During Charles's first months as White Sands National Monument custodian he oversaw roadbuilding. The day-long dedication gala, finally held on Sunday, April 29, 1934, was known as "Old Settlers Day," with prizes for "the oldest and longest-resident Hispanic, Anglo, and Indian attendee." The estimated 4,650 visitors who arrived in 776 vehicles watched their home team win a baseball game between the Alamogordo Black Sox and the El Paso Monarchs, two all-black teams who played for money donated by spectators. They listened to speakers on "early days" in southern New Mexico, including George Coe's "Recollections of Billy the Kid." A highlight came when an infirm, clearly failing Albert Bacon Fall, whom Hoover had released from federal prison early, delivered his "Reminiscences of Early Days." The *Alamogordo Advertiser* reported his "stunning reversal of form that few listeners could detect": "He told of various attempts to exploit the Sands commercially, all ending in futility, and stated his opinion that very appropriately they are now put to the best use possible, reserved for their scenic beauty and attractiveness" (Welsh 1995, 39, 40).

So successful was the occasion that the next year Charles inaugurated an early May "Play Day" for Otero County schoolchildren, teachers, and parents, including among the 3,500 in attendance 35 students from the Mescalero Apache school. Originally a way to reward Tularosa Basin Supporters of the monument, the annual Play Day soon expanded to include schoolchildren and college students from across southern New Mexico and west Texas.

Play Day was not part of Carl P. Russell's August 1935 *National Geographic* article, "The White Sands of Alamogordo: A Dry Ocean of Granular Gypsum Billows Under Desert Winds in a New National Playground," in which he notes that "last year 33,900 persons visited the area, although the White Sands National Monument was opened only on April 29, 1934, and is rather more difficult of access than some of the government's older recreation regions" (Russell 1935, 258). Publicity like Russell's article brought White Sands an impressive tourist traffic. State Tourist Bureau Director Joseph A. Bursey (1936a, 19) notes that "shortly after the [*National Geographic*] article appeared, tourists began arriving at the White Sands with copies of the magazine tucked under their arms. Some had traveled a thousand miles off their originally planned course just to visit a national monument which had been given the stamp of approval by a famous magazine." On October 19, 1935, Carlsbad Caverns National Park Superintendent Thomas R. Boles wrote Tom Charles at White Sands: "I have always felt that the Caverns' biggest competitor in the Southwest was the Grand Canyon," but after seeing the 1935 tourist figures "perhaps my real competitor is much closer," the more so when "you get a paved highway between Alamogordo and Las Cruces" (Welsh 1995, 45).

By the beginning of World War II this competition for visitors was altered by the military. In June 1941 the U.S. Army petitioned "to secure 1.25 million acres of public and private land in the Tularosa basin for a bombing range." It did not pursue that claim until after Pearl Harbor on December 7, but White Sands Custodian Johnwill Faris "wrote of the increase in visitation of uniformed personnel from Fort Bliss and Biggs Field, in and near El Paso. By July 1941, soldiers and their families comprised 15 percent of visitors to the dunes, and nearly 2,000 other soldiers stopped at park headquarters to see the exhibits in the museum" (Welsh 1995, 99). Secretary of the Interior Harold Ickes recommended that President Roosevelt grant the army's request and sign Executive Order No. 9029, "Withdrawing Public Lands for Use of the War Department as a General Bombing Range, New Mexico," on January 20, 1942. "The order contained a clause calling upon the Army to 'consult' with Interior officials about bombing targets. In addition, the order promised to restore the lands to Interior 'when they are no longer needed for the purpose for which they are reserved'" (Welsh 1995, 100).

In 1942 Alamogordo Army Air Field (later Holloman Air Force Base, then Holloman Air Development Center) was established six miles west of Alamogordo. White Sands Proving Ground was developed west, south, and north of the air field. It was officially designated on July 9, 1945, one week before the Trinity detonation. The Department of the Army renamed it White Sands Missile Range on May 1, 1958. According to historian Dietmar Schneider-Hector (1993, 138–39):

Trinity Site
July 16, 1945

"The effects could well be called unprecedented, magnificent, beautiful, stupendous, and terrifying. No man-made phenomenon of such tremendous power had ever occurred before. The lighting effects beggared description. The whole country was lighted by a searing light with the intensity many times that of the midday sun."   **Brig. Gen. Thomas Farrell**

A national historic landmark onWhite Sands Missile Range -- www.wsmr.army.mil

Trinity Site July 16, 1945, *front cover,*
U.S. Government Printing Office booklet, 2000.

Lt. Col. Harold Turner, the post's first commander, has received historical recognition for establishing the White Sands prefix, thereby associating the range with the most prominent geological feature in the Tularosa Basin. The military established a neutral position by refraining from associating the range by name with one of the surrounding communities. . . . From the first rocket launching on 25 September

1945 through 31 March 1980, 32,019 missile firings have been recorded at White Sands Missile Range. The steadily growing number of launches, accompanied by a corresponding increase of military and civilian personnel, brought economic prosperity for the tri-city area (Alamogordo, Las Cruces, and El Paso). The three chambers of commerce actively supported and endorsed the military's presence.

White Sands National Monument benefitted from the military during World War II:

Where civilians could not fill the dunes as they had in years past, military personnel rushed in by the thousands. The Army brought its Military Police (MP's) to supervise uniformed troops, and the White Sands staff remarked more than once about the good behavior of such large groups. The United Services Organization (USO) also planned activities at the dunes, among which were Tuesday breakfasts for soldiers' wives, and use of the museum lobby on winter evenings. Custodian Faris paid special attention to the "weekly visit of convalescent patients from the Air Base hospital as a means of outdoor recreation." The soldiers expressed great appreciation for the services provided at White Sands, taking as much park literature as Faris could provide, as well as gypsum that they sent home for Christmas gifts. They in turn promised to bring their families to the dunes at war's end. Evidence of this regard for White Sands came in November 1942, when the *National Parks Magazine* printed an article in its winter issue entitled, "Soldier's Paradise." Isabelle Story of the NPS information office decided that White Sands exhibited the type of service that the NPS wished to provide the military, and made the dunes the cover story for this nationwide publication. (Welsh 1995, 103)

After the war: "For White Sands, the triangle of Cold War, military spending, and family recreation caused visitation to multiply exponentially, starting in the spring of 1946. From its low point of 35,000 visitors in 1944, the park saw a doubling within two years, then doubling again in three more years (1949). By 1957, visitation had doubled once more (to 304,000), or ten times the war-era low" (Welsh 1995, 130).

The postwar situation is reflected in William Belknap Jr.'s July 1957 *National Geographic* article, "New Mexico's Great White Sands: Feathery Dunes of Snow-white Gypsum in a 140,000-acre 'Sandbox' Make This Area Unique Among National Monuments." Play Day that year was held on the second Saturday in April, and Belknap devotes a section, "Sandstorm Fails to Stop Play Day," to it. The festivities' end was signaled by a fly-over of four Air Force jets. This is pictured in a two-page photograph by the author (Belknap 1957, 132–33) showing the crowds on the dunes and the parked cars with the jets overhead. Each page carries a different caption:

Jets Roar over Play Day Spectators in a Show from Hollomon Air Development Center/ During World War II the armed forces used part of the gypsum desert as a bombing range. When planes crashed in the monument, Park Service men often assisted in the rescue. These F-94's thrill the crowd with rolls and loops.

The World's First Atomic Bomb Was Exploded in 1945 on a Near-by Wasteland/ White Sands testing range is the largest all-land installation in the Nation for the firing of intermediate-range missiles. Deserts extending 100 miles permit firing, flight, and recovery of the weapons.

Holloman Air Development Center, "with an annual payroll of about $38,000,000," has been "a vital factor in Alamogordo's growth" and contributed to "nearly 300,000 visitors coming to near-by White Sands each year" (Belknap 1957, 125).

National Geographic readers are reminded that "missiles have long been associated with White Sands" since "several fluted stone projectile points—spearheads used by Folsom man some 10,000 years ago—have been found in the area." In the 1880s "near-by history" was "like a shoot-'em-up western" with the Lincoln County War, Indian battles at Dog Canyon, and the pursuit of Geronimo, while "not far from White Sands a young desperado cut down some of the 21 men he is credited with killing. His name: Billy the Kid." The very next and final paragraph of this section on Alamogordo, entitled "City Name Recalls First Atom Blast," apparently because it means "fat cottonwood," reassures:

Modern missiles affect visitors at White Sands only infrequently. Officers at the proving ground occasionally restrict traffic along the highway during important "shoots," but it is purely an ultra precaution. The rockets land many miles away and are seldom seen from the road. (Belknap 1957, 128)

Four years before Belknap's Play Day participation, in September 1953, the Alamogordo Chamber of Commerce and the White Sands Missile Range sponsored the first open house at Trinity Site. According to *Trinity Site*, a January 1994 publication by the United States Department of Energy's National Atomic Museum in Albuquerque:

On Sunday, September 9, 1945, Trinity Site opened to the press for the first time, mainly to dispel rumors of lingering high radiation levels there, as well as in Hiroshima and Nagasaki. Led by General [Leslie R.] Groves and [J. Robert] Oppenheimer, this widely publicized visit made Trinity front page news all over the country.

Trinity Site was later encircled with more than a mile of chain link fencing and posted with signs warning of radioactivity. In the early 1950s most of the

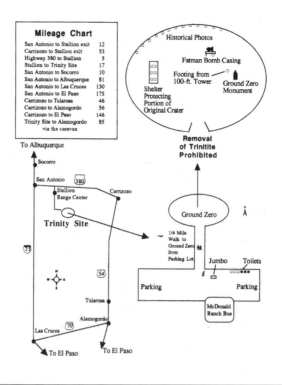

Trinity Site July 16, 1945, *site map, inside back cover,*
U.S. Government Printing Office booklet, 2000.

remaining Trinitite in the crater was bulldozed into a underground concrete
bunker near Trinity. Also at this time the crater was back filled with new soil. In
1963 the Trinitite was dug up, packed into 55-gallon drums, loaded into trucks
belonging to the Atomic Energy Commission (the successor of the Manhattan Project), and shipped somewhere. The site remained off-limits to military and civilian
personnel of the range and closed to the public for many years, despite attempts
immediately after the war to turn Trinity into a national monument [see Szasz
1984, 159–71].

By 1953, much of the radioactivity at Trinity had subsided. Later that year
[first Saturday in October], about 600 to 700 people attended the first Trinity Site
open house sponsored by the Alamogordo Chamber of Commerce and the Missile
Range. Two years later, a small group from Tularosa, NM visited the site on the 10th
anniversary of the explosion to conduct a religious service and pray for peace.

Historian Ferenc Morton Szasz (1984, 170) claims that the White Sands Missile Range
was late in acknowledging "the significance of the original Trinity Site": "For almost

twenty years following the detonation, the blast area was identified only by a worn wooden sign marked 'Zero.' It was not until 1965 that the army erected a modest marker at the site of Ground Zero." A metal plaque on that black lava rock obelisk monument reads: TRINITY SITE /WHERE /THE WORLD'S FIRST /NUCLEAR DEVICE /WAS EXPLODED ON /JULY 16, 1945 /ERECTED 1965 /WHITE SANDS MISSILE RANGE /J. FREDERICK THORLIN /MAJOR GENERAL U.S. ARMY /COMMANDING.

Trinity Site was designated a National Historic Landmark on December 21, 1965, and entered on the National Register of Historic Places (No. 66000493) on October 15, 1966. It was listed on the State Register of Cultural Properties (No. 30) in 1968. A bronze plaque below the 1965 one on the Ground Zero obelisk reads: TRINITY SITE /HAS BEEN DESIGNATED A /NATIONAL HISTORIC LANDMARK /THIS SITE POSSESSES NATIONAL SIGNIFICANCE /IN COMMEMORATING THE HISTORY OF THE /UNITED STATES OF AMERICA /1975 /NATIONAL PARK SERVICE /UNITED STATES DEPARTMENT OF THE INTERIOR.

The October (later also April) first-Saturday open houses began with minimal tourist markers. In her June/July 1967 *New Mexico Magazine* "Trip of the Month" Betty Woods (1973, 126) describes the October military-escorted, civilian caravans from Stallion Site on U.S. 380 and Oscuro Site on U.S. 54:

About twelve and a half miles from Stallion Site the caravan slows down and turns off the pavement and onto a dusty desert road. You'll see the short poles on which the wires were strung that set off the bomb. Three and a half miles later you'll come to a tiny green and very weathered sign on which you read the word TRINITY.

In the background, rising out of a slight depression is a slender monument built of lava rock. It marks GROUND ZERO where the bomb exploded on its two-hundred foot tower. This shallow crater, ten feet deep and a radius of 400 yards, shows the force of the explosion.

Most visitors quietly walk down to the monument. They read the simple bronze plaque.... They look around in awed silence trying to comprehend that cataclysmic explosion. There are the charred fence posts that were set afire by the blast. And on the ground are bits of greenish "trinitite" the rock hounds are swarming out to pick up. Atomic glass, some people call it. The atomic explosion was so hot that sand was turned to a glass-like solid.

Now you spread out a blanket and unpack your picnic basket. (Every one brings his own lunch.) You try to picture the intense activity of the last few hours before dawn on July 15 [*sic*], 1945, right where you are so safely sitting.... Around you desert grass is growing in the crater and insects are returning. Nature here has recovered from Man's most devastating force.

Woods's account contrasts with that of New Mexico State University graduate student Pierre Laroche (1989, 63) in the October 1989 *New Mexico Magazine:*

> A carnival atmosphere pervades Trinity now. Scores of tourists use a tall, rock pylon at ground zero as a handy landmark for snapshots. They pose, trade cameras, pose again and then move on to make room for more memory seekers. Although it is forbidden, some look for pieces of trinitite, which still contains measurable traces of radioactivity. Others content themselves with "Ground Zero" T-shirts on sale. Children, not aware exactly of what they are doing, frolic inside an enormous steel bomb casing as if it were a highway drainage pipe.

Entitled "Having a Blast," a photograph in the *Albuquerque Journal* of April 9, 1996, shows such "carnival atmosphere" on the part of German tourist Walter Strokosch, the man shown waving from atop the Ground Zero Monument.

Trinitite, the radioactive, pale green, molten rock, "named after the site itself, …an element formed in the few first milliseconds of the blast, when the desert floor encountered temperatures four times those at the center of the sun," figures in Greg Toppo's account of the April 1995 first-Saturday open house (in the *Albuquerque Journal*, July 16, 1995):

> Trinitite has always been something of a curiosity—radioactivity notwithstanding. According to Ferenc Morton Szasz, for years following the Trinity explosion, people sneaked onto the site and made off with handfuls of the stuff. At one time the El Rio Motel in Socorro sold it over the counter to tourists, and a Santa Fe bank gave away samples to new customers, with a warning attached: "Do not hold near body more than 24 hours."
>
> A 1967 report claimed that a person would have to eat 10,000 grams of trinitite, or hold a piece of it against one's skin for 83 straight days, to suffer any sort of radiation injury.
>
> Trinitite frequently is found in the homes of longtime Los Alamos residents. "Everybody's got some," said Berlyn Brixner, 84, a Los Alamos filmmaker who recorded the blast.
>
> Brixner said he has trinitite around his house somewhere, collected in those heady, post-bomb days. A year after Trinity, the Army made everyone sign hazardous material receipts. Today, an Army pamphlet says trinitite "is still radioactive and must not be picked up."

In the cover story of the September/October 2000 *New Mexico Journey*, Joe Nick Patoski (2000, 17) includes the army's pamphlet in his account of how "the infamous Trinity Site makes a strangely reassuring day trip":

Any fears concerning the lingering effects of the bomb blast are quelled by a pamphlet I am handed as I enter the main gate. Or are they? You get more exposure from a transcontinental airline flight than from standing around Ground Zero for an hour, the booklet reads. But a comment three sentences later about small children and pregnant women being "potentially more at risk than the rest of the population" is enough to give me pause.

And boy howdy, there's plenty of time for giving pause, long enough to appreciate the views of the stark white gypsum dunes of White Sands National Monument peeking above the scrub on the near horizon, the mildly majestic San Andres range looming to the west, and the snowcapped Sacramento range rising in the east. The military imposes only a few hard-and-fast rules: Observe the posted speed limit and all signs and personnel directing traffic, don't take photos en route, and don't pick up artifacts at the Trinity Site.

Patoski (2000, 18) notes that "in the parking lot, volunteers grill hamburgers for the approximately 2,500 expected visitors [and] Port-A-Potties line the perimeter." In a sidebar entitled "Where It All Came Together," he suggests:

> Before entering Ground Zero, board a bus at the southern edge of the parking area for the two-mile ride to the McDonald ranch house. This adobe structure is where J. Robert Oppenheimer and his Manhattan Project team assembled the plutonium core that triggered the atomic reaction.
>
> Built in 1913 by German immigrant Franz Schmidt and his wife, Esther Holmes, of Pearsall, Texas, the McDonald House was originally part of Schmidt Ranch, a working sheep and cattle operation. George McDonald purchased it in the mid-1930s; less than a decade later, the military appropriated the land....
>
> Behind the house are the ruins of the barn, off-limits due to the crumbling infrastructure and an abundance of snakes, and the concrete water tank that was transformed from a cattle feeder to a soaking pool for the more than 150 workers who gathered here in the long, hot summer of 1945.... A marker commemorates one of man's greatest technological conquests and bears a prophetic observation made in 1933 by Eugene Rhodes, a southern New Mexico writer: "Remember that in a thousand years or some such, historians will publicly offer their right eye to know what you can see now, at first hand." Buried nearby is a time capsule from 1984, the year the McDonald house was restored, to be opened in 2009.

An exception to the April and October first-Saturday open houses was granted on July 16, 1995, when Trinity Site was opened from 5:00 a.m. until 11:00 a.m. so several thousand visitors could bear witness to the birth of the nuclear age at 5:29:45 a.m. Mountain

War Time. According to an Associated Press release (*Santa Fe New Mexican*, July 17, 1995), that Golden Anniversary pilgrimage inspired "Sorrow. Fear. Anger. Awe." Some among the "uncounted hundreds" at Ground Zero "actually touched the spot at the time when the bomb exploded," while "many more waited eagerly outside the range in a line of cars that stretched for more than five miles—a multicolored metallic snake." Speaking through an interpreter, Japan Broadcasting Corporation Senior Director Koga Taketoshi, who "was trying to remain impartial while working on a documentary about the bomb's effects on Nagasaki," said: "I know many people died. When I see something like the Fat Man bomb, it's kind of an emotional feeling." Anti-nuclear protestors "in sandals, robes and flowing garments" circled the monument:

> The protestors, who remained peaceful despite occasional shouting matches with other visitors, displayed their feelings more tangibly [than Taketoshi]. They sang in an attempt to heal the earth's first "atomic wound." One splashed a vial of red liquid on the monument. As authorities moved to clean it off, another protester shouted "You can't wash the blood off. He merely made it visible."

For the tenth anniversary of the Trinity detonation Los Alamos Scientific Laboratory (now Los Alamos National Laboratory) "sponsored an unprecedented event . . . [opening] the Tech areas to newsmen, staff, and the family members of its work force" on July 17 and 18, 1955. A journalist "reported that two things impressed those around him: 'the hugeness of the entire installation and the safety precautions taken.'" Another concluded that, "although foot weary from the tour, most families decided it had been well worth their while 'seeing where Daddy works.'" No nuclear weapons were on display; "instead, the Open House offered a sophisticated science fair with nuclear reactors, remote-controlled arms, particle accelerators, and 'cooked' dimes" (Hunner 2004, 197, 198, 199). It was so successful that it became an annual event.

Residential Los Alamos was the last of the nation's atomic communities to dismantle its security fences. According to historian Jon Hunner (2004, 219):

> At noon on February 18, 1957, under an overcast sky and lightly falling snow, the guards at the main gate were relieved of their duties, and New Mexico's Governor Edwin L. Mechem became the first person to enter Los Alamos without a pass. Paul Wilson, manager of Los Alamos for the AEC [Atomic Energy Commission], escorted Mechem into the town and addressed the assembled crowd with these remarks: "To me, this little ceremony is symbolic of several things. First, it indicates the continued desire and effort to make Los Alamos part of New Mexico and

to make it a more normal community. Second, it is symbolic of continuing effort on the part of the AEC to make available for public use information pertaining to the peaceful uses of atomic energy. Third, it is symbolic of the freedom of the American people and their desire to live without unnecessary restrictions."

That Los Alamos is no longer "a well-guarded secret" is illustrated by the "Welcome to Los Alamos" in the Chamber of Commerce 1994 Visitors Guide, the cover of which carries the slogan: "We've Got Enchantment Down to a Science!":

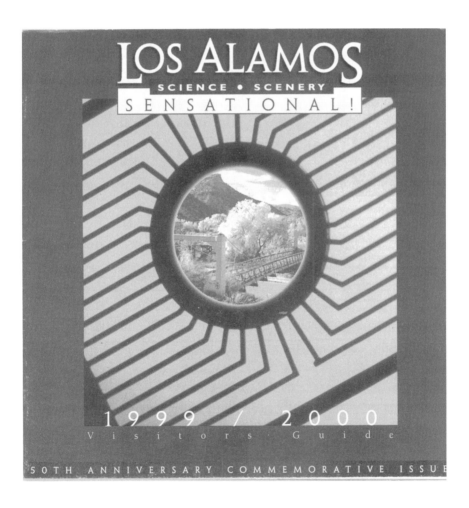

Los Alamos 1999/2000 Visitors Guide, *Los Alamos County Meeting and Visitor Bureau booklet, 1999. The fiftieth anniversary commemorated is for "History Contest Entries Fair at Fuller Lodge, October 15–17, Categories for Composition, Performing Arts & Visual Arts."*

Well-informed travelers are discovering a multitude of reasons not only to visit this small town in the beautiful Jemez Mountains but why they should make it a travel destination, and maybe even home. Los Alamos is an affordable place to stay and live, yet it is central to many of the desirable historical and cultural sites in the area. These include Bandelier National Monument, the eight northern Indian pueblos, 350 year old Spanish settlements, the cultural attractions of Santa Fe and Taos and the other sought-after sights of northern New Mexico, southwestern Colorado, eastern Arizona and southeastern Utah—the Four Corners area.

We invite you to enjoy the many activities available in and around Los Alamos. Make our reasonably priced accommodations your home base while traveling to nearby areas. If you are looking to relocate, ask us about our community—our schools, sports facilities, museums, churches, cultural life and community activities. You too may be fortunate enough to be one of the discoverers of the secret. Surprise! Los Alamos.

193

Conclusion

New Mexico's Engineered Nineteenth- and Twentieth-Century Enchantment

Five or six days after our [1831] arrival [in Santa Fe], the caravan at last hove in sight, and, wagon after wagon was seen pouring down the last declivity at about a mile's distance from the city. To judge from the clamorous rejoicings of the men, and the state of agreeable excitement which the muleteers seemed to be laboring under, the spectacle must have been as new to them as it had been to me. It was truly a scene for the artist's pencil to revel in. Even the animals seemed to participate in the humor of their riders, who grew more and more merry and obstreperous as they descended towards the city. I doubt, in short, whether the first sight of the walls of Jerusalem were beheld by the crusaders with much more tumultuous and soul-enrapturing joy.

—*Josiah Gregg*, Commerce of the Prairies, *Chapter V, 1844*

Territorial New Mexico the Tourists' Shrine that became the Land of Sunshine and, after 1934 but not officially until 2003, the Land of Enchantment was conceived along the Santa Fe Trail. Josiah Gregg reports members of his 1831 expedition who climbed Round Mound near what is now Clayton simply to enjoy the panorama "of the surrounding country, in some directions to the distance of a hundred miles or more" and to look down on the "very fine and imposing spectacle" of their caravan "passing under [its]

northern base." By the time their "first sight" of Santa Fe rivaled the crusaders' "tumultuous and soul-enrapturing joy" at first beholding the walls of Jerusalem, they had passed
through Pecos Pueblo and mission, abandoned by 1838 and according to local and travelers' lore the birthplace of the Aztec ruler Montezuma. Gregg claims to have seen Montezuma's subterranean "consecrated fire, silently smoldering under a covering of ashes, in
the basin of a small altar." A little over a century later, the stratospheric consecrated fire
of Trinity Site at 5:29:45 a.m. Mountain War Time on the morning of July 16, 1945, illu-
minated the birthplace of the nuclear age.

In 1839 Matt C. Field and his fellow Santa Fe Trail traveler Dr. David C. Waldo stayed
overnight at the Pecos Pueblo mission church in the care of an "old man," who fed them
supper and regaled them with the Montezuma tale told "in glowing words and with a rapt
intensity." Since they had to leave too early in the morning to "gratify our curiosity by
descending the cavern ourselves," they paid their host "a few bits of silver" for his hospitality and "each pocketed a cinder of the sacred fire and departed." In this they are like
the transcontinental traveler described in the 1924 Little Blue Book *The Indians of the
Pueblos* as alighting from his train to pace the southwestern railway station platform: "His
eye is attracted by the bright garb of the Indian woman who is offering bits of pottery for
sale. A coin makes him possessor of an oddly-shaped jar or jug; when the puff of the train,
a moment later, recalls him to his green plush seat, he carries with him in addition to the
souvenir the impression that he has made the acquaintance of the Pueblo Indian in his
native home." Their souvenir cinders also echo in the radioactive trinitite that annual and
later biannual tourists to Trinity Site since 1953 at first collected and then were forbidden
to remove by military order.

The Montezuma Legend fashioned by William G. Ritch, from 1873 until 1884 secretary of the Territory and from 1880 until 1889 the first secretary of the Bureau of Immigration, included a "tradition" noted in his *The Legislative Blue-Book of the Territory of
New Mexico* for the Twenty-fifth Session in 1882: " ...that Pecos pueblo was the birth-place
of Montezuma; that after he had grown to man's estate he showed himself possessed of
supernatural powers; that he at a certain time assembled a large number of his people and
started from New Mexico on a journey south [there to found the City of Mexico in 1325],
Montezuma riding on the back of an eagle; and thus riding in advance, was to his people,
as was the star to the wise men of the East." The eagle-borne Montezuma is depicted in
some of Ritch's many promotional pieces. These appeared after the February 1880 Oriental balloon over Galisteo Junction and anticipate the mushroom cloud of July 1945, the
Roswell Incident of July 1947, the Albuquerque Balloon Fiesta begun in 1972, and the
invitation-only Shiprock Balloon Rally begun in 1990.

Other airborne are in the southern borderland town of Columbus. Its attractions and
Pancho Villa State Park, the only public one in the country named for a foreign invader

"March of the Caravan," Round Mound, *lithograph in Josiah Gregg,*
Commerce of the Prairies, *1849 edition.*

(Mexican General Francisco Villa, on the night of March 9, 1916) and site of the United States Army's "first operational airbase in the United States" and the first "grease rack installed to service United States Army equipment engaged in field operations," are touted in an undated (probably late 1980s or early 1990s) Department of Tourism-labeled brochure, *Columbus, New Mexico, A Surprise in an Historic Setting: Visitors Guide*. Its counterpart is the northern mountain secret Atomic City of Los Alamos, opened in 1957 and proclaimed "a travel destination, and maybe even home" in the 1994 Chamber of Commerce brochure announcing that "We've Got Enchantment Down to a Science!": "You too may be fortunate enough to be one of the discoverers of the secret. Surprise! Los Alamos."

The Atchison, Topeka and Santa Fe Railroad and the Fred Harvey Company bought the hot springs and hotel at Gallinas near Las Vegas in 1880 and built a spur line there. On April 17, 1882, the corporations opened a new 270-room luxury Fred Harvey resort hotel, the Montezuma, so named because the Aztec ruler supposedly had bathed in those hot springs. Like "medieval" Chimayó with its Lourdes of America, the Gallinas hot springs had long been used by Native Americans and Hispanos for curative purposes. Las Vegas Hot Springs billed itself as the Karlsbad of America, and in 1899 the city of Eddy changed its name to the Americanized Carlsbad to capitalize on its own healing waters. A century later, a decidedly unhealthy Carlsbad was opened on March 26, 1999, at nearby WIPP, the Department of Energy's nuclear Waste Isolation Pilot Project. Tourism touting WIPP's safety played a role in gaining its acceptance, just as tours of the Farmington-Shiprock area's Four Corners Power Plant are geared to reassure about its pollutions.

Sometime after 1895 the Santa Fe Railway "erected on the north side of the tracks opposite the ruins an immense signboard proclaiming Pecos a wonder of the Southwest." As with the hot springs, Carlsbad vied with its caverns, the Eighth Wonder of the World, which in turn competed with the Grand Canyon and the White Sands. Shiprock, the towering northwestern Round Mound that was forbidden to climbers after May 12, 1971, is among the thirty-six sites in the 2000 Navajo Tourism booklet *Discover Navajo: The Official Navajo Nation Visitor Guide*. It is not, however, among the "Seven Wonders of the Navajo Nation" (Monument Valley, Canyon de Chelly, Little Colorado River Gorge, Rainbow Bridge, Grand Falls, Betatkin, and Window Rock) identified in the undated brochure *Four Corners Monument Navajo Tribal Park*, obtained there in May 2001.

In 1926 the Santa Fe Railway and the Fred Harvey Company launched chauffeured and guided automobile Indian Detours "to make you feel the lure of the real Southwest that lies beyond the pinched horizons of your train window." A November 1930 booklet claims that "we of the Harveycar courier corps" lead guests to "buried cities that flourished when Britons crouched in caves, reach medieval Spain dreaming away the centuries in the mountains of America, and string together age-old Indian pueblos where one may 'catch archaeology alive.'" Pecos was a stop on the first tour of three days and two nights from the Castañeda station-platform Harvey House in Las Vegas to the Santa Fe Plaza's La Fonda Harvey House to the Alvarado station-platform Harvey House in Albuquerque.

The archaeology caught alive at Pecos is dominated by the work of Alfred Vincent Kidder, who with his wife Madeleine and Model-T Ford "Old Blue" was interred on October 21, 1981, at the Forked Lightning Ruin a mile from the mission and once part of the Forked Lightning Ranch started in 1925 by cowboy Tex Austin and later owned by Texas oilman Colonel E. E. (Buddy) Fogelson and his wife actress Greer Garson. The Kidders' gravesite thus takes its place with those of Black Jack Ketchum in Clayton, Billy the Kid in Fort Sumner, Eugene Manlove Rhodes in White Sands, and the "two huge stone obelisks" erected in 1997 by Hub Corn on his alien crash "Universal Site" ranch near Roswell. The trail-side archaeological ruins of Pecos may also be seen as an engineered enchantment Ground Zero, where the obelisk, erected on White Sands Missile Range in 1965, marks "Trinity Site Where the World's First Nuclear Device Was Exploded, July 16, 1945."

A Pecos National Historical Park souvenir patch "Made in China" and purchased at the Fogelson Visitor Center on March 12, 2001, shows the church ruins and nearby kiva ladder with the plumed serpent head from a sixteenth-century Pecos pot in the sky overhead. It recalls the Manhattan Project military personnel patch shown on the inside back cover of the 2000 government-issued tourist booklet *Trinity Site July 16, 1945:*

The background of the patch was blue which represented the universe. A white cloud and a lightning bolt form a question mark which symbolizes the unknown results and the secrecy surrounding the project. The lightning bolt extends down to split a yellow atom, which represents atomic fission and the expected success of the test. A red and blue star in the center of the question mark is the insignia for the Army Service Forces to which soldiers working on the Manhattan Project were assigned.

Except, perhaps, for "O, Fair New Mexico," the official state song written in 1915 by Pat Garrett's daughter Elizabeth and adopted in 1917, Montezuma is no longer iconic. That contemporary trinity is depicted in a Roswell Convention & Visitors Bureau ad in the *Albuquerque Journal* of March 22, 1998, under the heading "Aliens, Artists and Outlaws … not your usual spring break crowd." The lefthand figure of an alien's face tops a column with the International UFO Museum and Research Center, "the definitive exploration of 'The Roswell Incident' including tours of the actual 1947 crash site," and The Great UFO Mystery, "a multimedia presentation in the largest planetarium in New Mexico." The central figure is a cow skull atop notice of the Roswell Museum and Art Center, "one of the southwest's great museums, featuring the works of Peter Hurd and Georgia O'Keeffe as well as the Robert H. Goddard rocketry collection." At right is the face of Billy the Kid over Billy the Kid Country, "Historic Lincoln Town, site of the Lincoln County Wars and Billy the Kid's last escape."

This year [1941], of all years, you'll want to get away to a vacation that will really relax and refresh you—and in New Mexico's peace and quiet you'll find just what you are looking for. Where else in America can you find such quaint and fascinating spots, such picturesque color, such majestic scenery? Where else can you be so sure of wonderful sunshiny days and crisp cool nights even in midsummer? Where else will you find the spirit of romance and adventure still so strong, lingering in the footprints of the Spanish Conquistadores and in the grass-grown wagon ruts of the old Santa Fe Trail? In New Mexico you can be as active or as lazy as you choose…. In New Mexico you are as near to the rushing world as your telephone, yet you can be as far away from strife and turmoil as on another planet. Come to New Mexico this year for the grandest vacation you've ever had!
    —New Mexico *"Land of Enchantment,"* State Tourist Bureau, *1941*

A turn-of-the-century telephone figures in Lilian Whiting's 1906 *The Land of Enchantment: From Pike's Peak to the Pacific*, which she toured on the Atchison, Topeka & Santa

New Mexico "Land of Enchantment,"
cover by W. H. Andrews, State Tourist Bureau booklet, 1941.

Fe Railway, enjoying the Fred Harvey accommodations. She notes Albuquerque's station-platform Alvarado Hotel and next-door Indian Building with its associated sales venues that "enable the traveller to purchase any souvenir from a trifle, to the costly baskets, richly colored Navajo blankets, the strange symbolic pottery, or the objects of religious rites." In New Mexico, "Land of the Sun King," Montezuma, and "Land of the Turquoise Sky": "When, on December 15, 1905, the first long-distance telephone in Santa Fé established communication *viva voce* with Denver, while within a radius of fifty miles, ruins of prehistoric civilization fascinated the tourist,—surely the remote past and the latest developments of the present met and mingled after the fashion of 'blue spirits and gray.'"

The Territorial Land of Sunshine that Whiting visited became the Sunshine State after being admitted to the Union on January 6, 1912. In its July 1929 booklet *Roads to Cibola: What to See in New Mexico and How to Get There* the New Mexico State Highway Commission highlights the "artists of international repute" and "a large group of writers whose names are household words" who sought that sunshine and "make New Mexico their home." After Florida became the Sunshine State in 1934, Albuquerque advertising executive Ward Hicks and freelance writer Joseph A. Bursey, who became the first director of the State Tourist Bureau when it began in 1935, appropriated Lilian Whiting's sobriquet for New Mexico. The first "Land of Enchantment" ad campaign was launched on May 20, 1934, and the "slogan" first appeared on license plates in 1941, "this year, of all years, [when] you'll want to get away to a vacation that will really relax and refresh you," and the year that brought Pearl Harbor on December 7. The Department of Tourism again invoked Whiting in its Essence of Enchantment spirituality ad campaign, launched in the fall of 2001, two months after September 11.

In 1821 Captain William Becknell and his Santa Fe Trail pack train left Franklin, Missouri, on September 1 and arrived in Santa Fe on November 16. In 1863 U.S. mail coaches made the trip in thirty days. In 1882 excursionists celebrating the completion of Atchison, Topeka and Santa Fe Railroad track to New Mexico's capital made a five-day round trip to the Missouri River. In 1946 guidebook writer Jack D. Rittenhouse made the U.S. 66 round trip from Los Angeles to Chicago at 35 miles per hour. And in 2000 Department of Tourism writers of the Diamond Jubilee of Route 66 *2001 New Mexico Vacation Guide* promised:

> Today, Interstate 40 more or less traces the east-west path of the old Route 66, with small sections of the old road still evident on some of its various flanks. And Interstate 25, another major thoroughfare that follows the general north-south path of both the extinct El Camino Real and sections of the Santa Fe Trail, crosses I-40 [in Albuquerque] at nearly the geographical heart of the state....

2001 New Mexico Vacation Guide, *Department of Tourism, 2000.*
Cover photo by Steve Larese: "Tom Jackson and Shantel Mandagaran, both of
Grants, drive Jackson's 1970 Ford Mustang past 'Dead Man's Curve.'"

While today's modern roads accommodate much faster speeds than any given period of the past, it is actually the slow pace of the Land of Enchantment that endears it to so many. Route 66, like its predecessors and successors, was only but a means to an end. Although New Mexico is situated toward the middle of the route's multistate path, this state was the final destination for many travelers who couldn't resist the allure of the landscape, no matter what the speed.

References Cited

Albright, Horace M., as told to Robert Cahn. 1985. *The Birth of the National Park Service: The Founding Years, 1913–33*. Salt Lake City and Chicago: Howe Brothers.

Arellanes, Kathy, ed. n.d. *New Mexico Scenic & Historic Byways: A Travel Guidebook to New Mexico Roads of Distinction*. New Mexico Highway & Transportation Department and Federal Highway Administration.

Austin, Mary. 1932. "Frank Applegate." *New Mexico Quarterly* 2: 213–18.

Baars, Donald L. 1995. *Navajo Country: A Geology and Natural History of the Four Corners Region*. Albuquerque: University of New Mexico Press.

Babcock, Barbara A. 1990. "'A New Mexican Rebecca': Imaging Pueblo Women." *Journal of the Southwest* 32: 400–37.

_____. 1996. "First Families: Gender, Reproduction and the Mythic Southwest." Pp. 207–17 in *The Great Southwest of the Fred Harvey Company and the Santa Fe Railway*, ed. Marta Weigle and Barbara A. Babcock. Phoenix: The Heard Museum.

Baca, Elmo. 2001. "Saving the Mother Road." *New Mexico Magazine*, February, 30–38.

Barrett, William P. 1996. "Unidentified Flying Dollars: P. T. Barnum Is Alive and Apparently Living in Roswell, N.M." *Forbes Magazine*, July 15, 49–51.

Beachum, Larry. 1982. *William Becknell: Father of the Santa Fe Trail*. Southwestern Studies Monograph No. 68. El Paso: Texas Western Press.

Belknap, William Jr. 1957. "New Mexico's Great White Sands." *National Geographic*, July, 113–37.

Bennett, R. W. 1933. "Motoring New Mexico." *New Mexico*, June, 7–9, 53.

Berke, Arnold. 2002. *Mary Colter: Architect of the Southwest*. New York: Princeton Architectural Press.

Bezy, John V., and Joseph P. Sanchez, eds. 1988. *Pecos Gateway to Pueblos & Plains: The Anthology*. Tucson: Southwest Parks and Monuments Association with assistance from The Friends of Pecos National Monument.

Birdseye, Roger Williams. 1926. "Selling New Mexico Right." *New Mexico Highway Journal*, September, 7–9.

Bowman, Jon, ed. 2002. *Montezuma: The Castle in the West*. Santa Fe: New Mexico Magazine.

Braddy, Haldeen. 1965. *Pancho Villa at Columbus: The Raid of 1916*. Southwestern Studies Monograph No. 9, vol. 3, no. 1. El Paso: Texas Western College.

Bryant, Keith L. Jr. 1974. *History of the Atchison, Topeka and Santa Fe Railway*. Lincoln: University of Nebraska Press.

Bryant, Robert. 1985. "Cashing in on the Caves." *New Mexico Business Journal*, November, 53–58.

Bunting, Bainbridge. 1983. *John Gaw Meem: Southwestern Architect*. A School of American Research Book. Albuquerque: University of New Mexico Press.

Bursey, Joseph A. 1932. "Carl B. Livingston." *New Mexico*, May, 9–10, 40.

_____. 1936a. "High Roads to Romance." *New Mexico*, January, 18–19, 37–39.

_____. 1936b. "New Mexico State Tourist Bureau." P. 68 in *New Mexico Blue Book, 1935–1936*. Santa Fe: Office of the Secretary of State.

Cameron, S. M. 1977. "Pueblo Pots – for Thirteen Cents." *New Mexico Magazine*, May, 38–39, 47–48.

Carroll, Curtis. 2001. "Enchantment or Bust: State Highway Maps Reflect the Times and Spirit of New Mexico." *New Mexico Magazine*, January, 25–27.

Cather, Willa. (1927) 1999. *Willa Cather Scholarly Edition: Death Comes for the Archbishop*. Historical Essay and Explanatory Notes by John J. Murphy; Textual Editing by Charles W. Mignon with Frederick M. Link and Kari A. Ronning. Lincoln: University of Nebraska Press.

Charles, Mrs. Tom [Bula Ward]. 1953. *Tales of the Tularosa*. Alamogordo, NM: Pass to the North, Carl Hertzog.

_____. 1959. "Gene Rhodes Pilgrimage." *New Mexico*, June, 57.

Chávez. Thomas E. 1997. "Reflections on Our Long, Glorious Past." *New Mexico Magazine*, July, 6–11.

Chilton, Lance, Katherine Chilton, Polly E. Arango, James Dudley, Nancy Neary, and Patricia Stelzner. 1984. *New Mexico: A New Guide to the Colorful State*. Albuquerque: University of New Mexico Press.

Christman, Al. 2001. "The Atomic Admiral." *New Mexico Magazine*, December, 73–75.

Coke, Van Deren. 1963. *Taos and Santa Fe: The Artist's Environment, 1882–1942*. Albuquerque: University of New Mexico Press.

Crane, Candace. 2000. *Carlsbad Caverns National Park: Worlds of Wonder*. Carlsbad, NM: Carlsbad Caverns-Guadalupe Mountains Association.

Crumpler, Larry S. 2001. "Land of Volcanoes." *New Mexico Magazine*, January, 60–67.

Davis, W. W. H. (1857) 1973. *El Gringo; or, New Mexico and Her People*. New York: Arno Press.

DeHuff, Elizabeth Willis. 1931. "The Santuario at Chimayó. *New Mexico Highway Journal*, June, 16–17, 39.

Delgado, Deane G. (1984) 1990. *Historical Markers in New Mexico: A Traveler's Guide*. Rev. ed. Santa Fe: Ancient City Press.

D'Emilio, Sandra, and Suzan Campbell. 1991. *Visions & Visionaries: The Art and Artists of the Santa Fe Railway*. Salt Lake City: Peregrine Smith Books, Gibbs-Smith Publisher.

Dorsey, George A. 1903. *Indians of the Southwest*. Chicago: Passenger Department, Atchison Topeka & Santa Fe Railway.

Drabanski, Emily. 1997. "Editor's Note[s]." *New Mexico Magazine*, July, 5, 44.

Dunleavy, Julie. 1984. "New Mexico: A Pioneer in Southwestern Tourism." *New Mexico Magazine*, November, 61–65.

Dye, Victoria E. 2005. *All Aboard for Santa Fe: Railway Promotion of the Southwest, 1890s to 1930s*. Albuquerque: University of New Mexico Press.

Ellis, Erl H. 1983. *Colorado Mapology*. Frederick, CO: Jende-Hagan Book Corporation.

England, Terry. 1999a. "Science Hot Spots." *New Mexico Magazine*, February, 36–38.

_____. 1999b. "Science and Space Museums." *New Mexico Magazine*, February, 64–67.

Fiske, Turbesé Lummis, and Keith Lummis. 1975. *Charles F. Lummis: The Man and His West*. Norman: University of Oklahoma Press.

Flower, B. O. 1914. *Progressive Men, Women, and Movements of the Past Twenty-Five Years*. Boston: The New Arena.

Foote, Cheryl J., and Sandra K. Schackel. 1986. "Indian Women of New Mexico, 1535–1680." Pp. 17–40 in *New Mexico Women: Intercultural Perspectives*, ed. Joan M. Jensen and Darlis A. Miller. Albuquerque: University of New Mexico Press.

Fox, Stephen D. 1983. "Healing, Imagination, and New Mexico." *New Mexico Historical Review* 58: 213–37.

Frost, Richard H. 1980. "The Romantic Inflation of Pueblo Culture." *The American West* January/February, 5–9, 56–60.

Gibbs, William E. 1993. "The Roswell Incident: An 'Unsolved' or 'Unsolvable' Mystery?" Pp. 145–60 in *Great Mysteries of the West*, ed. Ferenc Morton Szasz. Golden, CO: Fulcrum Publishing.

Gish, Robert Franklin. 1996. *Beautiful Swift Fox: Erna Fergusson and the Modern Southwest*. College Station: Texas A&M University Press.

Grand Canyon of Arizona, The: Being a Book of Words from Many Pens, about the Grand Canyon of the Colorado River in Arizona. 1906. Chicago: Passenger Department, The Santa Fe.

Grant, Blanche C. 1928. *Cavern Guide Book: Carlsbad Caverns, Carlsbad, NM*. Topeka, KS: Crane & Company.

Grattan, Virginia L. 1980. *Mary Colter: Builder Upon the Red Earth*. Flagstaff, AZ: Northland Press.

Gregg, Josiah. (1844) 1954. *Commerce of the Prairies*, ed. Max L. Moorhead. Norman: University of Oklahoma Press.

Hales, Peter B. 1988. *Henry Jackson and the Transformation of American Landscape*. Philadelphia: Temple University Press.

Hall, Ruth K. 1983. *A Place of Her Own: The Story of Elizabeth Garrett*. Santa Fe: Sunstone Press.

Hallenbeck, Cleve. (1949) 1987. *The Journey of Fray Marcos de Niza*. Dallas: Southern Methodist University Press.

Hammond, George P. (1956) 1979. "The Search for the Fabulous in the Settlement of the Southwest." Pp. 17–33 in *New Spain's Far Northern Frontier: Essays on Spain in the American West, 1540–1821*, ed. David J. Weber. Albuquerque: University of New Mexico Press.

Handy, Bruce. 1997. "Roswell or Bust: A Town Discovers Manna Crashing from Heaven and Becomes the Capital of America's Alien Nation." *Time*, June 23, 62–67.

Harlow, Francis H. 1983. *Pueblo Art: Southwestern Indian Pottery*. Dallas: The Somesuch Press.

Hartwell, Dickson. 1949. "Let's Eat with the Harvey Boys." *Collier's Magazine*, April, 9, 30, 32.

Hassrick, Peter H., ed. 1997. *The Georgia O'Keeffe Museum*. New York: Harry N. Abrams Publishers, in association with The Georgia O'Keeffe Museum.

Henderson, Alice Corbin. 1937. *Brothers of Light: The Penitentes of the Southwest*. New York: Harcourt, Brace and Company.

_____. 1938. "E. Dana Johnson: June 15, 1879–December 10, 1937." *New Mexico Historical Review* 13: 120–25.

Henderson, James David. 1969. *"Meals by Fred Harvey": A Phenomenon of the American West*. Fort Worth: Texas Christian University Press.

Hillerman, Anne. 1974. "A Magazine in Evolution: 50 Years of *New Mexico*." *New Mexico Magazine*, January/February, 29.

Hoebel, E. Adamson. 1979. "Zia Pueblo." Pp. 407–17 in *Handbook of North American Indians, Volume 9: Southwest*, ed. Alfonso Ortiz. Washington, DC: Smithsonian Institution.

Horgan, Paul. 1979. *Josiah Gregg and His Vision of the Early West*. New York: Farrar Straus Giroux.

Houk, Rose, and Michael Collier. 1994. *White Sands: National Monument*. Tucson: Southwest Parks and Monuments Association.

Howard, Kathleen L. 1996. "'A most remarkable success': Herman Schweizer and the Fred Harvey Indian Department." Pp. 87–101 in *The Great Southwest of the Fred Harvey Company and the Santa Fe Railway*, ed. Marta Weigle and Barbara A. Babcock. Phoenix: The Heard Museum.

_____, and Diana F. Pardue. 1996a. *Inventing the Southwest: The Fred Harvey Company and Native American Art*. Flagstaff, AZ: Northland Publishing.

_____. 1996b. "Making Art, Making Money: The Fred Harvey Company and the Indian Artisan." Pp. 168–75 in *The Great Southwest of the Fred Harvey Company and the Santa Fe Railway*, ed. Marta Weigle and Barbara A. Babcock. Phoenix: The Heard Museum.

Hungerford, Edward. 1923. "A Study in Consistent Railroad Advertising: What Twenty-seven Years of Advertising Have Accomplished for a Great Railroad System." *The Santa Fe Magazine*, March, 43–48.

Hunner, Jon. 2004. *Inventing Los Alamos: The Growth of an Atomic Community*. Norman: University of Oklahoma Press.

Hutchinson, W. H., ed. 1975. *The Rhodes Reader: Stories of Virgins, Villains, and Varmints.* 2d ed. Norman: University of Oklahoma Press.

Hyslop, Stephen G. 2002. *Bound for Santa Fe: The Road to New Mexico and the American Conquest, 1806–1848.* Norman: University of Oklahoma Press.

Jones, Billy M. 1967. *Health-Seekers in the Southwest, 1817–1900.* Norman: University of Oklahoma Press.

Jones, Paul M. 1985. *Memories of Santa Rita.* Silver City, NM: Southwest Offset.

"Joseph A. Bursey, Principled Politician." 1961. *The Santa Fe Scene: Weekly News and Features,* January 28, 4–7, 9.

Julyan, Robert. 1998. *The Place Names of New Mexico.* Rev. ed. Albuquerque: University of New Mexico Press.

Kay, Elizabeth. 1987. *Chimayo Valley Traditions.* Santa Fe: Ancient City Press.

Kessell, John L. 1979. *Kiva, Cross, and Crown: The Pecos Indians and New Mexico, 1540–1840.* Washington, DC: National Park Service, US Department of the Interior.

Kincade, Kathy, and Carl Landau. 1990. *Festivals of the Southwest: Your Guided Tour to the Festivals of Arizona and New Mexico.* San Francisco: Landau Communications.

Kosik, Fran. 1996. *Native Roads: The Complete Motoring Guide to the Navajo and Hopi Nations, Self-guided Road Tours Featuring the History, Geology, and Native Cultures of Northern Arizona.* Tucson: Rio Nuevo Publishers.

Kramer, Barbara. 1996. *Nampeyo and Her Pottery.* Albuquerque: University of New Mexico Press.

Krza, Paul. 2002. "State Promotion Enchantment & Economics: Agencies Push 'Spirituality' and Quality of Life." *New Mexico Business Journal,* April, 15–17.

Lang, Herbert H. 1976. "The New Mexico Bureau of Immigration." *New Mexico Historical Review* 51: 193–214.

Larcombe, Samuel. 1983. "Plaza del Cerro, Chimayó, New Mexico: An Old Place Not Quite on the Highway." Pp. 171–80 in *Hispanic Arts and Ethnohistory in the Southwest: New Papers in Honor of E. Boyd,* ed. Marta Weigle with Claudia Larcombe and Samuel Larcombe. Santa Fe: Ancient City Press; Albuquerque: University of New Mexico Press.

Laroche, Pierre. 1989. "Trinity Site Still Triggers Emotion." *New Mexico Magazine,* October, 61–64.

Lavender, David. 1980. *The Southwest.* Albuquerque: University of New Mexico Press.

Lears, T. J. Jackson. 1994. *No Place of Grace: Antimodernism and the Transformation of American Culture, 1880–1920*. New ed. Chicago and London: University of Chicago Press.

Levine, Frances. 1999. *Our Prayers Are in This Place: Pecos Pueblo Identity over the Centuries*. Albuquerque: University of New Mexico Press.

Lewis, Nancy Owen, and Kay Leigh Hagan. 2007. *A Peculiar Alchemy: A Centennial History of SAR, 1907–2007*. Santa Fe: School for Advanced Research Press.

Linford, Laurance D. 2000. *Navajo Places: History, Legend, Landscape*. Salt Lake City: University of Utah Press.

Livingston, Carl B. 1934. "The Eighth Wonder." *New Mexico*, March, 10–12, 41–46.

Long, Haniel. 1941. *Piñon Country*. American Folkways, ed. Erskine Caldwell. New York: Duell, Sloan & Pearce.

Lummis, Charles F. 1892a. *Some Strange Corners of Our Country: The Wonderland of the Southwest*. New York: Century.

_____. 1892b. *A Tramp Across the Continent*. New York: Charles Scribner's Sons.

_____. (1893) 1966. *The Land of Poco Tiempo*. Illus. fac. ed. Albuquerque: University of New Mexico Press.

Lynes, Barbara Buhler, Lesley Poling-Kempes, and Frederick W. Turner. 2004. *Georgia O'Keeffe and New Mexico: A Sense of Place*. Princeton and Oxford: Princeton University Press; Santa Fe: Georgia O'Keeffe Museum.

Lynn, Sandra D. 1999. *Windows on the Past: Historic Lodgings of New Mexico*. Albuquerque: University of New Mexico Press.

"Marking the Old Trails." 1931. *New Mexico*, September, 34, 51.

Marshall, James. 1945. *Santa Fe: The Railroad That Built an Empire*. New York: Random House.

McCutcheon, Chuck. 2002. *Nuclear Reactions: The Politics of Opening a Radioactive Waste Disposal Site*. Albuquerque: University of New Mexico Press.

McDonald, William F. 1969. *Federal Relief Administration and the Arts*. Columbus: Ohio State University Press.

McLuhan, T. C. 1985. *Dream Tracks: The Railroad and the American Indian, 1890–1930*. With photographs from the William E. Kopplin Collection. New York: Harry N. Abrams.

Merrill, Christopher, and Ellen Bradbury, eds. (1992) 1998. *From the Faraway Nearby: Georgia O'Keeffe As Icon*. Albuquerque: University of New Mexico Press.

Miles, John E. 1941. "Greetings from Governor John E. Miles." *New Mexico*, January, 11.

Miller, Michael. 1985. "New Mexico's Role in the Panama-California Exposition of 1915." *El Palacio* 91, 2 (fall): 12–17.

Moneta, Daniela P., ed. 1985. *Chas F. Lummis: The Centennial Exhibition Commemorating His Tramp Across the Continent*. Los Angeles: Southwest Museum.

Morris, Juddi. 1994. *The Harvey Girls: The Women Who Civilized the West*. New York: Walker and Company.

"New Mexico at 'A Century of Progress.'" 1934. *New Mexico*, May, 19.

Newcomb, Franc Johnson. 1964. *Hosteen Klah: Navajo Medicine Man and Sand Painter*. Norman: University of Oklahoma Press.

Nieto-Phillips, John M. 2004. *The Language of Blood: The Making of Spanish-American Identity in New Mexico, 1880s–1930s*. Albuquerque: University of New Mexico Press.

Nims, F. C. (1881) 1980. *Health, Wealth and Pleasure in Colorado and New Mexico*. Fac. ed. Santa Fe: Museum of New Mexico Press.

Nymeyer, Robert, and William R. Halliday, M.D. 1991. *Carlsbad Cavern: The Early Years*. Carlsbad, NM: Carlsbad Caverns-Guadalupe Mountains Association.

Page, Jake. 1995. *The Smithsonian Guides to Natural America: The Southwest (New Mexico and Arizona)*. Washington, DC: Smithsonian Books; New York: Random House.

Pardue, Diana F. 1996. "Marketing Ethnography: The Fred Harvey Indian Department and George A. Dorsey." Pp. 102–109 in *The Great Southwest of the Fred Harvey Company and the Santa Fe Railway*, ed. Marta Weigle and Barbara A. Babcock. Phoenix, Ariz.: The Heard Museum.

Parezo, Nancy J. 1983. *Navajo Sandpainting: From Religious Act to Commercial Art*. Tucson: University of Arizona Press.

Parker, John L. 1964. "San Juan's Black Gold." *New Mexico Magazine*, February, 12–15, 31, 40.

Patoski, Joe Nick. 2000. *New Mexico Journey*, September/October, 16–19.

Patton, Phil. 1986. *Open Road: A Celebration of the American Highway*. New York: Simon & Schuster.

Penkower, Monty Noam. 1977. *The Federal Writers' Project: A Study in Government Patronage of the Arts*. Urbana: University of Illinois Press.

Pike, David. 2004. *Roadside New Mexico: A Guide to Historic Markers*. Albuquerque: University of New Mexico Press.

Polese, Richard L. 1968. "The Zia Sun Symbol: Variations on a Theme." *El Palacio* 75, 2 (summer): 30–34.

Poling-Kempes, Lesley. 1989. *The Harvey Girls: Women Who Opened the West*. New York: Paragon House.

"Ports of Welcome." 1937. *New Mexico*, April, 32.

Resources of New Mexico. (1881) 1973. Santa Fe: William Gannon.

Riley, Carroll L. 1975. "The Road to Hawikuh: Trade and Trade Routes to Cibola-Zuni during Late Prehistoric and Early Historic Times." *The Kiva* 41: 137–59.

Ripp, Bart. 1984. "Greetings from White's City." *Albuquerque Living*, March, 70–71.

Ritch, W. G., comp. (1882) 1968. *New Mexico Blue Book, 1882*. A complete facsimile of the first edition, with a new preface by Clinton P. Anderson, Senator from New Mexico. Albuquerque: University of New Mexico Press.

Rittenhouse, Jack D. (1946) 1989. *A Guide Book to Highway 66*. A facsimile of the 1946 first edition. Albuquerque: University of New Mexico Press.

Rothman, Hal K. 1998. *Devil's Bargains: Tourism in the Twentieth-Century American West*. Lawrence: University of Kansas Press.

Russell, Carl P. 1935. "The White Sands of Alamogordo." *National Geographic*, August, 250–64.

Russell, Mrs. Hal. 1943. "Memoirs of Marian Russell." *The Colorado Magazine* 20, 3: 81–95.

Rydell, Robert W. 1993. *World of Fairs: The Century-of-Progress Expositions*. Chicago: University of Chicago Press.

Sagar, Keith, ed. 1982. *D. H. Lawrence and New Mexico*. Salt Lake City: Gibbs M. Smith.

Sando, Joe S. 1992. *Pueblo Nations: Eight Centuries of Pueblo Indian History*. Santa Fe: Clear Light Publishers.

_____. 1998. *Pueblo Profiles: Cultural Identity through Centuries of Change*. Santa Fe: Clear Light Publishers.

Sarton, May. 1976. *A World of Light: Portraits and Celebrations*. New York: W. W. Norton.

Schaffer, Marguerite S. 2001. *See America First: Tourism and National Identity, 1880–1940*. Washington and London: Smithsonian Institution Press.

Schneider, Jill. 1991. *Route 66 Across New Mexico: A Wanderer's Guide*. Albuquerque: University of New Mexico Press.

Schneider-Hector, Dietmar. 1993. *White Sands: The History of a National Monument*. Albuquerque: University of New Mexico Press.

Schriever, George. 1976. "Preface to Re-Publication." Pp. i–iii in *Representative Art and Artists of New Mexico*, School of American Research, Museum of New Mexico, Santa Fe, 1940. Bronx, NY: Olana Gallery.

Scott, Quinta. 2000. *Along Route 66*. Norman: University of Oklahoma Press.

_____ and Susan Croce Kelly. 1988. *Route 66: The Highway and Its People*. Norman and London: University of Oklahoma Press.

Scott, Winfield Townley. (1957) 1976. "A Calendar of Santa Fe." Pp. 45–69 in *The Spell of New Mexico*, ed. Tony Hillerman. Albuquerque: University of New Mexico Press.

Shane, Karen D. 1981. "New Mexico: Salubrious El Dorado." *New Mexico Historical Review* 56: 387–99.

Sheppard, Carl D. 1988. *Creator of the Santa Fe Style: Isaac Hamilton Rapp, Architect*. Albuquerque: University of New Mexico Press in cooperation with the Historical Society of New Mexico.

Shuart, Harry E. 1934. "New Mexico Goes to the 'World's Fair': The State's Exhibit at A Century of Progress Is One of the High Spots in the Big Show." *New Mexico*, July, 10–12, 43.

Simmons, Marc. 1968. *Two Southwesterners: Charles Lummis and Amado Chaves*. Cerrillos, NM: San Marcos Press.

_____. 1982. *Albuquerque: A Narrative History*. Albuquerque: University of New Mexico Press.

_____. 1990. *When Six-Guns Ruled: Outlaw Tales of the Southwest*. Santa Fe: Ancient City Press.

_____. 1996. *The Old Trail to Santa Fe: Collected Essays*. Albuquerque: University of New Mexico Press.

_____. 2006. *Stalking Billy the Kid: Brief Sketches of a Short Life*. Santa Fe: Sunstone Press.

_____ and Hal Jackson. 2001. *Following the Santa Fe Trail: A Guide for Modern Travelers*. 3d rev. ed. Santa Fe: Ancient City Press.

Sinclair, John L. 1982. "George Fitzpatrick: Pioneer of Enchantment." *New Mexico*, July, 2–4, 6, 9, 14, 16, 37.

Smith, Toby. 2000. *Little Gray Men: Roswell and the Rise of a Popular Culture*. Albuquerque: University of New Mexico Press.

Snead, James E. 2001. *Ruins and Rivals: The Making of Southwest Archaeology*. Tucson: University of Arizona Press.

Spidle, Jake W. Jr. 1986. "'An Army of Tubercular Invalids': New Mexico and the Birth of a Tuberculosis Industry." *New Mexico Historical Review* 61: 179–201.

"Statehood Stamp." 1962. *New Mexico Magazine*, February, 35.

Steele, Thomas J., S. J., and Rowena A. Rivera. 1985. *Penitente Self-Government: Brotherhoods and Councils, 1797–1947*. Santa Fe: Ancient City Press.

Stensvaag, James T. 1980. "Clio on the Frontier: The Intellectual Evolution of the Historical Society of New Mexico, 1859–1925." *New Mexico Historical Review* 55: 293–308.

Stover, Dawn. 1997. "50 Years After Roswell: What Crashed Here in 1947 Is a Matter of Dispute. But Whatever Happened Then Is Good for Business Today." *Popular Science*, June, 82–88.

Szasz, Ferenc M[orton]. 1984. *The Day the Sun Rose Twice: The Story of the Trinity Site Nuclear Explosion, July 16, 1945*. Albuquerque: University of New Mexico Press.

_____. 2006. *Larger Than Life: New Mexico in the Twentieth Century*. Albuquerque: University of New Mexico Press.

Tatum, Stephen. 1982. *Inventing Billy the Kid: Visions of the Outlaw in America, 1881–1981*. Albuquerque: University of New Mexico Press.

Terris, Virginia R. 1982. "Whiting, Lillian [sic]." Pp. 399–400 in *American Women Writers: A Critical Reference Guide from Colonial Times to the Present*, vol. 4, ed. Lina Mainiero. New York: Frederick Ungar Publishing.

Thomas, D. H. 1978. *The Southwestern Indian Detours: The Story of the Fred Harvey/Santa Fe Railway Experiment in 'Detourism'*. Phoenix: Hunter Publishing.

Thompson, Mark. 2001. *American Character: The Curious Life of Charles Fletcher Lummis and the Rediscovery of the Southwest*. New York: Arcade Publishing.

Tingley, Clyde. 1935. "Greetings from New Mexico's Governor." *New Mexico*, January, 5.

Tissot, Debbie. 1997. "Focus on Harvey Caplin." *New Mexico Magazine*, July, 70–79.

Tórrez, Robert J. 1993. "State Seal Receives Eagle-Eyed Scrutiny." *New Mexico Magazine* December, 80–87.

_____. 2004. *UFOs Over Galisteo and Other Stories of New Mexico's History*. Albuquerque: University of New Mexico Press.

Troyan, Michael. 1999. *A Rose for Mrs. Miniver: The Life of Greer Garson*. Lexington: University Press of Kentucky.

Tumber, Catherine. 2002. *American Feminism and the Birth of New Age Spirituality: Searching for the Higher Self, 1875–1915.* Lanham, Boulder, New York, Oxford: Rowman & Littlefield.

Turner, Victor, and Edith Turner. 1978. *Image and Pilgrimage in Christian Culture: Anthropological Perspectives.* New York: Columbia University Press.

Ungnade, Herbert E. 1972. *Guide to the New Mexico Mountains.* 2d rev. ed. Albuquerque: University of New Mexico Press.

"U.S. 66 Opened to Travel: New Program Is Planned." 1937. *New Mexico,* December, 31.

Usner, Don J. 2001. *New Mexico Route 66 on Tour: Legendary Architecture from Glenrio to Gallup.* Santa Fe: Museum of New Mexico Press.

Wallis, Michael. 1990. *Route 66: The Mother Road.* New York: St. Martin's Press.

Walter, Paul A. F. 1916. "A New Mexico Lourdes." *El Palacio* 3, 2: 3–27.

Ward, Greg. 1997. *Southwest USA: The Rough Guide.* London: Rough Guides Limited, distributed by the Penguin Group.

Waters, L. L. 1950. *Steel Rails to Santa Fe.* Lawrence: University of Kansas Press.

Weigle, Marta. 1976. *Brothers of Light, Brothers of Blood: The Penitentes of the Southwest.* Albuquerque: University of New Mexico Press.

_____, ed. 1985. *New Mexicans in Cameo and Camera: New Deal Documentation of Twentieth-Century Lives.* Albuquerque: University of New Mexico Press.

_____. 1989. "Finding the 'True America': Ethnic Tourism in New Mexico during the New Deal." Pp. 58–73 in *Folklife Annual 88–89,* ed. James Hardin and Alan Jabbour. A Publication of the American Folklife Center at the Library of Congress. Washington, DC: Library of Congress.

_____. 1992. "Exposition and Mediation: Mary Colter, Erna Fergusson, and the Santa Fe/Harvey Popularization of the Native Southwest, 1902–1940." *Frontiers: A Journal of Women Studies* 12, 3: 117–50.

_____. 1994. "Selling the Southwest: Santa Fe InSites." Pp. 210–24 in *Discovered Country: Tourism and Survival in the American West,* ed. Scott Norris. Albuquerque: Stone Ladder Press.

_____. 1996a. "A Brief History of the Spanish Colonial Arts Society." Pp. 26–35 in *Spanish New Mexico: The Spanish Colonial Arts Society Collection, Volume Two: Hispanic Arts in the Twentieth Century,* ed. Donna Pierce and Marta Weigle. Santa Fe: Museum of New Mexico Press.

_____. 1996b. "'Insisted on authenticity': Harveycar Indian Detours, 1925–1931." Pp. 47–59 in *The Great Southwest of the Fred Harvey Company and the Santa Fe Railway*, ed. Marta Weigle and Barbara A. Babcock. Phoenix: The Heard Museum.

_____. 1997. "Canyon, Caverns, and Coordinates: From Nature Tourism to Nuclear Tourism in the Southwest." *Journal of the Southwest* 39: 165–82.

_____ and Kyle Fiore. 1982a. *New Mexico Artists and Writers: A Celebration, 1940*. Santa Fe: Ancient City Press.

_____. 1982b. *Santa Fe and Taos: The Writer's Era, 1916–1941*. Santa Fe: Ancient City Press.

_____, and Peter White. 1988. *The Lore of New Mexico*. Albuquerque: University of New Mexico Press.

Welsh, Michael. 1995. *Dunes and Dreams: A History of White Sands National Monument*. Professional Paper No. 55. Santa Fe: Intermountain Cultural Resource Center, Intermountain Field Area, National Park Service, Department of the Interior.

Wheeler, W. E. 1949. "When Will Rogers Visited the Caverns." *New Mexico*, February, 16, 40–41.

Whiting, Lilian. 1906. *The Land of Enchantment: From Pike's Peak to the Pacific*. Boston: Little, Brown and Company.

"William H. Simpson Passes On." 1933. *The Santa Fe Magazine*, July, 43–44.

Wilson, Alan, with Gene Dennison. 1995. *Navajo Place Names: An Observer's Guide with Audio Cassette*. Guilford, CT: Jeffrey Norton Publishers.

Wilson, Chris. 1997. *The Myth of Santa Fe: Creating a Modern Regional Tradition*. Albuquerque: University of New Mexico Press.

Wilson, John P. 1993. *New Mexico State Monument Lincoln*. Santa Fe: Museum of New Mexico Press.

Winship, George P. 1896. "The Coronado Expedition, 1540–1542." Pp. 329–613 in *Fourteenth Annual Report of the Bureau of American Ethnology for the Years 1892–1893*. Part 1. Washington, DC: Government Printing Office.

Woodman, Pierre. 1934. "New Mexico Bids for Summer Vacationists in 1934." *New Mexico*, June, 12–13, 48.

Woods, Betty. 1950. *Fifty Trips to Thrills*, ed. George Fitzpatrick. Santa Fe: New Mexico Magazine.

_____. 1973. *101 Trips in the Land of Enchantment*, ed. George Fitzpatrick. 4th rev. ed. Santa Fe: New Mexico Magazine.

Workers of the Writers' Program of the Work Projects Administration in the State of New Mexico, comps. 1940. *New Mexico: A Guide to the Colorful State*. New York: Hastings House.

Wroth, William. 1983. "La Sangre de Cristo: History and Symbolism." Pp. 283–92 in *Hispanic Arts and Ethnohistory in the Southwest: New Papers Inspired by the Work of E. Boyd*, ed. Marta Weigle with Claudia Larcombe and Samuel Larcombe. Santa Fe: Ancient City Press; Albuquerque: University of New Mexico Press.

Young, John V. 1984. *The State Parks of New Mexico*. Albuquerque: University of New Mexico Press.

Zeman, Scott C. 2003. "High Roads and Highways to Romance: *New Mexico Highway Journal* and *Arizona Highways* (Re)present the Southwest." *New Mexico Historical Review* 78: 419–38.

Credits

Pg. 19: courtesy Photo Archives (New Mexico History Museum/DCA), neg. no. 16296. Pg. 46: courtesy Photo Archives (NMHM/DCA), neg. no. 130798. Pg. 60: courtesy Photo Archives (NMHM/DCA), neg. no. 137336. Pg. 81: courtesy Photo Archives (NMHM/DCA), neg. no. 50131. Pg. 147: courtesy Photo Archives (NMHM/DCA), neg. no. 003160.

Pg. 25: courtesy Western National Parks Association.

Pp. 31, 35, 62, 86, 87, 97, 98-99, 108, 122, 128–29, 170: courtesy New Mexico Tourism Department.

Pg. 82, 105, 143: courtesy New Mexico Department of Transportation.

Pg. 160, 183, 186: courtesy White Sands Missile Range.

Pg. 173: due diligence has been exercised by the author to obtain reproduction permission.

Pg. 191: courtesy Los Alamos Chamber of Commerce.

Index

Page numbers in italics refer to illustrations.

Abeyta de Cháves, Carmen, 120
Abeyta, Don Bernardo, 120–21
Abiquiú, New Mexico, 106, 110, 112
Abreu, Margaret, 49
Acoma Pueblo, 46, *48*, *50*, 81, *83*, 88, 178
Adams, John P., 44
Adams, Marsha, 123
Ah-Kena-Bah, 50
air fields/bases, 167–69, 176, 184. *See also* specific names

Alamogordo Army Air Field. *See* Holloman Air Force Base/Development Center
Alamogordo, New Mexico, 161–62, 175–82, 184–86
Albright, Horace M., 133
Albuquerque, New Mexico, 146, 167; advertising agencies of, 95, 158; and Balloon Fiesta, 166; and Harvey Indian Detours, 21, 66, 71, 92–93; and health seekers, 57, 59; hotels in, 21, 71, 78–79, 92, 196, 199; and Indian Building, 71, 79–80; museums in, 162; and Sandia Lab, 161–62; and WPA NM Guide, 119
Alsberg, Henry G., 119
Alvarado Hotel, 21, 71, 78–79, 92, 196
Andrews, Willard H., 96–97, *99*, *154*, 198
Apaches, 40, 68. *See also* Mescalero Apaches
Apodaca, Jerry, 81
Applegate, Frank, 121
archaeology, 13, 109, 178; attractions, 43, 47, 65–66, 89, 94, 161; at Carlsbad Caverns, 131; and historic preservation, 157; history of, 72; at Pecos Pueblo, 27, 196; relics in museums, 38, 107
Archdiocese of Santa Fe, 123
architecture, 157; adobe, 38, 44, 74, 102, 120; and artists, 101, 106; defensive, 38; hacienda-style, 24; of Harvey hotels/stations, 66, 92; models of, 44; Native American, 21–22, 43, 74, 77–78; at Panama-Calif. Expo, 46–48; Pueblo-Revival style, 49–50, 69, 78
Arizona, 57, 61, 65, 69, 71, 73–74, 78–79, 91–92, 139–40, 145, 147–49, 153, 166, 192
Army of the West, 14
art colonies, 101, 103–04, 106–09
Artesia, New Mexico, 138, *180*
artists, 49–51, 68–69, 74, 77–78, 80–81, *83*, 88, 101–12, 140, 164, 178, 197, 199. *See also* specific names
Atchison, Topeka and Santa Fe Railroad/Railway: advertising by, 66–68, 196; and artists/photographers, 68; booklets by, 21–22, 54, 57, *72*, 74, 94–95, *115*, *118*, 134;

financial struggles of, 66–67; and Harvey Company, 21–22, 55–56, 59–60, 68–69, 71–72, 92, 195–96; and promotional material, 16; and Pueblo Indians, 78–80; and Route 66, 151–52; routes in New Mexico, 53–55, 140, 164–65; and souvenirs, 52
atomic bomb tests, 161, 179, 182–83, 185, 187, 189–90, 196. *See also* Trinity Site; White Sands Missile Range
Atomic Engergy Commission (AEC), 186, 190–91
Aubry, François (Francis) Xavier, 30
Austin, John "Tex", 22–24, 196
Austin, Mary, 74, 79, 121
automobile tours/touring, 21–22, 38, 71, 88–89, 134–35, 152, 155–57, 168, 178, *180*, *200*. *See also* Harveycars; Santa Fe/Harvey Indian Detour
Avery, Cyrus S., 151–52, 155
Aztecs, 17–18, 20, 44, 61, 77, 194–95

Baca, Elmo, 157
Bandelier, Adolph, F., 20–21, 73
Bandelier National Monument, 28, 161, 192
Baumann, Gustave, 104, 121
Beckey, Fred, 142
Becknell, William, 13–14, 30, 87, 199
Begaye, Kelsey, 149
Belknap, William Jr., 184–85
Bennett, Ray W., 88
Billy the Kid, 29, 34–42, 45, 60, 172, 181, 185, 196–97
Billy the Kid National Scenic Byway, 40–41
Birdseye, Roger W., 73–74, 115–16
Blakeley, D. Ray, 34
Blanchard, William H., 169
Blondin, Joseph, 166
Blumenschein, Ernest L., 107–08
Boles, Thomas R., 133–34, 182
Bonnichsen, Paul, 140
Bradbury Science Museum (Los Alamos), 162
Bradford, Cleal, 149
Brixner, Berlyn, 188
Broome, Bertram C., 88
Brower, David, 142
Browning, Elizabeth Barrett, 158–59
Buffalo Soldiers, 40
Bureau of Immigration. *See* Territorial Bureau of Immigration
Burges, Richard L., 127
Burnett Foundation, The, 110
Bursey, Joseph A., 91, 94–99, 182, 199
Butterfield Stage, *31*, 152
Bynner, Witter, 74, 104

Cabeza de Vaca, Alvar Núñez, 76, 116
California, *31*, 36, 43, 57, 91–92, 142, 152, 155
Capitán, New Mexico, 38, *180*
Caplin, Harvey, 140–41
Carlsbad Caverns, 49, 71, *99*, 125–38, 178, 182, 196
Carlsbad, New Mexico, 125–26, 135–36, 138, *180*, 195–96
Carpenter, Howard, 148
Carson, Kit, *35*, 68
Carter, Harvey, 142
Casa Grande, 28
casinos, 40–41
Cassidy, Gerald, *70, 72*, 88
Cassidy, Ina Sizer, 88, 119
Castañeda Hotel, 21, 71, 92, 196
Castañeda, Pedro de, 77
Cather, Willa, 106
Catron, Thomas B., 181
Cavern Guide Book (Grant), *130*
cemeteries, 29, 32–36, 45
Century of Progress Expo (Chicago), 47, 49–51
Cerletti, Michael, 123
Chaco Canyon, 28, 49, 162
Chamuscado-Rodríguez expedition, 77
Chapman, Jeff, 42
Charles, Tom, 179–82
Chaves, Amado, 116–17
Chaves County Historical Society, 38
Chávez, Thomas E., 109
Chicago, Illinois, 55, 66, 71, 78–79, 152. *See also* Century of Progress Expo; Chicago World's Columbian Expo
Chicago, Rock Island and Pacific railroad, 16
Chicago World's Columbian Expo, 50, 66, 117
Chicago World's Fair. *See* Century of Progress Expo
Chimayó, New Mexico, 49–50, *105*, 114, 119–24, 195
Cimarron Cutoff, 14, 30, 32
Clark, Willard F., 104–05
Clark, William, 24
Clarkson, Robert Hunter, 71, 73, 92
Clayton, New Mexico, 30–34, 193, 196
climate, 47, 49, 57–63, 74, 89, 91, 93, 95–96, 197
Cloudcroft, New Mexico, 177–78, *180*
Cochiti Pueblo, *19, 48*, 78, 80
Coe, George, 181
Cold War, 184
Colorado, 36, 43, 57–59, 73, 91–92, 94, 124, 139–40, 147, 149, 192
Colorado & Southern Railway, 30, 32
Colter, Mary Jane, 69, 79
Columbus Army Air Field, 167
Columbus, New Mexico, 163, 167–68, 194–95
Coolidge, Calvin, 126, 129
Corbin, Alice, 74, 106, 109, 117–19, 121
Corn, Martin Van Buren, 172
Corn, Miller "Hub", 172, 196
Coronado Cuarto Centennial, 37, *39*, 108, 119, 140
Coronado, Francisco Vásquez de, 20, 32, 37, 75–77, 87
cowboys, 41, 71, 127, *130*, 133, 162
Crassas, Jerassimos, 26
Cronyn, George, 119
Crosby, Stan, 171
Currier, W. C., 23–24
Curtis, Edward S., 79
Cutting, Bronson M., 179

Darling, Ehud H., 147
Daughters of the American Revolution, 80

Davis, Ray V., 127–33
Davis, W. W. H., 58
Davis, Wyatt, 96
Dawes, Rufus C., 49
De Huff, Elizabeth Willis, 74, 124
De Vargas, Don Diego, 87
Demaray, Arthur E., 133
Deming, New Mexico, *180*
Denison, Charles, 58
Dennis, Glenn, 169
Denver & Rio Grande Railway, 16, 59, 107, 114
Department of Energy (DOE), 125, 136–37, 178, 185
Department of Tourism, 121, 123, 152, 161, 199
Detroit Photographic Company, 68
Dillon, Richard C., 104
dinosaur tracks, 32, 34
Dorantes, Estéban de, 76
Dorsey, George A., 78–79
Drury, Newton B., 133–34
Duke, Bernice, 95–96
Dunton, Herbert, 108

Earhart, Amelia, 133
Eddy, Charles Bishop, 126
Eddy, John Arthur, 126
Eisenhower, Dwight D., 153
Elephant Butte Dam, 178
Enola Gay, 162
"Essence of Enchantment" campaign, 158–59, 199
Evans, Will, 144
Everist, Nancy, 123

Fall, Albert Bacon, 181
Faris, Johnwill, 182
Farmington, New Mexico, 144, 196
Federal Writers' Project (FWP), 119
Fergusson, Erna, 72–73, 88
Fergusson, Harvey, 88
festivals/fairs, 110, 144–45, 164, 166, 169, 171
Field, Kate, 158
Field, Matthew C., 18–19, 194
films, 46, 56, 69, 133, 142, 161, 188, 190
Fisk, Samuel A., 58
Fitzpatrick, George M., 88
Flower, B. O., 158–59
Fogelson, E. E. "Buddy", 24–26, 196
Fogelson, Gayle, 26
Fogelson, Greer Garson. *See* Garson, Greer
Forked Lightning Ranch, 22–24, 26–27, 196
Fort Sumner, 29, 34–37, 149, 162, 196
Fort Union, 30
Four Corners: Monument, 139, 146–50, 196; Power Plant, 145–46, 196; Trading Post, 149
Fred Harvey Company: advertising by, 66–69; hotels, 21, *52*, 55, 59–60, 67, 69, 92, 195–96, 199; and Indian/Mexican Building, 79–80; launches rail/motor tour, 71; souvenirs, 52. *See also* Harvey, Frederick H.; Santa Fe/Harvey Indian Detour
Fred Harvey Indian Building/Dept., 78–80
Frost, Max, 93
Fruitland, New Mexico, 145–46

Galisteo Junction (Lamy), 55, 164–65, 194
Gallegos, Hernán, 77
Gallinas, New Mexico, 195
Gallup, New Mexico, *52*
Garrett, Elizabeth, 43–45, 197

Garrett, Pat, 29, 40, 43–44, 172, 197
Garson, Greer, 24–26, 196
Gaspard, Leon, 108
Gayer, Jacob, 130
Geary, Fred, 80
Geronimo, 177, 185
Goddard, Robert H., 174–75, 197
Goddard Rocket Flights Mescalero Ranch (Roswell), 162, 174
Gore, Howard M., 152
Gorman, James, 149
Grand Canyon, 67–68, 71, 74, 134, 182, 196
Grant, Blanche C., *130*, 132
Grant County, New Mexico, 58
Great Depression, 49, 51
Green, Janet L., 158–59
Gregg, Josiah, 14, 18, 30–31, 102–03, 152, 193–95
Groves, Leslie R., 185
guidebooks, 14, 96; and artists, 68; for Las Vegas, 61–63; on the Navajos, 139; for Route 66, 152–53; on the Southwest, *135*, 146; WPA, 118–19. *See also* Territorial Bureau of Immigration; Tourist Bureau
Guzmán, Nuño de, 76

Hall, Edward H., 153
handicrafts, 49–50, 73, 84, 139, 149. *See also* Pueblo Indians: pottery/handicrafts by
Hannett, Arthur T., 131
Harding, Warren G., 181
Harris, Fisher Sanford, 116
Harvey, Ford, 79
Harvey, Frederick H., 55–56, 60, 66, 69. *See also* Fred Harvey Company; Harveycars; Santa Fe/Harvey Indian Detour
Harveycars, 65, 70–71, 196
Hassrick, Peter H., 110
Hatch, New Mexico, *180*
Haut, Walter, 169
health/health seekers, 13, 16, 47, 49, 57–63, 65, 89, 115, 126, 158, *180*
Henderson, Alice Corbin. *See* Corbin, Alice
Henderson, William Penhallow, 106, 179
Hendron, J. W., 38
Herzstein Memorial Museum, 34
Hewett, Edgar Lee, 72, 102, 109, 112
Hickey, Ethel, 73
Hicks, Ward, 91–92, 94–95, 199. *See also* Ward Hicks, Inc.
Higgins, Charles A., 67, 78
Higgins, Victor, 108
Hiroshima, 162, 185
Hispanic villages, 16, 21, 49, 74, 107, 110, 113, 119–24, 192, 195
historic: landmarks, 35, 38, 40, 47, 51, 66, 68, 89, *98*, 101, 107, 141, 156–57, 163, 187, 197; markers, 89; preservation, 51, 66, 121, 157
Historical Center for Southeastern New Mexico, 164, *173*
historical pageants, 37
Historical Society of New Mexico, 72
Hockenhull, Andrew W., 47, 49, 51
Hodel, Donald P., 24
Hodge, Frederick Webb, 72
Holley, Robert A., 126–29
Holliday, Cyrus Kurtz, 54, 164
Holloman Air Force Base/Development Center, 176, 182, 185
Hoover, Herbert, 134, 179, 181

Hopis, 56, 67, 71, 76, 78–81, *83*
horses/horse racing, 40–41
hot air balloons, 165–66, 194
hot springs, 16, 21, 47, 58–63, 134, 178, *180*, 195–96. *See also* Las Vegas Hot Springs
hotels/inns, 21–22, 32, 47, *52*, 55, 60–63, 67, 96, 101, 125, 171, 177, 199. *See also* motels/motor courts; specific names
Hovenweep, 28
Hubbard Museum of the American West, 40–41
Hubbard, R. D., 41–42
Huckel, John F., 79
Huckel, Minnie Harvey, 79
Hurd, Peter, 37, 88, 110, 164, 169, 197
Hurley, George H. H., 140

Ickes, Harold, 182
Indian and Mexican Building (Albuquerque), 79–80, 199
Indian-detour. *See* Santa Fe/Harvey Indian Detour
International Space Hall of Fame (Alamogordo), 161–62, 175–76
International U.F.O. Museum and Research Center (Roswell), 164, 169–72, 197
Isleta Pueblo, 71, 78

Jackson, William Henry, 68
Jemez Mountains, 104, 161, 192
Jemez Pueblo, 18, 78, 84, 93
Jennings, Thomas E., 173–74
John Wheatley Studio, 32–33
Johnson, E. Dana, 121
Johnson, Gary, 100, 151
Johnson, Lyndon B., 157
Jorgensen, O. T., 49

Kansas, 54–55, 164
Kay, Elizabeth, *111*
Kearney, Stephen Watts, 14
Kellock, Katherine, 119
Ketchum, Thomas "Black Jack", 32–34, 196
Kidder, Alfred V., 27, 72, 196
Kidder, Madeleine, 196
Kimmell, Everett H., 148
Kindel, Frank, 132
Kit Carson House (Taos), *35*, 68
Klah, Hosteen, 49–51
Koehler, A. E. Jr., 45–46, *48*
Koshare Tours, 73
Kozlowski, Martin, 23

La Fonda Hotel (Santa Fe), 21, 69–71, 196
La Posada Hotel (Winslow, AZ), 69
Lamy, Jean Baptiste, 106
Lamy, New Mexico, 103. *See also* Galisteo Junction
Landmarks of the Santa Fe Trail (exhibition), 44
Langmuir Laboratory for Atmospheric Research (Socorro), 162
Las Cruces, New Mexico, 63, *180*, 182, 184
Las Vegas Hot Springs, 53, 57–63, 195
Las Vegas, New Mexico, 16, 21, 59–60, 71, 92, 164, 195–96
Lawrence, D. H., 94, 102
Leck, Bert, 132
Lee, Charles, 135–36
Lee, Dana, 131
Lee, Elizabeth, 131
Lee, Willis T., 127, 129–32

Legislative Blue-Book of the Territory of New Mexico, The,
   12, 15, 17, 55, 194
Lentz, James M., 148
Lincoln County, New Mexico, 29, *35*, 37–42, 45, 172, 185,
   197
Lincoln National Forest, 177, 180
Littell, Max, 169
Livingston, Carl B., 131–32
Long, Abijah "Bige", 127
Long, Alice, 103
Long, Haniel, 103, 134
Long Walk, 149
Lordsburg, New Mexico, *180*
Los Alamos National Laboratory, 137–38, 161–62, 190
Los Alamos, New Mexico, 104, 188, 190–92, 195
Lummis, Charles F., 72, 74, 113–17

Madalena, James Roger, 84
Madrid, Patricia, 138
Manhattan Project, *160*, 162, 186, 189, 196–97
maps, 82, 88, 96, 140, *143*, 148–50, 152, 154–55, 162
Marion, Anne and John, 110
Martinez, Maria and Julian, *82*
Mayer, Robert, 26
McBride, "Big John", 36
McDonald House, 189
McDonald, William C., 44–45
McGary, Dave, 41
McIlwain, W. F., 127
McKim, Harry, 132
McManus, John, 98–99
Mechem, Edwin L., 190
medievalism, 117–19, 124, 195
Medina, Ramon and Saranita, 120
Meem, John Gaw, 23–24, 69
Melgares, Don Facundo, 14, 87
Mera, Harry P., 80
Mera, Reba (Mrs. Harry P. Mera), 80–81
Mesa Verde, 28
Mescalero Apaches, 38, 127, 177, 180–81
Mexican heritage, *31*, 74. *See also* Hispanic villages
Mexican War, 14
Mexico, 13–15, 17, 20, 43, 54, 75–76, 87, 168, 194
migration/immigration, 14–16, 45–47, 54, 89, 93, 153,
   155
Miles, John E., 38, 89, 98
Military Institute, 169
Mimbres culture, 161
mineral springs, 125–26. *See also* hot springs
mining, 47, 65, 127, 145–46, 175
Minton, Charles Ethrige, 119
mission churches, 24, 43, 46–48, 96, *99*, 107, *122*, 194,
   196
Missouri, 13–14, 21, 199
Montezuma, 15, 17–21, 43–44, 60, 77, 94, 194–95, 197,
   199
Montezuma Hotel (Las Vegas), 60–63, 195
monuments: national, 126–27, 132–33; state, 38, 40, 42
Moore, Gilbert, 175
Moran, Thomas, 68
Morgan Lake, 145–46
Morley, Sylvanus Griswold, 72
Moseley, Manuel F., *39*
motels/motor courts, 153, 156, 174. *See also* hotels/inns
Museum of Art (Santa Fe), 47, *50*, 107. *See also* Museum of
   New Mexico

Museum of Natural History and Science, 140
Museum of New Mexico, 37–38, 44, 69, 80–81, *83*, 109,
   114. *See also* Museum of Art
museums, 66, 79–80, 92, 107, 110, 112, 121. *See also* specific names

Nagasaki, 185, 190
Nampeyo, 79
National Atomic Museum (Albuquerque), 162, 185
national forests, 40, 95, 177, 180
National Geographic Society, 130–31
National Historic Preservation Act, 157
National Park Service, 24–27, 132–34, 136–37, 182, 185,
   187
National Register of Historic Places, 42, 187
National Solar Observatory (Alamogordo), 162
Native Americans, 53, 76–77, 96, 195. *See also* individual
   tribes; Pueblo Indians
Navajos, *35*, 49–50, 56, 68, 71, 80, 92, 139–50, 196, 199
Nevada, 138
New Mexico Endowment for the Humanities, 34
New Mexico Highway Journal, 88, 109, 124, 180
New Mexico Magazine, 88–89, 109–10, 140, 148–49, 157,
   162, 174, 187–88
New Mexico State University, 179
New York World's Fair, 98
Newcomb, Franc J., 50–51
Newsom, John D., 119
Nicholson, Frank E., 132
Nicholson, George T., 67
Nims, F. C., 59
Nohl, Mark, 121

"O, Fair New Mexico" (song), 43–45, 197
Ojo Caliente, New Mexico, 63
O'Keeffe, Georgia, 106, 110–12, 164, 197
Oklahoma, 152, 154–55
Ollinger, Bob, 40
Olona, Richard, 123
Oppenheimer, J. Robert, 185, 189
Otero County, New Mexico, 179–81
Otero, Miguel Antonio, 21
Owen, Bill B., 164

Page, Hubert D., 148
Palace of the Governors, 15, *50*, 107, 109
Panama-California Expo (San Diego), 44–48, *50*, 80, *82*
Panic of 1893, 63, 66
Parsons, William S. "Deak", 162
Pecos National Historical Park, 23–25, 27, 196
Pecos Pueblo, 17–25, 27, 44, 71, 77, *105*, 165, 194, 196
Penitente Brotherhood, 106–07, 113–14, 116–18, 120
penitentiary, 32, 98–99
Pershing, John J. "Black Jack", 167
Peshlaikai, Fred, 49–50
Petroglyph National Monument, 161
Phillips, Bert G., 107–08
photographers, 68, 78, 130, 155. *See also* specific names
photography studios, 32–33, 133
Pino, Peter, 84–85
Polk, James K., 14
postal stamps, 81, *83*, 140–41, 149
postcards, 68, 152
Potter, Jack, *33*
pottery, *19*, 25, 27, 75, 77–83, 92, 94, 161, 194, 196, 199
Pratt, Chuck, 142

prehistoric: artifacts, 185; culture, 94; period in NM, 43, 159; ruins, 13, 17, 27–28

promotional literature/programs, 16–17, 58–59, 68, 73, 89, 95–98. *See also* advertising; guidebooks; Tourist Bureau

Pueblo Indians, 20, 43, 49; artists' portrayals of, 108; description of, 61, *99*; and Panama-Calif. Expo, 46–47; pottery/handicrafts by, 77–84, 92, 94, 194, 196, 199; and tourism, 16–17, 65–69, 73–75, 77, 84, 93–94, 98, 106, 113–14, 116, 159, 192. *See also* specific tribes, pueblos

Pueblo Revolt, 22

Pueblo ruins, 27–28, 38, 78, 89, 94, 159, 196

Puyé cliff dwellings, 71

railroad, 51, 53–54, 65, 75, 107, 113, 115, 126, 162, 168. *See also* specific company names

ranches, 22–24, 26, 42, 47, 96, 126, 131, 172, 174, 181, 189, 196

Rapp, Isaac Hamilton, 46–47, 69

Rapp, Rapp, and Hendrickson, 46, 69

Raton, New Mexico, 55, 71

Raton Pass, 14, *31*, 53, 55, 151

recreation, 87, 89, 145

religious processions, 120–21, 123

Representative Art and Artists of New Mexico (School of American Research), 109, 112

resorts, 43, 47, 58, 60, 62–63, 145

resources, 15, 45, 47, 50–51, 89, 91, 93, 104

restaurants/food service, 55–56, 67, 92, 132–33, 144, 156–57

Rhodes, Eugene Manlove, 74, 94, 178–79, 189, 196

Richards, Jon, 26

Richardson, Bill, 100

Richter, Conrad, 88

Rick Johnson & Co., 158

Ripley, Edward Payson, 66–68

Ripley, Robert, 133

Ritch, William G., *12*, 15–17, 20, 55, 194

Rittenhouse, Jack D., 153, 199

roads/highways, 87–89, 116, 120, 124, 152–53, 168, 181–82, 201. *See also* Route 66

Robbins, Chandler, 147–48

Robbins, Royal, 142

Robert Goddard Planetarium, 164, *173*

rock art, 161

Rocky Mountains, 54, 71, 106–07, 140

rodeos, 23, 169

Rogers, Will, 133

Romero, Orlando, 123

Roosevelt, Franklin D., 47, 179, 182

Roosevelt, Theodore, 44

Rosebrough, Bob, 142

Roswell Incident, 162, 164, 169–72, 174, 194, 196–97

Roswell Museum and Art Center, 164, *173*, 197

Roswell, New Mexico, 38, 45, 168–74, *180*

Round Mound (Mount Clayton), 30–32, 193, *195*

Route 66, 151–59, 199–201

Rowe, New Mexico, 22

Ruffner, E. H., 107

Ruidoso Downs Racetrack, 40–41

Ruidoso, New Mexico, 40–42, *170*, 178

Russell, Carl P., 182

Russell, Marian Sloan. *See* Sloan, Marian

Ruthling, Ford, 80–81, *83*

Sacramento Mountains, 177, 189

San Diego, California, 44–47

San Felipe Pueblo, 78

San Ildefonso Pueblo, 81–83

San Juan Pueblo, 71

San Mateo, New Mexico, 116–17

Sanchez, Alfred, 42

Sandia Man Cave, 161

Sandia National Laboratories, 161–62

Sandia Pueblo, 78, 93

sandpaintings, 50–51, 144, 149

Sangre de Cristo Mountains, 101, 106–07, 110

sanitariums, 60, 63. *See also* health/health seekers

Santa Ana Pueblo, *50*, 78, 93

Santa Clara Pueblo, 71

Santa Fe Chamber Music Festival, 110

Santa Fe/Harvey Indian Detour, 21–22, 65–74, 78–80, 92, 94–95, 115–18, 124, 152, 178, 196; courier guides, 71-73

Santa Fe Institute, 162

Santa Fe New Mexican, 24, 67, 84–85, 93, 102, 108–09, 112, 121, 123, 136

Santa Fe, New Mexico: artists of, 49, 69, 80–81, 101–06; attractions of, 61, 63, 74, 101–02, 107, 192; early history of, 14; hotels in, 69–71, 196; and Indian-detours, 70–71; and Montezuma legend, 20; preservation of, 26; railroad arrives at, 53, 55, 164–66, 199; remodeling of, 78; restaurants in, 24; and tourism, 21, 71, 93, 116, 119, 138, 178

Santa Fe Plaza, *50*, 69, 101

Santa Fe Railway. *See* Atchison, Topeka and Santa Fe Railroad/Railway

Santa Fe Trail, 13–14, 18, 21, 30–32, 44, 53, 55, 69, 74, 101, 107, 151–52, 156, 193–94, 197, 199

Santa Rita, New Mexico, 162, 175

santeros, 123

Santo Domingo Pueblo, 71, 78

Santo Niño de Atocha, El, 120

santos, 120–21

Santuario de Chimayó, El, 114, 120–24

Sarton, May, 103–04

Scenic and Historic Byways Program, 156

scenic attractions, 43–44, 47, 49, 65–66, 71, 73–74, 89, 91, 93, 106–07, 114, *180*, 197. *See also* individual sites

Schmidt, Franz, 189

Schmitt, Harrison H., 175

School of American Research (School for Advanced Research), 109, 112

Schweizer, Herman, 79

Scott, Winfield T., 103–04

See America First League, 116

Service Bureau, 88–89

Seven Cities of Cibola legend, 32, 75–77, 87

Seymour, Flora Warren, 75

Sharp, Joseph H., 108

Shiprock, New Mexico, 139–45, 194, 196

Shuart, Harry E., 88

Shuster, Will, 49, 104, 109

Silver City, New Mexico, 29, 63, *180*

Simpson, William H., 67–68, 78

Sloan, Marian, 29–30

Smithsonian Institution, 77

Society for the Preservation and Restoration of New Mexico Churches, 121

Socorro County, New Mexico, 94, 161–62, 188

Solly, Samuel E., 58

souvenirs, *52*, 56, 75, 77, 92, 132, 144, 194, 196, 199

Space Center (New Mexico Museum of Space History), 175

Spain, 13, 43, 65, 75–76
Spanish Colonial Arts Society, 121
Spanish heritage, 16, 20–22, *25*, *31*, 37, 40, 43–44, 49,
   66, 74–77, 87, 107, 114, 196–97
sports, 42, 47, 49, 89, 145, 177
St. Louis Exposition, 45, 47
Stamm, Roy A., 166
Staples, Berton I., 49
state: flags, 45–46, 75, 80–81, 84–85; official question,
   100; parks, 163; seals, 45, 149; songs, 43–45, 197; sym-
   bols, 91, 100
State Cultural Properties Review Committee, 89
State Highway Commission/Dept., 39, 49, 87–89, 95–97,
   104–05, 107, *143*, 148, 156, 199
State Legislature, 80, 84, 99–100, 168, 179
state nicknames, 119; "Land of Enchantment", 80, 87, 91–
   100, 151, 159, 162, 193, 199, 201; "Sunshine State",
   45–46, 88, 92, 95, 119, 148, 193, 199
State Register of Cultural Properties, 187
statehood, 45, 51, 140, 181
Stedman, Wilfred, 140, *143*
Steinbeck, John, 152
Stevens, Walter B., 126
Stevenson, James, 77
Story, Isabelle, 184
Street, Gordon, 49

Taft, William Howard, 45
Taos, New Mexico: and artists, 49, 101, 106–08, 132, 178;
   attractions of, 101, 192; highway to, 124; and Kit Carson
   House, *35*, 68; tours to, 71; and WPA NM Guide, 119
Taos Pueblo, 77, *105*, 107
Territorial: fairs, 15, 166; governors, 15, 21; history, 29, 44;
   legislature, 14–15, 17, 107, 116; New Mexico, 20, 193–
   94; railroad, 54–55; seal, *12*, 15
Territorial Bureau of Immigration, 13–17, 20, 58, 89, 93,
   194
Tesuque Pueblo, 61, 71
Thorlin, J. Frederick, 187
Three Rivers Petroglyph Site, 161
Tingley, Clyde, 87–88, 96
Toddy, Jimmy, *147*
Toribio, William, 84
Toulouse, Betty, *81*
tourism, 104; and atomic bombs, 196; boosters of, 58, 178;
   establishment of, 16; in Europe, 92, 119; and the Navajo,
   150; and outlaws, 32, 34, 36–40; as profitable industry,
   16, 74, 84, 87, 126, 171–74; and Pueblo Indian ruins,
   28; and the railway, 66; and ranches, 22–23; and reli-
   gion, 121, 123–24; and roads/highways, 86–88; and
   Santa Fe Trail, 30–32; and state's attractions, 46–47; in
   the West, 116, 153; and the WPA, 118–19. *See also*
   resorts; Santa Fe/Harvey Indian Detour; souvenirs
Tourist Bureau, *31*, *35*, 80, 86–88, 91, 95–97, *99*, *108*,
   122, 125, *170*, 182, 197, 199. *See also* Department of
   Tourism
trade/traders, 13–14, 18, *25*, *31*, 50–51, 78, 144, 147–49
Trever, John, 137
trinitite, 178, 186–88, 194
Trinity Site, 160–62, 178, 182–83, 185–90, 194, 196–97
Troup, Bobby, 156
Tularosa Basin, 176, 181–83
Tularosa, New Mexico, 180, 186

Turner, Harold, 183
Twitchell, Ralph Emerson, 45

Ufer, Walter, 108
U.F.O.s. *See* Roswell Incident
University of New Mexico, 37, 119
UNM Fine Arts Museum, 110
U.S. Army, 30, 60, 107, 167, 182–85, 187–89, 195
U.S. Bureau of Land Management (BLM), 42
U.S. Congress, 14, 21, 136
U.S. Navy, 162
Utah, 139–40, 149, 192
Utes, 141, 149

Very Large Array Radio Telescope, 161–62
Vigil y Alaríd, Juan Bautista, 14
Villa, Francisco "Pancho", 163, 167–68, 194–95
Vroman, Adam Clark, 79

Wagner, Sallie, *147*
Waldo, David C., 18, 194
Walker, John B., 117
Wallace, Lew, 107
Walsh, Charles F., 166–67
Walter, Paul A. F., 43–44, 47, 72, 114
Ward Hicks, Inc., 95–97, *99*, *154*. *See also* Hicks, Ward
Warner, James N., 36
Waste Isolation Pilot Plant, 125–26
Waste Isolation Pilot Project (WIPP), 136–38, 196
weavings, 49–50, 79–80, 92, 94, 120–21, 124, 139, 144,
   199
White, Fannie, 127, 131
White, James "Jim", 127–32
White Sands Missile Range (Alamogordo), 162, 176, 182–
   87, 196
White Sands National Monument (Alamogordo), 49, 177–
   86, 189, 196
White, W. F., 66–68
Whiteskunk, Selwyn, 149
Whiting, Lilian, 91–95, 102, 158–59, 197, 199
Wide Ruins trading post, *147*
Wiley, R. W., 57, 59
Wilson, Paul, 190
Woods, Betty, 148–49, 187–88
Works Progress Administration. *See* Works Project Adminis-
   tration
Works Project Administration (WPA), 37–38, 114, 118–19.
   See also WPA New Mexico Guide
World War I, 124
World War II, 37, 89, 156–57, 182, 184–85
WPA American Guide Series, 118–19, 153
WPA New Mexico Guide (1940), 37, 121, 140–41, 145,
   168, 179
writers, 51, 68, 74, 78, 88, 101–04, 106–07, 109, 112,
   115–16, 119, 153, 155, 199. *See also* individual names
Wyeth, Henriette, 164

Young-Hunter, John, 108
Yucca Mountain nuclear waste facility (Nevada), 138

Zia Pueblo, 75–78, 80–81, 83–85, 93
Zunis, *52*, 76, 178